INFAMOUS LADY:
THE TRUE STORY OF
COUNTESS ERZSÉBET BÁTHORY

Kimberly L. Craft, Esq.

Infamous Lady:
The True Story of Countess Erzsébet Báthory
First Edition

For the girls....

PREFACE

World's Worst Female Serial Killer. Over 650 servant girls murdered. Vampire drinks and bathes in the blood of her victims. Witch, lesbian, and sadist. Walled up alive in castle tower.

Had she lived today, the media—including the tabloids—would most certainly offer headlines like this about a most unusual Hungarian countess who lived four hundred years ago. Years ago, I happened to overhear a conversation. A young lady made a remark in passing to her friend about this particular woman, Countess Erzsébet (Elizabeth) Báthory of Hungary. The friend had never heard the name before, and that caused the first young lady to explain: "She's the world's worst serial killer."

The world's worst serial killer? Names like Bundy, Dahmer, Manson and Gacy immediately come to mind, but Báthory?

"She killed over 600 people," the first woman continued. "She bathed in the blood of her victims and was finally walled up in her castle."

The friend remembered the story now, perhaps from an old horror movie.

"Yes, but was it true?" she asked.

"Yes, she was a real person, and she's in the Guinness Book of World Records."

Intrigued, I myself wondered why someone who had killed over 600 people—someone listed in, of all things, the Guinness Book (albeit as the world's worst *female* serial killer)—was not a household word, particularly given the public's fascination with "true crime" stories.

Some preliminary research quickly demonstrated that facts could not easily be separated from fantasy. Unlike other documented accounts of criminal personalities, the elaborate tales and legends woven around this particular figure had turned her into something of a caricature or cartoon character. On the one hand, she was a member of Hungary's ruling elite, the wife of a national war hero, and descended from an old and illustrious noble family. On the other hand, she was a lesbian vampire witch who bathed in the blood of 600 victims whom she had tortured to death before writing about each in her diary. She attempted to preserve her youth and beauty through sorcery and murder, and the story of her final punishment—being walled up alive within a tower—prompted both books and horror movies, all retelling the ghastly story. It is said that Countess Báthory inspired both the Brothers Grimm as well as Bram Stoker; even a metal band by the same name found its inspiration in her. Yet, it didn't make sense. The vampire stories could be brushed aside as superstition but, logistically, how would a member of the aristocracy, someone who managed vast estates, even have *time* to kill so many people? How could someone who attended the emperor's court maintain her position in polite society if so much killing was going on? Where would she even stash so many bodies? And why were so many of her victims young girls?

The more I researched the subject, the more I discovered how strange this story really was. Countess Báthory was truly an enigma: uncovering, or recovering, her story became something of an obsession. I was particularly interested in the legal aspect. Her accomplices were tried and convicted while she, herself, was never tried—yet still convicted. Over 300 witnesses testified, but only a handful claimed to have actually seen her do anything wrong. As for the body count, those with knowledge testified to perhaps 50 dead over a period of decades; one or two thought the count was possibly as high as 200. In fact, the allegation of 650 victims came only from a single source—an unknown servant girl, still in childhood, who based her entire claim on hearsay.

There was, indeed, apparently much more to this story, all of it buried under the rubble of history: ruthless politics, relentless religious wars, blood-feuds with Ottoman Turks, and the crumbling vestiges of feudal society struggling to retain its power. In the end, I discovered, as always, that truth was indeed more interesting than fiction.

That said, many decisions had to be made during the preparation of this work. Proper names, for example, posed a particular problem: should they be spelled in the original language or in English? Should variant spellings be given? Four hundred years ago, few people were literate, and recordkeeping was not an exact science. In official court documents and letters, the same person's name could be spelled two or three different ways and, in some cases, even phoenetically by the scribe. As far as possible, I decided to use formal spellings, in the original languages, for proper names; however, for the reader's convenience, I have also included all of the variant spellings whenever possible.

As for original source material, the question arose whether to use standard translations or render the material using new, literal translations. To this end, I decided to utilize literal translations. They are more accurate and, in many ways, more revealing than some of the former, romanticized versions.

Researching this project posed a particular challenge. Of all the material written about the Countess, much of it is fictional, speculative, or inaccurate. My challenge was to find as much original source material as possible. That said, the material would then have to be translated from Hungarian, Slovak, Latin, or German and finally reconstructed into a (hopefully) more accurate portrait of this woman and the events surrounding her life. Unfortunately, little information is available today. While other noble families of the time maintained and, to this day, still have historical archives in their names, none exists for

Countess Báthory. As for the actual trial transcripts, various versions were already in existence at the time when they were originally written, some even with marked differences.

We know without doubt that Erzsébet existed, but we cannot find the site of her burial today—crypts allegedly housing her remains have supposedly been found empty. Thus, researching this work became quite the treasure hunt. The mystery of the Countess grew deeper and deeper, and finding the elusive fragment of a letter, document, or some other original source was very much like striking gold. For the interested reader and fan of this subject material, however, I am sure you will experience the same excitement that I did upon discovering what I promise will be fresh and new material on the Countess. In many cases, the information presented here is being published for the very first time in English: well over a year was spent researching and translating original source material.

Finally, in an effort to keep the content interesting yet reliable, I have written some of the material in the form of literary vignettes—snippets of detail that read in story form—using as much original dialogue as possible. The dialogue and scenes have been recreated from trial transcripts and witness depositions. Some artistic liberty has been taken since we do not know every detail, but the reader can be assured that there is more fact than fiction.

In the end, I have attempted to put together the best documentary possible on the Countess. I apologize to the reader in advance, however, since it is not, and never will be, perfect. In addition, the work will never truly be finished, since it will continue to evolve over the years as more information comes to light. It is, however, an honest effort to provide new information on the riddle of Erzsébet Báthory, her alleged activities, and the various conspiracies surrounding her personally. In some ways, she herself was a victim, and that, more than anything else, may be the most interesting facet of the so-called Blood Countess.

Contents

Countess Erzsébet Báthory, c. 1585

1

OPENING VOLLEY

On the evening of December 29, 1610, a party of armed men arrived at the manor house of Castle Csejthe, in what was then the Kingdom of Hungary. The man in charge was the palatine (prime minister) of Hungary, György Thurzó. The other two nobles following behind him were Counts Nicolaus Zrínyi and György Drugeth de Homonnay, and the last, Squire Imre Megyeri. They were accompanied by a large party of armed guards. The men had been to this place before and moved in quickly.

Lying near the entryway, they found the body of a young girl who had been beaten to death. Struck by the mutilated condition of her body, they paused for a moment and then headed inside. They found two more young girls who had also been stabbed and beaten—one would die later, the other maimed for life. Moving through the manor house, they followed the sounds of screaming. Opening a door, they came upon three old women and a young man, all servants of Countess Erzsébet Báthory, in the midst of torturing one of the girls, with another sobbing child waiting to be taken next.

The beatings stopped suddenly as the men in arms quickly moved in to apprehend the four servants. Securing the suspects, they then made their way toward the private apartments of the 50-year-old Countess Erzsébet Báthory—also known to them as the Lady Widow Nádasdy. When they came upon her, she stared for a moment and then screamed at the crowd, "What is this intrusion? You shall all pay for this!"

And then slowly, in the dim light, she began to recognize exactly who these men were: the Prime Minister of Hungary, whom she affectionately called "cousin"; her two sons-in-law, Counts Zrínyi and Drugeth; and her son's tutor, Imre Megyeri.

"Lady Widow Nádasdy," the Palatine said, "In the Name of the King, you are hereby under arrest."

"That's ridiculous!" she laughed. But her expression quickly changed as the men came for her.

Hurling insults, the Palatine pulled her by the hair and rushed her through the manor house. He demanded that she take a hard look at the carnage and her four accomplices, now being put in chains. Disheveled but defiant, the Countess said nothing.

Furious, Thurzó turned to his men.

"Secure these four, and then take this bestial woman up to the castle. Search it from top to bottom!"

Outside, nearly thirty men from the town of Csejthe had gathered. The grim procession made its way toward the castle, determined now to discover the truth behind the rumors.

The day after her arrest, December 30, 1610, Palatine György Thurzó wrote to his wife:

My greetings and update, Beloved Heart!

I arrived here at Újhely yesterday evening in good health, thank God. I apprehended the Nádasdy woman. By now, she has been led away to the castle above. Now, those who tortured and murdered the innocent—those evil women in league with that young lad who in silent cruelty assisted with their atrocities—were sent to Bytča. They are under guard and will be held in strict captivity until, God willing, I arrive home to bring the strong justice they deserve. The women can remain imprisoned in the town, but the young lad must be confined at the castle.

As for our people and servants that I brought with me, when my men entered Csejthe Manor, they found a girl dead in the house; another followed in death as a result of many wounds and agonies. In addition to this, there was also a wounded and tortured woman there; the other victims were kept hidden away where this damned woman prepared these future martyrs.

I am just waiting until this cursed woman is brought to the castle and the others' destination is determined, and then I break away and hope, if the way permits, that I make it home by tomorrow. May God grant it!

I have written this in the greatest haste: 30 December 1610 in Vág-újhely.

Your loving Lord and spouse,

Count György Thurzó

Of all the many tales told about the Countess over the years, we shall turn now to the original source material, much of it written over four hundred years ago in Hungarian, Slovak, Latin, and German. It is here that we attempt to recreate Countess Erzsébet's life and the events leading up to her arrest and trial. Rather than indulge in legends, we will explore what she actually said and what was said about her by the people of her time: her accomplices, certainly, but also the testimony of her servants and other eye witnesses—estate managers, stewards, castle administrators, accountants, kitchen staff, huntsmen, clergy, doctors, nobles, and townspeople—306 people, in fact, were called to testify against her. Because her name was banned from polite Hungarian society, many of these words remained silent over the centuries. However, the fragmented and crumbling manuscripts have finally been exhumed, revealing a genuine human being rather than a mere legend: a complex figure, in fact, whose actual deeds are even more baffling than any legend or tale ever created about her.

2

THE BÁTHORY FAMILY

During the late Middle Ages and Renaissance, Erzsébet Báthory's family rose to prominence and exerted a great deal of influence over Central Europe. Its members, including several princes, a cardinal, and even the king of Poland, held positions of high authority in the Kingdom of Hungary and surrounding areas. The Báthory (Bathori, in Latin) family belonged to a clan of Hungarian nobles called the *Gutkeled* which, according to history, formed when two German brothers, Gut and Keled, moved to Hungary. History traces the technical beginning of the family, however, to András of Rakoméz, patron of the monastery of Sárvár in the county of Szatmár. In 1279, King László rewarded András' brother, Hados, as well as his sons György (d. 1307), Benedek (d. 1321) and Briccius (d. 1322) for their military service by granting them the estate located at Bátor in the county of Szabolcs. In 1310, Briccius took possession of Bátor. Soon after, he and his descendants referred to themselves as being *of Bátor* or Báthory.

The Báthory family later divided into two major branches, both descended from Briccius' sons. The elder branch of the family, the Báthory of Somlyó, descended from János, Count of Szatmár, Briccius' first-born son, through his eldest,

László (d. 1373). László, Count of Szabolcs, married Anna Meggyesi and received the Somlyó property as part of her dowry. The younger branch of the family, the Báthory of Ecsed, descended from Lukacs, the youngest son of Briccius. Lukacs possessed wide estates in Szatmár and was granted the lordship of Ecsed by the king. There, he built the castle called *Hrséy* (loyalty). Since they retained possession of Bátor, members of this branch were called either *of Bátor* (i.e., Báthory) or, as the younger branch, *Nyírbátor* (New Báthory).

The Báthory family recounted its own legend that placed the family's origin in the year 900, well before the brothers Gut and Keled came to Hungary. In this more romanticized version, a warrior named Vitus, of the first generation of the Gutkeled clan, went to fight a terrible dragon that lived in the swamps of Ecsed. Vitus killed the dragon with three lance thrusts and, as a reward, received both land and castle located there. He was also honored with the name *Báthory*, which means "good hero." The word for "brave" in Hungarian is also *bátor*. In reference to this legend, the Báthory coat of arms, granted in 1325 to the sons of Briccius, featured three horizontal teeth surrounded by a dragon biting its own tail.

The Ecsed branch rose to prominence when Lukacs' great-grandson, István III, was appointed Palatine (prime minister) of Hungary (d. 1444). István's sons also held high positions: László V (d. 1474) was Supreme Count of the counties Szatmár and Szarand; András III (d. 1495) held the estate at Buják; István V (d. 1493) was Voivod (Prince) of Transylvania, the first in a long line of Báthory rulers of that country; and the youngest son, Miklós III (d. 1506), was the bishop of Syrmia and Vác, serving also as counselor to King Matthias Corvinus.

In the 16th century, Hungary was divided over two competing claims to the throne: The Ecsed branch of the Báthory family sided with the Hapsburgs who organized the election of Archduke Ferdinand of Austria as King of Hungary. However, the Somlyó branch supported János Szapolyai, who had been elected king by the majority of Hungarian nobles. The two branches of the Báthory family were eventually united, politically, by Erzébet Báthory's own parents, György and Anna, when György Báthory of the Ecsed branch changed allegiance from the Hapsburgs to Szapolyai.

It is said that György renounced his allegiance to the Hapsburgs in order to marry his "Transylvanian cousin," Anna, of the Somlyó branch, but his intention was probably more political than romantic. In any case, when the Hapsburg king commandeered his castle at Buják as punishment, György was eager to strengthen his alliance with Anna's brother, István, who had been appointed Voidvod of Transylvania under Szapolyai. He accomplished this by marrying Anna and, in so doing, united the two branches of the Báthory clan.

Anna Báthory was the widow of the last descendent of the Dragffy family, and György took over the Dragffy castles when they married. Unfortunately, the Habsburgs forced him to yield those castles to them, as well. György and Anna withdrew to Csitsva in the county of Zemplén and later to the Báthory family estate at Ecsed. Tension between the Hapsburgs and Báthorys would continue for generations, however, as the rival families vied for power in Central Europe. Born amidst this conflict was a daughter who shared blood from both sides of the family tree: Countess Erzsébet Báthory.

3

ERZSÉBET BÁTHORY'S EARLY
YEARS (1560-1575)

Erzsébet Báthory was born August 7, 1560 at the Ecsed family
estate in Nyírbátor (Nagyecsed), Hungary.   Located today in the
Northern Great Plain region of eastern Hungary in Szabolcs-
Szatmár-Bereg County, Nyírbátor served as the Báthory family
seat, an administrative center, and family burial site. In fact, the
Báthory family owned the town from the time of its Gutkeled
ancestors in the late 1200's until the death of Gábor Báthory,
Voivod of Transylvania, in 1613.

As discussed, Erzsébet's parents came from two separate
branches of the Báthory clan—György (c. 1522-1570) from the
Ecsed branch and Anna (1539- c. 1574) from the older Somlyó
side of the family. With the separate Báthory clans merged by
this powerful union, the little Countess was born into one of
Central Europe's most illustrious families. Her uncles on both
sides of the family were Voivods (Princes) of Transylvania, as
was her maternal grandfather. Her uncle, István (1533-1586),
was also the king of Poland. Erzsébet's cousins, András, Gábor,
and Zsigmond, would someday become Transylvanian princes,
as well, and, in 1595, Prince Zsigmond would enter into a grand

ERZSÉBET BÁTHORY'S EARLY YEARS (1560-1575)

marriage with the Habsburg Archduchess, Maria Christina, helping to resolve tensions between the Habsburg and Báthory
families.

The young countess spent her childhood at the Báthory
family estate in the countryside of Nyírbátor near the Romanian
border. Erzsébet had an older brother, István (1555-1605), a
brother Gábor (unfortunately, we have no dates of birth or death
for him, or whether he was married or not—only his name, according to 19th century genealogist, Alexander v. Simolin) and
two younger sisters, Zsofiá and Klara. Despite the political and
social unrest surrounding the Báthory children, the family seat
was well protected and its countryside peaceful. Surrounded by
pastureland, misty forests, marshes, swamps, and foggy moors,
the land produced its share of legends from the days of dragons,
heraldry and magic. For the most part, it still slumbered in the
Middle Ages, and the Báthory family continued to rule its lands
and peasantry as it had done for hundreds of years.

Meanwhile, Turkish invaders were pouring throughout
Europe. During this time, Hungary was divided into three portions: northern Hungary and a large part of Transdanubia were
under the control of Turkish satraps; western Hungary fell under
Hapsburg control; and Transylvania remained largely independ-
ent, its rulers siding either with the Turks or the Hapsburgs as
the situation warranted. In addition to tension between the three
ruling powers governing Hungary, this nation, as well as most of
Europe, was caught in the midst of the Protestant Reformation.
Not only were Islamic Turks clashing with European Christians,
Catholic and Protestant Europeans were also engaging in bloody,
ideological battles with each other.

Protestantism was particularly popular in Transylvania,
as well as with the common people and some of the Hungarian
nobility, while the kings and other great lords of the region
maintained allegiance to the Catholic Church and Holy Roman
Emperor. Erzsébet's parents chose Protestantism. No doubt,
they still fostered hostility against the Catholic Hapsburgs who
had commandeered their lands some years back. Like many no-

bles, they likely supported the Reformation since it also put limits on the power of both King and Roman Catholic Church. Erzsébet herself was raised a Calvinist by her mother. Anna Báthory belonged to the first group of high nobility who supported the Reformation in Hungary and was a generous benefactor, even founding a Protestant school in Erdöd.

However, Erzsébet's uncle István, King of Poland, was a practicing Roman Catholic, and her uncle András was a Catholic cardinal who, on several occasions, served as an emissary to the Pope. The fact that a family could be divided in such a way was not unusual for the time, as Europe struggled to resolve its religious identity. No doubt, Erzsébet was quite familiar with the teachings of both Catholicism and Lutheranism, as well as Calvinism. This was typical of the nobility. We know that her future mother-in-law quoted Calvin at length in one of her letters, yet raised her son in the Lutheran faith, while her future father-in-law, though technically a Catholic, filled his court with Lutheran scholars. Everyone, including the common people, had an interest in the new doctrines being preached in those days, and allegiances shifted frequently in such turbulent times.

In 1566 when Erzsébet was six years old, Sultan Suleyman the Magnificent (1520-1566) died. His son, Selim ("the Sot"), temporarily turned his attention away from Hungary, creating a lull in the fighting for the next twelve years. During this time, Turks and Hungarians co-existed rather peacefully, even establishing some commerce. Raids still occurred, particularly near the tense border regions but, overall, travel and trade could be conducted again. Although not ideal, Erzsébet Báthory's childhood and first few years of married life were spent during this relatively quiet period of Hungarian history. The lull was much needed: prior conflicts had laid waste to the land and its people. Food shortages and famines were common, and a large portion of the male population had died in the fighting.

And yet, this same time period saw the maturation of the Early Modern or Renaissance Era across Europe: the arts and sciences were flourishing along with new inventions. The world was only a century away from the Industrial Revolution and Age of Enlightenment. Explorers were now conquering the oceans and reaching the New World, and printing presses were operating. Telescopes peered into the heavens, cannons and rifles changed the nature of warfare, and some of the world's greatest art and architecture came into being. This was the world of Galileo, Queen Elizabeth, Da Vinci, Luther, and Michelangelo. This was also the world—complex, dynamic, revolutionary, artistic, bloody, and brilliant—in which Erzsébet Báthory grew up. As a member of the high nobility, she would experience all of it.

Some commentators have speculated that Erzsébet suffered from insanity and exhibited sexual sadism later in life as a result of her formative years spent at the Báthory family estate. Some, in fact, described the place as if it were an insane asylum of dysfunctional, inbred lunatics. They claim her brother, István, for example, was a sadistic, lecherous sex fiend and drunkard who could be found running naked in marketplaces after a binge; her uncle, Gábor, dressed in armor and fought off invisible attackers while shouting in unknown languages and foaming at the mouth; her aunt, Klara, was a bisexual who practiced witchcraft, killed her husbands, and taught Erzsébet how to torture servants and make love to women; her father refused to leave a favorite chair, whether to sleep, eat or bathe; and, as a child, Erzsébet herself witnessed the bizarre execution of a peasant who, when accused of selling his child to the Turks, was sewn alive into the body of a horse.

The absolute validity of such stories is questionable. We know for a fact that this family rose to power and prestige both at court and on the battlefield not by means of patronage or luck but because of superior intelligence, cunning, and courage. While Erzsébet's brother, István, might have been a sex fiend, it apparently did not result much in the way of offspring: he had no children with his wife, Fruzsina Drugeth, and, according to commentators, only one illegitimate child. And while he might have been a drunkard as an adult, it probably had little impact on

Erzsébet. István was only five years her senior, and she had already moved out of the family estate by the age of eleven.

Regarding stories of a crazy uncle named Gábor, a review of both the Somlyó and Ecsed branches of the Báthory family genealogy indicates that Erzsébet did not have an uncle by the name of Gábor. She did, however, have a cousin on her mother's side by the name of Gábor, who died in 1586. His son, by the same name, would go on to rule Transylvania.

Erzsébet did have an aunt Klara on her father's side. Klara was married first to a man named István Drugeth of Homonnay (d. between 1538-40) and then to Antal Losonci (d. 1551). It seems questionable that Klara would have murdered either of her husbands, however, whether of the Drugeth or Losonci clans. More likely, she simply outlived them. Indeed, the Báthory clan had close ties to both the Drugeths of Homonnay and Losonci families: Erzsébet's mother had been married three times, the second of which was to Antal Drugeth of Homonnay; Erzsébet's brother, István, married Fruzsina Drugeth of Homonnay, and Erzsébet's daughter, Katalin, would later marry György Drugeth of Homonnay (also spelled variously as Homonna, Hommonay, and Homanna). Klara's own brother, Miklós, married Anna Fruzsina Losonci. The murder of prominent family members would certainly not have been tolerated, nor would intermarriage between the clans continue if something akin to homicide actually happened. In addition, it is unlikely that Erzsébet's Aunt Klara had very much time to tutor her niece, whether in the ways of torture, witchcraft, or lesbianism. Although her exact birth year is uncertain, it is known that Klara was alive by 1521, thus placing her at least in her fifties by the time Erzsébet was a mere ten years old.

Mental illness may, indeed, have run in the family, particularly from inbreeding, but some of the alleged insanities— temper tantrums, swordplay in the house, or an unusual allegiance to a favorite chair—were also typical of aristocratic eccentricities.

ERZSÉBET BÁTHORY'S EARLY YEARS (1560-1575)

It is known that Erzsébet suffered seizures and fits of rage as a child, however, and it is said that her father did, as well. In later years, her letters described both eye and head pain that caused her problems; likely, migraines and epilepsy.

It is true that servants were dealt with harshly in Erzsébet's time, and she likely witnessed brutal, public executions. Before her birth, a peasant revolt in 1514 had caused a drastic change in the laws, and István Werbőczy's Tripartium Bull of 1517 reduced the local workforce to "property" status by the time she was born. Nobles, such as the Báthory family, had the legal right to settle disputes amongst their peasantry and to serve as local judge and jury, dispensing judgment that included even the death penalty. Essentially, peasants lacked most legal rights and, on occasion, unusual punishments were meted out.

For example, György Dozsa, leader of the same 1514 peasant revolt, was executed by being roasted alive. It is interesting to note that Dozsa was finally routed and captured at Temesvár by the combined forces of János Szapolyai and Erszébet's uncle, István Báthory. An illustration from a 16th-century Hungarian almanac shows a group of reveling nobles placing a red-hot metal crown on the captured Dozsa's head. Bound half-naked to an iron throne, hot coals were shoveled beneath his seat and ignited. His accomplices who had not already been impaled all around him were force fed their commander's flesh before being broken on the wheel and hanged. (In the rather unlikely alternative, it has also been said that while Dozsa was dying, he was actually mobbed and eaten by six of his rebel followers who had been starved beforehand.) Such spectacular executions, however, were reserved for special criminals and unique situations: Dozsa and his men had gone on a killing and looting spree, impaling dozens of priests and nobles before being apprehended.

For a commoner, particularly a gypsy, the usual punishment was hanging or the cutting off of a hand or fingers. Gypsies, in particular, were viewed as sub-human and godless by the ruling classes of the time. The accusation that a gypsy sold off a child to the Turks would probably not raise an eye amongst the nobility, as the upper classes deemed such behavior typical. If anyone did care, a sentence of death by being sewn into a live horse would be most unlikely unless the animal were already dead or dying. In a time when horses were viewed as more valuable than most peasants, it was unlikely that a horse would be killed to accommodate the sentence of a gypsy commoner. On the other hand, Hungarian nobles were also well-known for a somewhat "unique" sense of justice: had the gypsy instead been accused of stealing the horse, then a certain degree of black humor might indeed have been used to create a punishment to fit the crime.

In any case, the story goes on to say that young Countess Báthory witnessed this unusual event. She was hardly traumatized by it, however. Upon seeing the gypsy stuffed and sewn into the horse's belly, his head sticking out of the animal's body, Erzsébet found herself giggling at the bizarre spectacle. The tale is recounted by the French writer, Maurice Périsset, in his book, *La Comtesse de Sang* (The Blood Countess).

Stories aside, we do know that Erzsébet received an outstanding education at her parents' home and that her family, as eccentric as they might have been, believed (rather progressively for the time) that it was permissible for a girl to be as well educated as a boy. In fact, she was trained in the classics, mathematics, and could read and write in Hungarian, Greek, Latin, German and even Slovak, the language of many of her servants. She also appears to have been interested in religion and occultism as well as the sciences, including astronomy, botany, biology and anatomy. Throughout her life, she ordered various books from merchants, requested copies of works from fellow nobles, and appears to have been what we would today call a life-long learner. It is even said that in her last years, spent under house arrest, she passed time by writing on the walls when parchment ran out. Various documents, written in her own hand, prove her ability to write fluently.

ERZSÉBET BÁTHORY'S EARLY YEARS (1560-1575)

In fact, her writing style was short and to the point, almost curt. She wasted few words, generally, and wrote in the controlled style of one trained in the classics, including logic, Latin and Greek. Her penmanship and tone, as well as scholastic achievement, all indicate that she grew up in a very controlled and disciplined environment rather than a house of chaos or perversion.

Such an education was exceptional, especially at a time when few aristocrats, whether male or female, could read or write. Most of the nobility simply dictated their correspondence to clerks and administrative staff. In addition, the existing letters from the period suggest that writing was time consuming, laborious, and even thought to cause physical exertion. This is probably true to some extent: the process of scratching ink onto parchment (often sheepskin) by quill without smearing or blurring, all the while maintaining proper penmanship (as well as posture), would certainly have taken more time and effort than it does today.

Young Erzsébet was what we would today call a "tomboy": she demanded to be treated as well as her male relatives and staff. She enjoyed dressing up like a boy, studying like a boy and playing boy's games, including fencing and horsemanship. She would also throw hysterical fits when she did not get her way. She was extremely studious and mature, however, and there is no question that she was brilliant. Given her magnificent education and early marriage into one of the most prominent families in Hungary, she likely turned heads even as a child. She was also a perfectionist who equally enjoyed dressing up like a young lady, adorning herself with jewelry, playing with animals, and engaging in philosophical discussions.

We do know that Erzsébet would travel back to her Ecsed family home many years later when her brother István died and, before that, she made periodic trips to visit. It is likely that she conducted business there and had at least a cordial relationship with her brother. Unfortunately, we do not know very much about her younger sisters or her relationship with them, except that both Klara and Zsofiá married what might be called "middle-class" noblemen. Klara married Mihály Várdai (Michaelis de Kisvardi or Michael de Kiswárda). Zsofiá married András Figedy (also spelled Figedyi or Fygedy) and had at least two children, István and Borbála Figedy. (Despite a romanticized tale to the contrary, Erzsébet's sisters were not murdered as children in a peasant revolt.)

It was typical for a young girl of the nobility to become engaged in childhood and then spend her adolescence at the estate of her future in-laws. There, she would learn how to run the household, manage its staff, and finish her social training before the wedding date. So it was for young Erzsébet Báthory. In the year 1571, the 11-year-old was engaged to 16-year-old Count Ferenc Nádasdy de Nádasd et Fogarasföld in what was essentially a business deal between the two families. Some time before the conclusion of the marriage contract in December of 1572, she left her family home at Ecsed to travel to Sárvár, the main residence and family seat of the Nádasdy family. There, she was entrusted to the care of her future mother-in-law, Countess Orsolya Kanizsai Nádasdy.

Neither of Erzsébet's parents would attend her wedding. Her father, György, passed away in 1570 when she was only ten, and we know that her mother, Anna, was also deceased by the time of the wedding in 1575. (György Báthory was approximately 50 years old when he died. Although his date of birth is uncertain, his siblings all appear to have been born in the 1520's, and he himself was named Lord of Castle Buják in 1522—likely the year of his birth. Born in 1539, Anna Báthory's date of death is uncertain. We do know, however, that she, too, was already dead by the time of Erzsébet's wedding in 1575, thus passing away in her mid-thirties.) By her wedding date, Erzsébet had inherited an enormous amount of property from both of her parents The family estate at Ecsed ceded to her older brother István, however, who would reside there for the remainder of his life.

16

4

THE NÁDASDY FAMILY

Although not as old or illustrious as her own, the young Countess would nonetheless marry into an incredibly wealthy and powerful family. Her future mother-in-law, Orsolya Kanizsai, was the daughter of László von Kanizsai and Anna Dragffy. Born in 1523, Orsolya was the last family heir to the massive Kanizsai fortune and was married off at the age of twelve to Tamás Nádasdy.

The town of Sárvár, where Orsolya and Tamás Nádasdy would establish their main residence and family seat, is located in the county of Vas, Hungary, some 80 miles southeast of Vienna. A large castle and manor dominate the town, even today. Both were originally donated by Sigmund of Luxemburg to Orsolya's ancestor, János Kanizsai. The Kanizsai family owned this property until 1535 when both castle and manorhouse transferred to Orsolya's new husband, Tamás Nádasdy, through marriage. Tamás would later rebuild the palace in a grand, new Renaissance style.

Baron Tamás Nádasdy de Nádasd et Fogarasföld (1498-1562), Erzsébet's future father-in-law, was quite senior to his barely-teenaged bride Orsolya, already 37 years old when they married. He was a true Renaissance man, however, having been educated at Graz, Bologna and Rome. He was a scholar, statesman, and warrior, determined to bring Hungary out of the Middle Ages and into the Modern Era.

His ambitions had always been high: at the age of 23, Tamás accompanied Cardinal Cajetan (whom the pope had sent to Hungary to preach a crusade against the Turks) to the city of Buda to act as his interpreter. Four years later, in 1525, he became a member of the Council of State and, two years after that, was made commandant of Buda, having sided with the Hapsburgs and Ferdinand. In 1528, with the help of Baron György Cseszneky, commander of Tata, Nádasdy occupied Győr for Archduke Ferdinand. (Ferdinand was the brother of the Holy Roman Emperor, Charles V, and, as mentioned, the Hapsburg choice for King of Hungary.)

Unfortunately, Tamás Nádasdy would soon face the difficult decision of most Hungarian nobles at the time: remain loyal to the Hapsburg family and its choice of Ferdinand for the throne, or side with János Szapolyai, the choice of Hungary's lesser nobility. Meanwhile, Szapolyai had been plotting behind the scenes with the Turkish Sultan, Suleyman the Magnificent. Both Szapolyai and the Turks wanted to end the Hapsburgs' control over Europe. In exchange for pledging allegiance to Suleyman, Szapolyai was given a massive Ottoman army. In 1528, he headed for Vienna with his Turkish forces in tow. Szapolyai had to pass through the territory of Buda which was under Nádasdy's control, however, and it is here that Nádasdy had to make his choice: either take a stand for Ferdinand, fighting Szapolyai and the Turks, or capitulate. Nádasdy chose the latter. After hiding out for a time, he finally emerged, switching his allegiance from Ferdinand to Szapolyai.

Whether through fear, clever negotiation, or a simple desire to save the city and its people from harm, Nádasdy virtually handed Buda over to Szapolyai. His Turkish forces marched in, took control of the city, and then headed for their primary target, Vienna. In 1529, they laid siege to the city to the horror of

Europe. Vienna managed to hold out against the Turks, but the damage to Tamás Nádasdy's reputation was done.

Although "imprisoned" by the Turks, Tamás Nádasdy meanwhile charmed his captors who knew he had given Buda to them. The following year, Szapolyai, now a powerful lord of the Sultan, honored Nádasdy by making him Master of the Treasury. This would suggest that Nádasdy had done his share of dealmaking before handing Buda over to Szapolyai. The honor was ultimately an embarrassment, however, for many of Szapolyai's followers still thought of Nádasdy as a dishonorable turn-coat who had betrayed Ferdinand. Tamás Nádasdy had to do something to save face; in other words, he would have to fight gloriously for Szapolyai and the Turks now. That said, he headed up an army of over 10,000 troops and attacked one of Ferdinand's holdings, the castle at Szigetvar. The siege was a success, and Szapolyai gave the 32-year-old Nádasdy the Fagaras region of Transylvania as a gift.

Tamás Nádasdy then used his connections on both sides to force Ferdinand and Szapolyai into a temporary truce for the sake of the country. It is during this brief period of relative calm that he also turned his attention toward getting a wife. Nádasdy now had some property and status, but he wanted more: the second daughter of László Kanizsai, a seven-year-old child named Orsolya, was the only remaining heir to the massive Kanizsai fortune. Marriage negotiations began and, that same year in 1530, the couple became engaged. Tamás would have to wait five more years for Orsolya to come of age, however, planning to marry her in 1535.

Only one thing now stood in the way of Tamás securing the massive Kanizsai holdings for himself: the Kanizsai family was still loyal to Ferdinand. If Nádasdy was to take possession of Orsolya's massive tracts of land, villages, and castles, he would have to change his allegiance yet again, back to Ferdinand and the Hapsburgs. Negotiations began; Tamás promised loyalty to his original lord, Ferdinand, in exchange for his wife's properties. Happy to have him back, Ferdinand agreed, promising Nádasdy additional grants of land from the Emperor as a wedding gift.

Angered by Nádasdy's treachery, however, Szapolyai and the Turks vowed revenge. In 1532, Turkish forces attacked Nádasdy's towns of Sárvár and Leka (Lockenhaus), acquired from Orsolya's family. In each instance, the small garrisons of both towns managed to repel the Turks (considered a miracle by the local people). Luckily for Tamás Nádasdy, the Hapsburgs and the Ottoman Turks began peace talks soon after and reached another cease-fire agreement in June 1533: Ferdinand acknowledged Sultan Suleyman as "father and suzerain," agreed to pay an annual tribute, and give up all Hungarian holdings acquired after the original Ottoman conquest. His rival, Szapolyai, was crowned king of central Hungary, serving under the sultan.

Peace restored, matters quieted for Tamás Nádasdy. So long as he paid tribute, he was left alone. Returning now to his vast estates, he married Orsolya in 1535 and immediately set about turning Sárvár into a true Renaissance city. He built a magnificent new castle on the marshes and established a cultural center in the crumbling, war-struck town. In 1534 he founded a school and, in 1537, a printing house in Újsziget. Nádasdy placed János Sylvester in charge of both, also appointing him teacher at the school. Sylvester promptly translated the New Testament into Hungarian and printed it in 1541, creating the first printed book in Hungary. Although a Catholic when he needed to be (particularly around Ferdinand and the Hapsburgs), Tamás Nádasdy also championed the new Protestant movement, inviting Lutheran scholars to Sárvár. He filled his palace with artwork and surrounded himself with scientists, doctors, humanists, theologians, musicians, and painters while rising steadily through the political ranks.

The peace between Ferdinand and the Turks was not to last, unfortunately, and even Szapolyai began to fear unchecked Turkish expansion. Clashes continued and diplomacy, as well as warfare, took Tamás Nádasdy away from home frequently. From 1537 onwards, he became one of Ferdinand's most influential counselors, spending much of each year at Court in Vienna and Prague. Subsequently, he defended the border provinces against the Turks. In 1540, the same year that János Szapolyai died, Tamás Nádasdy was appointed iudex curie regie (royal court judge); in 1547 he presided over the Diet of Nagyszombat, and finally, in 1559, was elected Palatine (Prime Minister) of Hungary by the Diet of Pozsony (now Bratislava, Slovakia).

5

THE LETTERS OF TAMÁS AND ORSOLYA NÁDASDY

As a result of her tutelage at Ecsed, Erzsébet Báthory learned to write in the controlled, classical style of Latin and Greek, typically avoiding any sort of flowery language or poetics. In later letters to her husband, in fact, she avoided any "kiss-and-tell" language, using only simple and respectful forms of address and conclusions, such as, "your loving wife," or "at your service." Indeed, her tone was often formal, with expressions such as: "Congratulations on your good fortune," or, "I have received your numerous letters. Let God keep you in good health."

This is in stark contrast to the often lyrical and even poetic letters between Tamás and Orsolya Nádasdy. Tamás, for example, would frequently tease about his age, calling himself "your old grey vulture," or "your old cod piece," and write in full phrases, such as, "Your letter caused me great pleasure." Although some commentators claim that Orsolya Nádasdy could neither read nor write, this is not true. The letters between Tamás and Orsolya Nádasdy are some of the finest examples of mid-sixteenth-century writing of the nobility, and a great deal of correspondence, written in their own hands, has been preserved to this day. Orsolya was unable to read and write when the couple first married; Tamás saw to it, however, that she received tutoring. Within a few years, she was fluent, although she still found it physically difficult to write, and it took her considerable time to do so.

From their letters, we also learn much about their relationship, including the ill health that Orsolya frequently suffered. The act of writing, apparently, was even thought to contribute to her weakened condition: "My beloved Orsolya," cautioned Tamás in 1552, "you have done well not to write with your own hand. You are not to do so henceforth either, because it is common knowledge that whereas three fingers are writing, the whole body is at work."

One month later, she dictated the following: "Why I cannot write myself, Your Honor, You must forgive me, for I dare not exert myself in bed, not even with writing."

Despite the time and (physical) effort required, it would appear that the two preferred the privacy of writing directly to one another rather than dictating their content to scribes. They reserved dictation only when rushed or ill. For example, in 1553, Orsolya apologized: "…Your Honor should forgive me for having this letter written in another hand, for I could not perform it myself, owing to the urgent departure of the post."

The Palatine himself also apologized for having been too busy to write: "Forgive me, therefore, my beloved kinswoman, for not writing this letter in my own hand, for the many activities I conduct."

On another occasion, Tamás urged, "Write to me every day, I beseech you, about your condition, but do not tire yourself, for whatever you may entrust either the estate steward or the castellan to write [have them do for you], but whatever is not becoming to be written about by them (such as women's maladies) you should have my woman sister take down when she has no headaches." (This "woman sister" was a relative of Tamás Nádasdy, the widow of István Majláth).

Orsolya was treated by the noted doctor and herbalist, Gáspár Körös. Apparently, his treatments helped. By 1560, she was able to write again by herself and used her letter to reassure her husband of her improving condition: "My handwriting is proof enough," she reasoned, "that a sick person cannot write this much."

The following day, he replied: "Do give me a reply to my letter, I beseech you. When you write that you are in good health and I can learn about this by seeing letters in your own hand, then I believe you, and I also rejoice because of your healthy state....I have also written to you more with my two hands in these days."

6

FERENC NÁDASDY

Although frequently separated by business deals, affairs of state, or warfare, Tamás and Orsolya Nádasdy tried repeatedly to have children: they had two sons, László and Márton, both of whom died young. By the mid 1550's, Tamás was nearing 60 years of age and, given the correspondence between them, Orsolya was apparently still in an on-and-off-again state of ill health. Time was running out.

Desperate for a male heir, the couple entered into a contract with nobleman Gábor Majláth so as to adopt from his family and thus consolidate the clans' fortunes. However, just as the agreement concluded, it was announced that Orsolya was pregnant. Although the news no doubt dashed the Majláth family's hopes of buying into a dynastic fortune, the birth of the Nádasdys' long-awaited heir, Ferenc, was obviously a source of great joy for them. Ferenc was born on October 6, 1555. Tamás was away at court and met his new son for the first time upon returning home for Christmas a few months later.

There is no question that Orsolya and Tamás doted over the boy who would someday become Hungary's national war hero and Erzsébet Báthory's husband. Orsolya maintained meticulous journals on his academic progress and filled pages of letters with commentary on his every move. Tamás wrote frequently to his son, often referring to himself as, "Your Old Daddy," or "Your Old Lieutenant." They gave their son the nickname, Ferkó.

Like any child, Ferkó frequently requested gifts of toys and food from his father. By the time the boy reached the age of five, it was determined that he should no longer expect to get something for nothing. Writing to Orsolya, Tamás said that he had bought the requested gift this time, but: "Unless he writes himself next time, I shall not send or give him anything."

That said, young Ferkó penned the following letter to his father:

> *Great and Respected, Reverend Sir, my Loving Father,*
>
> *At your service and mercy I write to you with love, my Father. May I ask that you not despise me and send me trumpet and drum kit. May I also ask your mercy and love, as my father, that you please send me pomagranates, small calamari...and that you write soon. I love you.*
>
> *Your son,*
>
> *Ferenc Nádasdy*

Both Tamás and Orsolya worried about the unstable political situation and the boy's future in an increasingly dangerous world. It is said that when Ferkó was less than a year old, his father ordered that the child be raised such that he never have "soft eyes." Tamás also felt that the boy was terribly spoiled by his mother. In another letter to Orsolya, he told her to entrust Ferkó to someone who would "spank him when necessary." It is likely that young Ferenc began military training at an early age.

THE ENGAGEMENT OF ERZSÉBET BÁTHORY TO FERENC NÁDASDY

Judging by the boy's letters, however, playing soldier was already one of his favorite games.

In 1560, when Ferenc was five, the Nádasdy family inherited a playmate for him—a little boy named Györkó Öry. In his will, the child's father left the boy to the Nádasdys as a permanent servant. Tamás sent Györkó to Sárvár with the message that "Ferenc should receive him into his court." The fact that Ferenc had his own court at the age of five was exceptional; being an only child, however, was also exceptional.

The couple would not live to see their only son grow up, however, nor have the pleasure of meeting their grandchildren. Tamás Nádasdy passed away first, in 1562, when Ferenc was only seven. After a lengthy period of mourning, including the erection of a massive memorial to her husband, Orsolya began to consider her son's future more seriously, as well as her own. Her young Ferkó was already studying with some of the greatest minds of the time at Sárvár, including the noted preacher and botanist, István Beythe (1532-1612). Ferenc studied with Beythe until the age of ten, when Beythe left Sárvár in 1565. From there, Demeter Sibolti (Tholnensis) assumed the role of primary tutor, from 1565-68. At the age of 12 (1567), Ferenc left for Vienna to further his education, accompanied by Demeter Sibolti and other Lutheran tutors. He would remain there for two years, until 1569. Ferenc must have enjoyed his work with Sibolti; in July of 1568, he wrote that he was a "grateful pupil." Ferenc also began formal military training as a cadet assigned to barracks set up along the Austro-Hungarian border. While at the King's Court, he met up with two boys that would also have notable careers in Hungarian history: István Bocskai (1557-1606), leader of the revolution in Transylvania, and the famous Hungarian poet, Bálint Balassi (1554-1594).

However, as his mother recounted, her son was growing up to be a skilled athlete and warrior, popular with the other boys, but "no scholar." She worried more than once over what would become of him when his strength failed. For the time being, though, a military career seemed nearly certain: by the time Ferenc reached his teen years, border skirmishes and raids with the Turks were occurring again.

Meanwhile, young Ferenc freely came and went, enjoying his school friends and pursuits, while his mother continued to obsess about his future and her own. Orsolya's health problems continued, and she would need to find a wife for him soon. Soon, the business of managing the vast Kanizsai-Nádasdy estates would fall upon him, and it was clear that he needed a strong—and intelligent—helpmate. In addition, in order to preserve the vast family fortune, he would also require a young lady of equal or better wealth and social status.

The choice seemed obvious: young Erzsébet Báthory was already known for her superior intelligence even as a child, and, more important, her illustrious family name held even more prestige and status than that of the Kanizsai-Nádasdys. In addition, Erzsébet's mother, Anna, and Orsolya Nádasdy were related through marriage on the Dragffy side of the family. Talks between the families began with the goal of a marriage contract.

While some marriage proposals amongst the nobility were spontaneous, most were negotiated heavily with great emphasis placed on following strict rules and lengthy periods of courtship. Property terms were also carefully crafted, considering that vast tracts of land, possessions and money would either transfer hands or stay within a family, as clans united politically as well as economically. Beneficiaries had to be considered, as did the preservation and enhancement of power on both sides. In some cases, families even negotiated the unthinkable: an assassination or "mysterious death" of a party to the marriage contract could result in a forfeiture or reversion of assets.

On December 21, 1572, with the wedding contract concluded, the now 12-year-old Erzsébet Báthory was formally engaged to 17-year-old Count Ferenc Nádasdy de Nádasd et

THE ENGAGEMENT OF ERZSÉBET BÁTHORY TO FERENC NÁDASDY

Fogarasföld at Castle Csicsva. Around this time, she left her family home in the countryside to travel to the Nádasdy family seat at Sárvár. We cannot be sure if Erzsébet ever visited Sárvár before this, but we can say with relative certainty that she must have been somewhat awed, if not culture shocked, upon arrival. Unlike the Báthory family, steeped in its long history that emphasized classical training and the traditions of the Middle Ages, the Nádasdy family's palace at Sárvár was bursting with all that was new—music, art, books, inventions, and religion—with an eye clearly toward the future.

In Erzsébet's time, the castle at Sárvár was approached by a long rampart and surrounded by a moat as wide as a river. The town and castle sat amidst wetlands with a few homes situated on boggy islands that accommodated staff. In the summer, the stench of swamp water, along with clouds of mosquitoes, plagued the residents, while biting insects tormented the horses in their stables. It is no wonder that, in the future, Erzsébet would typically spend summers at her other estates, preferring to reside at Sárvár court only in the colder months of winter. The young Countess was probably used to these conditions, however; her own family estate at Ecsed also sat amidst its share of bogs, marshes, and wetlands.

Although much has been made of the terrible relationship between young Erzsébet and her mother-in-law, Countess Orsolya Nádasdy, that they hated each other and that Erzsébet learned various methods of cruelty from watching her future mother-in-law discipline servants at Sárvár, such animosity—or lessons in cruelty—could not have lasted very long. Orsolya Nádasdy died in the spring of 1571—possibly before the young Erzsébet even arrived at Sárvár. How well the child knew her prior to the engagement is questionable, but they certainly did not spend any meaningful amount of time together.

Without Orsolya's watchful eye, and with her fiancé off at school or away on adventures with friends, Erzsébet probably had considerable free time. The Nádasdy court flaunted its money on parties and patronizing the arts: artists, philosophers, schools, and libraries flourished there. It is likely that young Erzsébet indulged at least a few of her intellectual passions here, studying with some of Europe's great tutors on staff at Sárvár. If nothing else, she was certainly exposed to the most contemporary thought of her time.

On the other hand, she may also have been quite unhappy there. The culture at Sárvár was quite different from her upbringing at Ecsed. The Báthory family appears to have either indulged or simply ignored young Erzsébet, in any case permitting her to engage in her male pursuits and frequent temper tantrums. At Sárvár, however, it was a different matter. She was being groomed now to be a wife and noblewoman of high station, which included eating, dressing, walking, and speaking like a lady. The showdowns between this strong-willed country girl and her courtly tutors must have been formidable, to say the least.

Sárvár was also a large and well-run estate, and there may have been long stretches of time in which Erzsébet went unsupervised with little to do. Likely, she got into trouble. That may explain a story that has persisted to this day: in 1573, two years before her wedding, the thirteen-year-old became involved in an illicit affair with a young man while staying at the Nádasdy manor in Trnava. The gossip of history tells us that his name was Ladislav Bende. The property in Trnava does indeed exist, and a certain László, or Ladislav, Bende did, indeed, live there.

Located on the Danube in the fortified walls of Trnava, the bride-to-be occupied a small manor house during that summer. There, she became attracted to a young man named László Bende. He supposedly had a magnetic personality and heroic manner. Some commentators state that he was a servant and table waiter; others claim that he was a young nobleman.

In 1894, Ferdinand von Strobl Ravelsberg authored a biography of the Countess entitled, *Die Blutgräfin (Erzsébet Báthory): Ein Sitten und Charakterbild* (The Blood Countess (Elizabeth Bathory): A Study and Character Portrait). Writing under the pen name, R.A. von Elsberg, he wrote that her virginity was robbed (*virginitatem suam*) and she was brought into perpetual infamy (*in perpetuam infamiam*). According to the story, Erzsébet became pregnant by Bende and gave birth to a daughter. The baby immediately disappeared, taken somewhere into Sedmohrad (Transylvania), probably Wallachia (today, part of Romania). Accordingly, the Báthory family did everything possible to cover up the scandal, including hush money to raise the child in secret; as etiquette dictated, the wedding with Ferenc Nádasdy proceeded in spite of the bride's transgression. Legend also has it that the furious bridegroom had László Bende castrated, throwing his severed private parts to the dogs.

Von Elsberg provided the additional details that a pregnant Erzsébet Báthory actually appeared before the priests at the Cathedral Chapter of Esztergom on the day before the Feast of St. Martin (November 11) to lodge a formal complaint and admission that seven months prior, during Holy Week, she had been forcibly abducted by Ladislav Bende and then raped. The seducer had also drugged her with an extract of hempseed. Von Elsberg speculated that a failed abortion was initially attempted when the pregnancy was discovered. Moreover, to appease the bridegroom's family and permit the wedding to proceed, both complaint against Bende and documentation of the rape were required from the church. The future bride's reputation now cleared, she was "in an instant made a countess, and as such, imposed as the wife of Ferenc Nádasdy." Von Elsberg states that two documents, both with the same date, were prepared by church authorities: *Protestaria Elisabethae Bathory*, sub fol. 210 Liber II, and *Civitate libera regia Tyrnavense feria II, proxima ante festum S. Martini episcope et confessoris 1609.*

If this indeed true, then one can only wonder about the strange date of both church records: 1609. This is because in November of the year 1609, when the teenaged countess supposedly made her accusation against the rapist, Erzsébet Báthory was *49 years old*—hardly a virgin maiden. (Von Elsberg, unfortunately, does not seem to notice the bizarre discrepancy.)

In 1932, the Slovakian author, Jožo Nižňanský, wrote his own biography of the Countess, "Lady of Csejthe" (*Cachtická Pani*). With all the trappings of a great Gothic novel, he brought serialized legends of the so-called Bloody Lady back to life, thrilling a new generation who had never heard of Countess Báthory. Whether its details are true or not, Nižňanský also rekindled interest in the story of Erzsébet's torrid love affair with László Bende and lost baby.

7

THE WEDDING (1575)

Pre-marital affair or not, the wedding took place according to plan. On May 8, 1575 (months before either of their birthdays), 14-year-old Erzsébet and 19-year-old Ferenc married at Varanno Castle in Vranov (present-day Slovakia) in a celebration that went on for days. At this point, the parents of both bride and groom were deceased. However, the alliance of these two powerful families was essentially an affair of state conducted by legions of courtiers and remaining aunts, uncles, and cousins. By all accounts, its lavishness rivaled that of a king's wedding, with 4,500 invited guests, including an invitation to the Holy Roman Emperor himself, Maximillian II (son of Tamás Nádasdy's on-and-off-again protector, Ferdinand). Nothing suggests that Maximillian wished to avoid the event; however, fearful of traveling through Turkish-occupied lands from his court in Prague, the Emperor sent his apologies along with an official delegation and lavish gift.

Two weeks before the wedding, in an imperial, hand-written letter addressed to the Hungarian Court Chamber in Vienna, the Emporer wrote:

We have respectfully asked Ferenc Nádasdy, after he proposed marriage to the late Count György Báthory's daughter, Erzsébet Báthory—to be joyfully celebrated on Sunday the 8th, in the coming month of May at Varanno—to know that it is our delight and desire to send our wedding envoy delegation. And (we) graciously granted, in accord with his obedient request, an order for a master craftsman to build a decorative credenza. We commend their mercy that they receive a silver-overlaid goblet or a picher and basin valued at 200 Thaler to be brought to them instead of our appearance at their wedding, the delivery of which is to be ordered. In addition, we graciously want you to know that the Roman Empress, our amiable, beloved spouse, thought Nádasdy should also receive a goblet worth 100 Thaler, and we desire to allocate the money for that. So we have also graciously granted that our amiable, beloved sons, Rudolph, King of Hungary, and Archduke Ernst of Austria, should also provide cups worth 150 Thaler, as well as have the credenza inscribed, and issue this gracious command: Your choice will certainly be honored, whether they bring the serving cups with them and herewith order them, or you have the craftsman make them in a style similar to our Spanish Court (as otherwise will not pay for it). This indicates our gracious will and opinion. Prague, 26 April 1575.

Amidst the roar of trumpets, drums, and ceremonial cannon and musket firing, the wedding festivities began with a joust and tournament. Cantoring past field banners and flags, the young groom rode in to the cheers of the attending visitors, including his bride-to-be. Here he attempted to prove not only his athletic ability but also his loyalty by securing the wreath or garter that would be worn by his new bride. It is certain that he won the tournament, presenting his Lady with her prize at the end of the event.

Later, his retinue would meet up with the bridal party where the young people exchanged jokes, flirtations, and gifts. It was here that Ferenc formally presented his bride with her wedding gift: Castle Csejthe (Hung.: Csejte; Slovak: Čachtice) and its 17 accompanying villages. The property had been acquired by his mother in 1569, and she had given it to Ferenc as a gift. He now transferred it to Erzsébet. We are not certain of her reaction; perhaps, the 14-year-old girl would have preferred something more whimsical or personal than property she had likely never seen. In any case, she accepted.

As the guests moved on to the halls and temporary pavilions to enjoy the first round of feasting and music, the final ritual took place before the wedding ceremony: Ferenc would have to prove his loyalty and love for his new bride. The bride, along with members of the bridal retinue, covered their faces with veils, and each girl paraded before Ferenc pretending to be the bride-to-be. In a comic show, the young ladies imitated the bride with dramaticized gestures and movements, and it was up to him to select the true bride over her imitators. Upon selecting the correct young lady, Erzsébet lifted her veil, revealing her face to a round of applause and a kiss from the groom.

Now, the actual religious ceremony could take place. In those days, the bride did not wear a white wedding gown. Young ladies from common families wore traditional, brightly-colored dresses. A noble like Erzsébet wore an elaborate gown ladeled with silks, embroidery, and jewels. (She would keep this gown her entire life and actually mentioned it in her Will of 1610.) As Ferenc had been raised a Lutheran, the Protestant service was somewhat similar to a Catholic Wedding Mass. A blue ribbon united the hands of the couple as the union was blessed.

Now married, the young couple was escorted to the banquet hall where they and their retinue were seated at a long table on a raised dais. The most important guests were seated in the hall with them at long tables; other guests dined in ancillary pavilions outside. Feasting, drinking and music went on for hours, including traditional Hungarian, Spanish, Italian and Polish dances. For the invited clergy who were not permitted to touch the bride yet still desired a dance with her, they circled around her or touched the blue ribbon in her hand. At the end of the day, the groom's retinue escorted the bridal couple by torchlight to the bridal chamber. They would stand vigil to ensure that the couple consummated the marriage before retiring themselves or continuing with the festivities.

Although the specifics are lost to us today, we do have some idea of how elaborate the wedding must have been and what was typical for the high nobility of the time. For example, when György Thurzó's daughter Zsuzsanna wed in 1603, records detail the tremendous amount of food required for the festivity. Spices and fruit were purchased in Vienna, while animals, produce, and oats were obtained from surrounding estates. Thurzo purchased 200 pounds of pepper, 50 pounds of ginger, 25 pounds of garlic bulbs, 4 pounds of hazelnut, 1000 lemons, 500 oranges, and 253 pounds of honey. From his barons, Thurzo demanded, among other things, 36 bulls, 118 calves, 103 sheep, 58 lambs, 119 pigs, 185 rabbits, 526 geese, 381 capons, 785 chickens, 420 ducks, 5,333 eggs, 1,600 trout, countless crayfish, and 35 carts of oats. And the wedding of Ferenc and Erzsébet was likely similar—perhaps even larger—than this.

Commentators mention that Erzsébet chose to retain her maiden name rather than take her husband's, citing the fact that hers was older and more prestigious. They go on to say that Ferenc even added her name to his own, thus becoming Ferenc Báthory-Nádasdy. Documents from the period indicate that Countess Báthory signed correspondence, as well as her last will and testament, in her own name. Her contemporaries, however, did not always acknowledge the Báthory surname—nor did her husband. In public addresses and court documents, she was typically referred to as "Lady Nádasdy" or, in later years, "Lady Widow Nádasdy." Letters, as well as a portrait of Ferenc, lists his name not as Báthory-Nádasdy but as Ferenc Nádasdy or Ferenc Nádasdy de Nádasd et Fogarasföld.

Both Ferenc and Erzsébet inherited their parents' vast properties, generating enormous wealth for the new couple. Collectively, they would own thousands of acres of land throughout various counties, along with dozens of towns and more than 20 castles across present-day Hungary, Slovakia, Austria, Romania, and the Czech Republic, including: Lánzser, Léka (or Lockenaus, the burial place of Tamás and Orsolya Nádasdy) and Sopronkeresztúr in present-day Austria; Beckó (Beckov), Csejthe (including castle and 17 villages), Csicsva, Dévény, Nagybicse, Rozgony, and Varannó in Slovakia and the Czech Republic; Fogaras, Somlyó, and Szátmar in present-day Romania; and Buják, Egervár, Füzér, Kapuvar, Nagyecsed, Nagykanizsa, Onod, and Sárvár in present-day Hungary. In a short time, in fact, they would possess more wealth than the King of Hungary.

THE EARLY YEARS OF MARRIAGE
(1575-1585)

It is hard to know the exact relationship between Ferenc and Erzsébet, except from what we learn through witness testimony and the couple's correspondence. By all accounts, Erzsébet was a good wife and mother, at least publicly. With the exception of her alleged pre-marital indiscretion, she did nothing to raise eyes in the early years of her marriage. She attended official functions with her husband, publicly practiced religion, gave money to the poor, protected widows, and even assisted with the administration of health care for her staff and surrounding villagers. Based on her own letters, we know of several instances where she intervened on behalf of destitute women, including one whose husband was captured by the Turks and another whose daughter was raped and impregnated. In fact, György Thurzó, later Palatine of Hungary and the man who would someday apprehend the "Bloody Countess," commented to one of his own daughters that she "should be more like" Erzsébet.

In 1578, three years after their wedding, Ottoman Turks were again conducting open raids across the countryside. Mindful that Ferenc' father, Tamás, had betrayed both Szapolyai and the Turks, the younger Nádasdy now set about refortifying the family properties and collecting an army in preparation to meet the enemy. He had prepared for this moment his entire life, and the thrill of finally riding off to battle must have been exhilarating for him. Ferenc, together with his military comrades, Zrínyi, Erdödy, Batthyányi, and Palffy, would come to be known as the "unholy quintet," and clash repeatedly with the Turks over the years. Ferenc would soon earn the title, "High Stable Master" in 1587, as well as "The Black Bey" (a Turkish title, meaning "chieftan" or "lord") and "The Black Knight of Hungary" from his enemies. In his role as Captain of the Hungarian Army, he would eventually spend his entire life engaged in warfare against the Ottoman Turks.

For his 18-year-old wife, however, Ferenc' departure left her alone for long periods of time in the huge family home at Sárvár. The couple had not yet had children, and Sárvár, by all accounts, continued to be well staffed and well run. Until she fully established herself as mistress of the house and chief administrator of the vast estates in her husband's absence, she probably had little to do.

Commentators suggest that, during this time, Erzsébet made frequent trips to visit her bisexual aunt, Klara, with whom she learned witchcraft, torture, and how to make love to women. Given Klara's estimated date of birth some time around the early 1520's, she would have been nearly 60 years old now in an age when few people survived to 50. We are not certain if she was even alive at this point, but would have at least been in her waning years. How instructive she was to her young niece is questionable, if the stories are true at all.

While Erzsébet's aunt is reputed to have practiced witchcraft, we also know that many women accused of such during the period were actually practitioners of folk art and herbal medicine. Such practices were not limited to the peasantry or so-called "forest witches," but popular amongst the nobility, as well. Ironically, folk medicine was fairly tolerated during

Erzsébet's time; some years later, during the witchhunts that blazed across Europe, such practices would come under intense scrutiny.

Commentators also suggest that a bored Erzsébet spent her free time engaging in sexual horseplay with male servants, particularly a man named István Jezorlay. However, in the legions of trial documents and testimony of approximately three hundred servants and eyewitnesses, no emphasis is placed on any sort of repeated or blatant sexual misconduct on the part of Erzsébet. Only one witness, in fact—Janós Felon—accused her of having an affair once with a young soldier and servant, Vitus Trombitás, before he was killed at the front fighting for Ferenc Nádasdy. This is not to say that Erzsébet never engaged in illicit activities; however, if she did, she and her servants were exceptionally discreet. Even when under lock and key years later, her servants both past and present probably still feared her. However, many servants were no longer in her direct employ by then and, during the last round of depositions, knew that she had little hope of ever being released. Thus, apart from fear or healthy respect, they had little to lose by disclosing past misdeeds. The fact that they said so little on the matter, particularly in an age when women, in general, were routinely accused of sexual misconduct or some form of witchcraft—no matter the main charge—is significant.

Also significant is that the four accomplices who participated in the most heinous deeds near the end of Erzsébet's life— all of whom had their testimony extracted under torture—made no mention of sexual misconduct on her part either. Witnesses, particularly amongst the Sárvár staff, do mention that certain portions of Sárvár Castle were under guard and that access was forbidden. Nevertheless, the witnesses believed that such secret chambers were used for torturing servants rather than illicit sex play.

There are also signs to indicate that Erzsébet was, at least at times, a passive partner in the marriage: Ferenc clearly did as he pleased, often without telling his wife about his activities or dealings. In 1596, for example, she discovered through a third party that he had gone off to Transylvania with no clear purpose for the trip. She rebuked him angrily, although it thinly disguises hurt feelings:

> *I found out from a letter of His Majesty that you went from Vas (the county in which Castle Sárvár was located) to Transylvania, and I find that very surprising, since nothing good can come from Transylvania. The same land from which we collect the harvest is also the land from which we receive bad news. All are surprised about this, because you did not take possession of any property in Transylvania. You live from the yield and fat of this country, so why did you leave this country? We do not understand this, as we have learned from the first letter of our friend, about which I wrote, who highly questions me. This has affected me very much, and when I heard it, I was very bitter. God maintain your health.*

Ferenc Nádasy, on the other hand, never appeared to speak ill of his wife in public and, on more than one occasion, defended her honor against what would soon become an increasingly critical clergy. In correspondence with others, he spoke either lovingly of her or simply referred to her state of health.

9

COMING OF AGE (1585-1600)

By her mid-twenties, Countess Báthory had finally settled into a routine. Ferenc was routinely away fighting the Turks now, and it became clear even to his family staff that the Lady Nádasdy was there to stay. She was now the one to whom they would report. During these years, she spent the majority of her time at Sárvár and Kereszstúr castles, the centerpieces of the Nádasdy family holdings. However, she visited all of the other properties at least once a year. She also resided periodically at the family manor in Vienna, co-owned with the Batthyányi family. When Castle Sárvár underwent a substantial reconstruction, the Countess chose to spend more time at her other residences.

We can say that her lifestyle was typical of noblewomen of her time. Upon arising, she would begin a rather lengthy process of dressing, typically with the assistance of her ladies in waiting. If attending a formal event or receiving visitors, she would have to rise very early, even before sunrise, to begin a more elaborate process that involved extensive hair and makeup work. On an ordinary day, the process could take two to three hours; for affairs of state, possibly four to six. Breakfast might be taken during or after the procedure, depending on time constraints.

COMING OF AGE (1585-1600)

On a typical day, she would spend time looking after the estate, managing staff, consulting with her court officials and supervisors, dictating or writing letters, paying bills, reviewing documents, making rounds both inside and outside the manor, and receiving visitors. Lunch would be taken around 11:00 a.m. In later years, after the birth of her children, she would look in on them and meet with their nannies and tutors. She would also spend time at chapel and religious services.

Depending on how many appointments she had scheduled, some free time might be available. Leisure time included horseback riding, picnics, hunts, drives into town, and reading. We know that the Countess enjoyed going to the spa at Piešťany, as well as shopping and attending concerts in Vienna. Some noblewomen played musical instruments and created elaborate handicrafts, although we have no record of Countess Báthory engaging in either pursuit. In addition to affairs of state and appearances at court, parties were common; the nobility entertained frequently. Also, traveling musicians, entertainers, acting troupes and poets often came to town to perform.

Dinner would be served around 6:00 p.m. She had the option to eat in the formal diningroom or have dinner brought up to her by staff. If no visitors or parties were scheduled for the evening, the Countess would retreat to her bed chamber by dark. According to witnesses, her "evening entertainments" could go on for hours after that.

In Erzsébet's time, the household staff was divided primarily into male servants who answered to the Lord (e.g., the castellan, steward, house manager, stable master, etc.) and the female servants who answered primarily to the Lady (kitchen staff, washer women, seamstresses, and so forth). Both Lord and Lady also had personal attendants who waited on them, helped them dress, and kept them company. When the Lord was away, administrative direction for the entire staff came from the Lady of the House who also took charge in his absence.

In the case of the vast Nádasdy holdings that included dozens of castles, manor homes, villages, thousands of acres of land

and hundreds of staff members, Erzsébet was ultimately responsible for running all of it when Ferenc was away. She was also responsible for arbitrating disputes for servants and locals, maintaining defenses against the Turks along the border, and even conducting sensitive matters of diplomacy.

For example, in 1587, her uncle, Cardinal András Báthory, sent a private message to Erzsébet who, apparently, was running the estate by herself at the time:

> *Let this present letter be delivered by hand to my beloved sister...I desire everything be well for my beloved sister. I had to depart to Rome and inform them of the sad news of the death of King István (Báthory, King of Poland and Silesia). I pray that the man who delivered this letter to you remains lodged at your court unknown, for his mission requires that he meet at the first opportunity. My man escorted the noble lord from Venice. He is a large supporter of our family and thus, I ask your pardon on this, that you take care of him. I trust that your court has enough of everything which he requires.*

(The reader will notice that the term *sister* was used in those days as a term of endearment.)

More than ten years into the marriage, there are still no obvious signs that Erzsébet was on a collision course to becoming one of the worst serial killers of all time. On May 12, 1588, for example, she wrote a short letter in her typically curt style. However, it is courteous and completely normal by all accounts, demonstrating that she had at least a cordial relationship with a certain Mrs. Ponticzka:

> *So then, how are you, dear Mrs. Ponticzka, our good sister. Greetings. I wish to say that, if you*

so desire, send me at once a book about ailments of the back, and that you write and tell me how Lord Ghuczi is, and about yourself, if you are happy or not.

Her Ladyship, Erzsébet Báthory (by her own hand)

Another letter sent off by the Countess, now 29 years old, was dated November 5, 1589. This one was written to a family servant, Imre Vasvari:

...We have received your letter along with the supplies of food. We especially thank you for the delivery. Be advised that even if my husband does not return home, you should know, sir, that these provisions should still be sent to us. Accordingly, heed us, that you are to send on Saturday as usual whatever you have on hand and the rest later on or else, behold, I will be angry because I expect to entertain when my husband himself returns home. For tomorrow evening, send cod and crawfish. I understand that you distributed food to the poor, but accordingly, we establish that you care for the estate and act in accordance to adjust the kitchen for whatever we need. Let God provide for you.

While Erzsébet Báthory typically wrote in a formal style, and Vasvari might have deserved her anger, there is a certain tone of lofty or superior impatience that can now be found in her writing. This same sort of imperious tone can also be observed in letters to her Court Master, Benedikt (Benedek) Deseö, whom she rebuked several times, and in other examples of Erzsébet's correspondence, which she herself maintained. Indeed, several of these logs or journals of her conversations were used as source material by hostile witnesses testifying against her in later years. By the 1580's, Erzsébet Báthory was clearly the Lady of the House and running a tight ship.

From her letter, there is also a suggestion that she felt tension to make certain everything was in perfect order for Ferenc' arrival home and that the estate be well supplied with provisions. Lord Nádasdy's homecomings were cause for great pomp and circumstance. Accompanied by his lieutenants and attending retinue, Hungary's Chief Captain of the Army arrived amidst a flurry of trumpets, drums, banners and battle flags. In some cases, hundreds of his troops came along as well, pitching tents and setting up camp outside the castle on the estate property.

Ferenc brought with him the spoils of war, including captured horses and livestock, and wagon trains loaded down with anything that he and his men could carry off: tapestries, carpets, furniture, weapons, musical instruments, kitchenware, silks, jewels, and gold. The inner rooms of his castles were a cross between a museum and a storage room. When the plundered spoils overflowed, they were moved down into cellars and underground tunnels.

Dozens of pigs, chickens, sheep, and game were slaughtered for the feasting that followed. Often, neighboring nobility and family members would be invited to visit, many staying on for days. Reveling went on all night. After the presentation of various speeches, toasts, and entertainments, the Lord and his closest guests sat drinking and laughing in front of the fire long after the Lady and her retinue went to bed. For the staff, it was a grueling marathon of keeping cups filled, plates full, beds made, stables cleaned, garments washed, and halls cleared. Both Lord and Lady's staff were on high alert until the last guest finally departed. After that, the long clean-up process began.

Before departing himself, Ferenc and Erzsébet sat together or with their administrators to discuss household business: taxes that needed to be paid, paperwork requiring signatures and seals, decisions regarding salaries and stipends, upkeep on property, and funds needed to run the estates during Lord Nádasdy's coming sojourn. Directives were issued, and then the Lord and his men began loading up their wagons with provisions, buckling on swords, and saddling up their horses. The front was never far from Ferenc Nádasdy's properties, and his military services were in constant demand from both King and Emperor. Likely, he didn't mind; prior to and throughout the course of the Fifteen Years War, or so-called "Long War" (1593-1606), Ferenc was present at nearly every battle, fighting continuously even when in ill health until his death in 1604.

10

THE NÁDASDY CHILDREN

One matter still remained open, however: the issue of children and heirs to the family fortune. There is no record of a child until the birth of their daughter, Anna, around 1585, ten years after the couple wed. It is not completely clear why Erzsébet and Ferenc waited so long to have children: commentators have speculated the obvious, that Ferenc was away at war so often that it was a physical impossibility.

Others have speculated that Ferenc resented his deflowered bride for years after their wedding. It may also be that the two secretly hated each other, with even the possibility that both ultimately preferred the company of the same sex. Again, however, any hatred between them was either kept private or, at least, their servants remained discreet regarding the matter. Eyewitness testimony does not dwell on any obvious or open hostility between the couple.

This would be typical of the time, however. Since marriages amongst nobles were arranged for them as children and established primarily for business or political reasons, couples rarely married for love. Many kept lovers on the side. Legally, the marital arrangement demanded that the couple attend public functions together, have children, and exhibit polite courtesy to the other. Behind closed doors, however, it was quite a different story. The love expressed between Tamás and Orsolya Nádasdy was the rare exception; the typical aristocratic couple slept in separate bedrooms, maintained separate personal staff and, with rare exception, had little to do with the other.

It may also be, however, that Erzsébet had fertility problems. At the time, much of the Hungarian nobility suffered from problems of sterility and infertility, including related problems of venereal disease; the birth rate, in general, was low. Some aristocratic couples turned to religious or magical sources for assistance: one could purchase a translation of the *Book of Magic* from a bookdealer in Venice, or perhaps try a Persian or Turkish potion disseminated from oral tradition out of Transylvania. Folk remedies included the licking of genitals in the manner of a cat; expensive alternatives included the purchase of a holy relic or a magical stone such as a green emerald or aquamarine talisman to enhance the marriage, protect the wearer from infidelity, and grant fertility.

We know that during this time, Erzsébet sought out the assistance of Countess Eva Poppel Lobkovitz, wife of family friend, Ferenc Batthyányi. Countess Eva was reputed to be an excellent herbalist and practitioner of folk medicine. In general, Countess Báthory preferred herbal and spa treatments throughout her life rather than the traditional medical treatments of the day. Likely, the orthodox methods of leeching, cutting, and barbering would have done her little good, anyway.

In any case, children were eventually born. By mid-1596, we know that the couple had three living children: daughters Anna, Orsolya (Orsika), and Katalin (Kata), and that Erzsébet was pregnant with son András. Anna was born roughly in the year 1585. We are not certain as to Orsika's year of birth, although it was probably some time around 1590, and daughter Katalin followed in approximately 1594. It is likely that Anna and Orsolya were named after Erzsébet's and Ferenc' mothers, respectively, and Katalin perhaps after Erzsébet's aunt on her mother's side.

INFAMOUS LADY

We find from her letters that Erzsébet Báthory was a good wife and mother. In May of 1596, for example, she mailed a letter to Ferenc on their three girls' well-being:

> *At your service, I write to you as my beloved husband,*
>
> *Regarding the children, I can report that Anna and Orsika are healthy. Regarding Kata, however, there is a problem in her mouth: namely, rot has spread there, such that even the jawbone is infected. The Barber poked about the middle of the tooth with an iron—he says it was a stroke of luck that not a single tooth fell out. I do not know how the Lord will bring the matter to an end but right now, it is, in any case, very bad for her. About myself, I can write that things are now going much better than in the past few days....*
>
> *Written at Sárvár, On Friday after the Ascension of the Lord (May 24), 1596*
>
> *Your Servant,*
> *Erzsébet Báthory (by her own hand)*

Two months later, she also wrote:

> *At your service, I write to you, my beloved Lord,*
>
> *Regarding the children, I can report that Anna, thank God, is healthy, Kata has eye pain, and Orsika the mouth rot. I am healthy, thank God; only the eyes hurt me. God keep you.*

THE NÁDASDY CHILDREN

Written at Sárvár, on the 8th day of the Month of
St. James (July), 1596

Your Servant,
Erzsébet Báthory (by her own hand)

In the latter half of that same year, 1596, son András was born. Two years, later, son Pál arrived in 1598. András lived briefly until the age of seven, passing away in 1603, and daughter Orsika was also deceased by 1610. By the date of her Will in 1610, Countess Báthory would identify only three surviving children, to whom she left her entire estate: daughters Anna and Kata, and son, Pál. As the only surviving male heir, the primary estate at Sárvár would ultimately go to Pál.

Some chronicles also indicate that the couple had another son, albeit a lesser-known child, named Miklós, although this cannot be confirmed at present. Records indicate that a certain Miklós Nádasdy de Nádasd et Fogarasföld married Countess Zsuzsanna Zrínyi. We are not certain of his birth year or date of death, unfortunately, although it appears that Miklós was within the same generation as Pál and the other Nádasdy children. We are not certain of his lineage, either, given the somewhat scanty genealogical records left to us today. He might have been a cousin.

By the time of Pál's birth, Erzsébet was already 38 years old, and her mothering days were nearing an end. Miklós bore the surname and title Nádasdy de Nádasd et Fogarasföld like the rest of her children. However, he did not appear to grow up at the family seat at Sárvár. It also appears that he was not placed under the guardianship of Imre Megyeri, like brother Pál. Nanny and wetnurse Ilona Jó testified to having raised the Nádasdy girls and Pál, but made no mention of Miklós (although she might simply have been too old by then to care for him). Finally, in her Will of 1610, the Countess references only three children—Anna, Kata, and Pál —making no mention of Miklós.

This would suggest then that, as mentioned, he was either a cousin of the Nádasdy children or, although formally recognized by Ferenc Nádasdy in order to avoid scandal, the child was not his and, thus, raised quietly at one of the lesser estates with a surname but without any substantive birthright.

Typical of the time, noble mothers did not nurse or, for the most part, raise their own children. The Nádasdy children were entrusted to the care of a nurse, or *dajka*. In this case, her name was Ilona Jó, the wife of coachman István Nagy. Some say that she was also Erzsébet's nurse, as well. Although she would ultimately assist in running the torture chambers of her Ladyship's Castle at Csejthe (Cachtice), there is no record that she in any way mistreated the children of her Lord and Lady. And Countess Erzsébet, by all accounts, cared about her children and provided well for them. She made certain that her daughters received lavish wedding celebrations, partnering them with illustrious young men from the Drugeth de Homonnay and Zrínyi families, two of the few remaining dynasties of comparable importance. She also made certain that her son Pál received a fine education and that he acquired the family seat of her estate, despite later legal complications.

On April 17, 1605, Erzsébet's eldest daughter, Anna Nádasdy, married Count Miklós Zrínyi at Csepreg, a town not far from Sárvár. A fragment of a letter from Anna to her mother survives, written December 22, 1605. Anna writes about life with her new husband, Count Zrínyi, at his castle in Csáktornya (Cakovec, now in Croatia). The letter is polite and even has a spontaenous postscript, rather rare in those times, indicating intimacy. She writes:

> *Thank God we arrived easily, and our health, happily, is in order. My lord, my husband, came[a distance] across, and we are all in good mood and health. Only his hand [was hurt], as he fell from the act. But it is nothing too serious; the hand will soon be in order. Regarding my du-*

ties, I will listen, obey, and do what they say. Do not worry about me. Everything is fine with us, and his family respects me. May God grant happiness.

Your loyal servant and sister, Anna Nádasdy

P.S. I sent you and my beloved brother a basket of figs (clams?). I would have sent you more, but that's all we received from the sea.

Before Ferenc' death, Countess Erzsébet had been moving about the various castles and manor homes under her control to settle administrative matters, conduct inspections, and host social affairs. It appears that when not at war, Ferenc preferred coming back to his boyhood home at Sárvár, while Erzsébet spent increasingly more time in the countryside at the other castles and manor homes, particularly at Csejthe. Located in what is today Western Slovakia, Csejthe Castle was a 13th-century fortification situated on a hill that came with a fiefdom of 17 villages. The Nádasdy family acquired the property in 1569 and, as mentioned, Ferenc received it as a wedding gift from his mother before giving it, in turn, to Erzsébet. He later redeemed the property in 1602 from the Emperor for 5,000 forints, thus securing permanent title for her. In time, it would become the site of her gruesome murders and, ultimately, the final prison of Lady Erzsébet.

It is likely that Erzsébet Báthory was never completely well-received, or well-liked, at Sárvár. Her son Pál was entrusted to a tutor and governor there, a squire named Imre Megyeri (or Megyery), nicknamed "Red." Megyeri would later be appointed Pál's legal guardian after his father's death and during the Countess' legal proceedings. Megyeri clearly disliked the Countess, ultimately filing formal charges against her with the king for her alleged torturing and murdering of servants. She certainly had no great affection for him either (according to witnesses, he appeared on the receiving end of her "evil spells" and even a plot to poison him). In addition, Erzsébet began to clash with the local clergy. It is clear that by the 1590's, something very unusual was going on not only at Sárvár but also at the other Nádasdy estates that the Countess periodically visited, including Beckó (Beckov), Keresztúr, Csejthe, Kosztolány, and the manor in Vienna.

11

STRANGE GOINGS ON (1585-1604)

At first, no one seemed to notice anything unusual. A young servant girl died suddenly in the night in the women's section of Castle Sárvár. Her body was placed in a casket, and the local pastor, István Magyari, was summoned. When he arrived, he was a little surprised to find that the girl had already been placed into the box with the lid sealed. Ordinarily, he would have expected to find her lying out on a bed. The Countess quietly took him aside.

"I'm afraid that we have a case of cholera on our hands," she confided. "I don't want to alarm the other servants or create a panic in town."

The pastor nodded quickly. These things happened, even in a wealthy household.

The casket was brought out and loaded onto a wagon at the gates, where it was met by the pastor and a group of seminary students. A few servants nearby glanced up from their work as the students opened their hymnals and began singing funeral hymns. The little procession made its way out of the estate towards the cemetery.

Inside Castle Sárvár, however, the female staff members were unusually quiet that day. They looked around nervously and, when the Countess walked past, immediately lowered their heads or moved quickly out of her way. When no one was in sight, they whispered incessantly.

. . . . .

In his role as Castellan (Warden) of Sárvár, Benedek Bicsérdy was in charge of estate security, administration, serving as deputy assistant in dispute settlements, and overseeing the household staff. Bicsérdy was apparently close to both Ferenc and Erzsébet Nádasdy: he even named his own children after both Lord and Lady as well as the various Nádasdy children.

But something seemed rather unusual about this particular request.

The Countess took him aside and motioned to a door that led to a series of inner rooms.

"Post an armed guard here," she ordered. "Inform the staff. I do not want anyone going in there without my express permission."

"Yes, Ladyship."

Her hand suddenly tightened on his wrist. Surprised, he looked into her eyes, suddenly black with intensity.

"Do you understand, Benedek?"

"Yes, Ladyship," he said again.

Her hand relaxed.

"Good," she said as she walked away. "Do not disappoint me."

. . . . .

The Sárvár clergy was again summoned. Pastor Magyari was unable to attend that day and so the assistant pastor, Michael Zvonaric (Hung.: Mihály Varga Zvonarics), took the call. Servants had already brought up a casket to the church when he arrived, this one a bit larger than usual. Zvonaric asked the men to wait a moment. Rumors had already gone around that three girls had been nailed inside. Asking the servants to wait, he went to the castle to find the Lady.

"Ladyship, may I ask why there are three bodies in a single casket?"

Countess Erzsébet looked somewhat miffed by his question.

"There are only two," she said evenly. "You may bury them together in one grave site."

He pressed further.

"But what happened to them? Why did all three die together so quickly—one after the other?"

To this, she repeated, "There are only two. One had already died and the other was near death, and so we waited to put them together into a single coffin. If two coffins had been brought out one after the other, it would have caused even more gossip."

Later, the belfry master, who had been listening, took the young minister aside.

"Father," he said quietly, "It's best not to say anything or question the Lady about these things."

When Zvonaric went to protest, the belfry master warned, "It will go badly for the servants if you do."

• • • • •

What began as an isolated incident slowly turned into an ever-increasing stream of dead bodies that began to follow Countess Báthory wherever she went. In the preliminary investigation against the Countess that took place in October of 1610, the first deposed witness was Sárvár Castellan, Benedek Bicsérdy. By the time of this inquest, he stated that he knew of at least 175 girls and women who had died. He knew nothing regarding how they died, however, because "unless she called for him, he was not permitted to go into the house of the Lady."

Once, however, he did glimpse a bloodstain on one of the walls, and said that when he walked the outside of the castle, he could hear the "noises of a lashing from inside…through the walls." He knew of beatings that would sometimes go on for six or more hours. The Lady kept a series of inner rooms under guard where "the tortured people were kept hidden."

If Bicsérdy's estimate of the death toll seemed high, another confirmed: Baltazar Poby (also sp. Balthasar Poky), another man who had served as Castellan at Sárvár, testified that he had heard the number of victims, dead from the after-effects of torture, actually numbered over 200, "if not already amounting to nearly three hundred."

Other servants, nobles, clergy and townspeople from Sárvár and the surrounding areas would come forth. They all said the same thing: burials and funerals took place at an alarming rate there; the dead were almost always young servant girls; access was forbidden to a certain part of the estate under heavy guard; and, although no one actually saw much of anything, all had heard tales that these girls died from torture.

Another witness, Gergely Balás (Gregor Balasz), also agreed that the bodies of girls were taken out by cart, accompanied by clergy members singing funeral songs, but did not know how they had died.

Rev. Michael Zvonaric claimed that when the Lady was in the house, it was not possible to see anything unusual since the staff had been highly warned not to enter certain rooms. One entrance, in particular, was always highly guarded by a man named Drabont, and that no one could enter without permission. Somewhere behind there was an inner, secret room, however, and he'd heard from servants that girls were tortured in there. He himself saw nothing, though.

Evidently, the Countess was meticulous in covering her tracks. Benedek Bicsérdy said that, when he was called, everything had already been cleaned up by the time he entered the secret areas. Michael Zvonaric agreed that if he, or someone else, went into the Lady's house, "everything was cleaned and there was nothing to see. She demanded great care to be taken by her people."

The death of a few staff members in and of itself was not unusual in a time when disease and poor hygiene claimed its daily share of victims, even in a wealthy household. At first, no one seemed to notice a few dead girls. The ordinary answer was that these poor souls had succumbed to cholera—quite common at the time—and that their hasty burial, with closed coffin, was performed so as not to create a panic amongst the staff or townspeople. The local clergy willingly accepted the explanation. Students studying for the ministry walked beside the casket-bearing wagons, singing funeral songs to the grave site. The local pastor performed the rites, and brief eulogies were given. Countess Báthory herself even attended the services.

But then the numbers started to multiply. More stories of death, and even rumors of torture and bizarre behavior, began to surface. At about the same time, the knight, Paul Boëd, who worked as assistant manager (Vice Castellan) at Sárvár Castle, also claimed to have seen, at the gates, the bodies of girls being buried amidst funeral singing. While he didn't personally witness their deaths, he had also heard from other staff members that the girls died from torture. In 1602, Boëd met with Captain János Mogyórssy and Gergely Jánossy, both senior professors at Sárvár, as well as Pastor István Magyari.

Magyari was a distinguished member of the Lutheran clergy and noted theologian who worked as chaplain under Tamás Nádasdy and continued at his post, after Tamás' death, for Ferenc and Ezsébet. Despite his advancing age, Magyari remained outspoken and principled. He engaged in literary warfare, for example, with Catholic Archbishop Péter Pázmány, publishing a work entitled *Az Országokban Valo Sok Romlásnak Okairol* ("The Causes of Hungary's Ruin") in 1602 that declared Catholicism the principal cause. Pázmány replied with his own work, *Felelet Magyary Istvannak* ("Reply to Istvan Magyary"). The two would fire back and forth for years with their respective replies and counter-replies. (Pázmány also worked tirelessly for decades to try and convert, or re-convert, Hungary's Protestant nobility to Catholicism.)

The men collectively put the burden on this minister to report these strange activities, telling him, "It is feared that the Lord God will punish us along with you. Either let us all go and get away from here, or you, good Mr. István—since you are a man of the church and would otherwise be guilty—must warn her. If she does not stop, then you must announce her deeds from the pulpit, because it offends the Lord God, and He will not tolerate it."

Nobleman Ferenc Bornemisszy (Bornemissze) recounted how Magyari took on the challenge, publicly confronting Countess Báthory when his conscience could no longer tolerate the disturbing events taking place at Sárvár.

.   .   .   .   .

The service that morning was unusual. Pastor Magyari seemed upset, even grave, and his fingers continued to move restlessly over his missal. When it came time to deliver the sermon, he gripped the railings tightly while speaking. He cleared his throat several times throughout, apparently distracted.

"My Brothers and Sisters," he finally said, at the conclusion, "in order for me to remain at the pulpit, I must disclose something of the utmost importance to you."

The congregation at Sárvár, made up of nobles, servants, and townspeople, had all heard the rumors by now. The gossip had spread that yet another girl had died of torture. Some looked over to the reserved pew of the Lord and Lady Nádasdy. The Lord was away in Vienna on this particular morning, but the Lady was present. Her eyes locked on Magyari now. No one made a sound.

"It is said about us as a preacher," Magyari began, "that we know other people complain," --he turned to face the Lady directly-- "but that Your Grace is not reproached. Therefore, I cannot conceal it. It must be even moreso announced that, regarding the girl, Your Grace should not have so acted because it offends the Lord, and," his voice began to rise now, "we will be punished if we do not complain to and criticize Your Grace."

Her nostrils flared slightly, but the Countess remained silent and upright in posture.

"In order to confirm that my words are true," Magyari challenged, "we need only exhume the body."

He brought his hand down on the pulpit, perhaps a bit too hard. The noise echoed throughout the church, and a few flinched.

"You will find that the marks identify the way in which death occurred!"

Countess Nádasdy turned to face him fully now.

"See here, Minister István," she said firmly, "You will soon see that I will make you pay for this. My husband and I have relatives who will not tolerate that you bring such shame on me and denounce me so. You have introduced me to an outrageous situation in which I am subjected to the pulpit, including even the indictment of my husband!"

She stood up now, and her attendants rose with her.

"I will write to my husband!"

"If Your Grace has relatives," Magyari called after her, "then I also have a relative: the Lord God! But for better proof of what I say, let us dig up the body, and then we will see what you have done!"

Immediately after this altercation, the Countess stormed back to the palace and wrote a furious letter to her husband in Vienna. She demanded that he punish the pastor for his insults and behavior. Her invective was so severe, in fact, that Ferenc Nádasdy immediately set out for home.

Pastors Magyari and Zvonaric, meanwhile, did report the strange rumors, much to Count Ferenc Nádasdy's anger and embarrassment upon his return. On March 27, 1602, a letter was sent to Rev. Gregor Phythiaräus (Gergely Piterius), the pastor at Keresztúr, for guidance. Zvonaric informed Rev. Phythiaräus that he and his colleague at Sárvár had come to the conclusion that they "should warn His Majesty (Count Ferenc Nádasdy) and his wife regarding the atrocities that they have committed. And this also applies to an evil woman, Anna Darvolya, whom everyone knows," who has "assisted Erzsébet Báthory in inhuman atrocities."

Anna Darvolya (Darvulia) is an interesting figure. She was apparently a Croatian woman who lived in the town of Sárvár. She clearly served the Countess between the years 1601-1609 but, based on letters of the clergy and witness testimony, likely served the Nádasdy family even before that. She began to make more frequent appearances at court and eventually took up a permanent residence with the Countess at Csejthe. She was described by locals as a "wild beast in female form" who taught Erzsébet and the other servants elaborate—and deadly—methods of torture. Anna's favorite method of torture including beating someone repeatedly—up to 500 times in some cases—until death finally occurred. She served as "gate keeper" for the Countess, as well as a personal advisor. She, in fact, was reputedly the one who had advised the Countess to take on only peasant girls "who had not yet tasted the pleasures of love." This appears in line with Erzsébet's *modus operandi*: the disappearance of a few Slovak peasant girls would not have been a political bother to Erzsébet nor merit the attention of authorities.

Rumors of Anna's cruelty—including allegations that she was running a torture chamber and executioner's butcher shop within Sárvár palace—began to circulate by 1601. In addition, rumors that the Lord and Lady Nádasdy knew exactly what she was doing, including their tacit as well as tangible approval, followed. The servants were in agreement that both Lord and Lady participated with her, more than once. It is likely that Ferenc also shared his own techniques, discovered on the battlefield: Anna Darvolya soon learned how to strangle servants in the "Turkish" style of execution.

By March of 1602, with the Easter Service approaching, the Sárvár clergy was particularly concerned over a theological point; namely, whether or not to deny the Eucharist at the coming service and possibly even excommunicate the female accomplice, Anna, for her actions. In letters to their colleagues and superiors, the Sárvár clergy bristled at the thought that Anna Darvolya would brazenly approach the communion rail on Easter Sunday. Both she and the Countess routinely attended services as though nothing had happened.

During this time, excommunication was the subject of dispute between Lutherans and Calvinists. Upon agreement by a council of Lutheran elders, the Sárvár pastors were advised to make clear to the Lord and Lady the gravity of their sins, as well as consequent results.

As it happened so often, upon his hasty return home, Ferenc Nádasdy ultimately managed to appease the ministry, likely through a substantial donation. In fact, Ferenc's considerable donations to the Lutheran Church, as well as scholarship funds for students at Wittenberg University, continued even after his death. To our knowledge, the question of excommunication was never actually taken up or debated any further, and witnesses recounted that Lord Nádasdy and Pastor Magyari reconciled shortly thereafter. (In fact, when Catholic Cardinal Peter Pázmány suggested, shortly after Lord Nádasdy's funeral, that Hungary's war hero would not be going to heaven because of the violent life he led, Rev. Magyari himself engaged in a heated literary debate with Pázmány, defending the future of the Count's soul.)

The allegations of torture and murder slowed somewhat, for the time being. However, torture and murder had by now been tied to a secret location on Count Nádasdy's property, and word was spreading amongst his peers and subjects that something was very wrong.

Although Ferenc Nádasdy was probably furious with his wife for creating a public scandal, he himself was not innocent of the accusations. As mentioned, stories already circulated amongst the servants that he, too, enjoyed torturing servants and teaching his wife ways in which to discipline them. He was already known to be ruthless on the battlefield and sought retribution against his enemies in atrocious ways. At least once, he ordered the execution of captured prisoners "in the most heinous way possible." He was also known to dance with the dead bodies of his enemies and throw their severed heads into the air or play "catch" and kickball with them.

Ferenc Nádasdy could also be ruthless with his own men. In 1600, French and Flemish mercenaries, working for the Hapsburgs under Nádasdy and Adolf Schwarzenberg, were garrisoned in the market town of Pápa, not far from Sárvár. The general staff owed these men over 60,000 ducats in back pay. After making numerous demands without any luck, the troops then asked their Hungarian masters for the money. When refused, the men sent a secret delegate to the Turks, promising to turn over the town to him if the Turkish pasha could provide their money. The pasha sent 10,000 ducats, at which point, the troops took the money and began plundering the town for the rest.

Schwarzenberg and Nádasdy rode in to put down the rebellion; when Schwarzenberg was killed in action, Ferenc Nádasdy assumed command. Securing a nearly immediate surrender, he then rounded up the rebel troops and ordered that they be "hanged with inhuman cruelty" to make an example of them. (For this, he received special honors in Vienna.)

One particular gift Ferenc allegedly brought home to his wife was a device that resembled a hand of sharp claws that could be fitted over the fingers to cut, slash, and stab a victim. Ferenc would reputedly order servant girls to stand naked before him. It was reported that he once covered the younger sister of nursemaid, Ilona Jó, with honey and made her stand in the summer sun so as to be attacked by swarms of insects. When servant girls passed out or were thought to be lazy, Ferenc taught Erzsébet how to insert pieces of oiled paper between their toes and then light the papers on fire.

STRANGE GOINGS ON (1585-1604)

It seems, however, that Ferenc stopped just short of murdering his own staff. János Újváry testified that, while Lord Nádasdy knew of what went on regarding the death of servant girls, he disapproved of their murder and actually forbade it. For Ferenc Nádasdy, image was everything. His wife followed his orders to some extent; the number of dead girls accrued in relatively small increments but then, after his death in 1604, escalated dramatically.

One wonders what exactly provoked the Countess to torture and kill her adolescent servant girls. We do know that, at that particular time in Hungarian history, the series of wars and blood conflicts that had ravaged the land left a glut of young, unmarried women and a shortage of men. Historically, females were already viewed as less important than men and one might wonder if, in an odd way, the Countess actually felt as though she were doing a service for her lands by maintaining a sort of population control.

It is also possible that the pathology began in the early to middle years of her marriage. As an adolescent, Erzsébet may very well have been brutalized herself at Sárvár in an effort to force her compliance into the role of a proper—and submissive—young wife and lady. Her husband likely brutalized her behind closed doors, as was customary at the time. Husbands were freely permitted to torture their wives into submission, to punish any act of disobedience, and to maintain their status as lord and master of the household. The effects of warfare at such a young age likely traumatized Ferenc himself. The stress of combat probably caused him to drink heavily when home on leave and to act out his aggression on family and servants.

Erzsébet's torturing seemed to start out slowly and progressively; first, with pinching, biting, and kicking, and then increasing in intensity and amount. Later, she advanced to pricking or sticking pins and needles into lips and under fingernails. After that, she progressed to inflicting burns on her victims, or cutting them with knives. These were all acts of meanness and cruelty, still adolescent in many ways, but not fatal.

It appears, however, that when Erzsébet acted in concert with others, she found the courage to push the limits farther. She eventually learned how to torture in a serious way from her husband and Anna Darvolya. The profile of Erzsébet's victims was almost always the same. The hundreds of witnesses who testified agreed that men were not targets of the Countess' attacks and, for the most part, mature women generally were not, either. It was always an unmarried, adolescent girl.

That is not to say, however, that older women were completely exempt from capital punishment for disobedience. Witness Ferenc Török, a yeoman (squire) and juror at Sárvár, along with a number of others, swore before the court that the Countess also murdered a married woman who once refused to follow orders. It was customary, at that time, to use unmarried virgin girls to work as table attendants during a certain festival. When she didn't have enough young girls on hand, the Countess ordered an older woman to pretend to be one of the virgins and dress up like a young girl. It appears that she had ordered the woman to dress up as a girl on other occassions, as well. The lady's name was Modl (or Modli). She had come either from Vienna, Bratislava, or Germany (witness accounts varied), and had been described as full-figured or matronly. Up until that point, she had actually been a favorite of the Countess and worked as a milliner.

According to witnesses, however, the woman finally could no longer abide by the request to play the part of a child and apologized, "But certainly, my dear high and gracious Lady, I cannot be a girl since I already have a husband and a son, my little Ferenc."

The Lady became enraged at this. In her anger, she went and brought in a small log, commanding her to put it in diapers and carry it with her around the castle, saying, "Suckle your child, you whore. Don't let it cry!" The Lady even woke her up at night, violently forcing the piece of wood to her breast as though it were a baby. Later, the witnesses said that the Lady tortured her in a variety of ways until she finally died.

Although Sárvár Pastor István Magyari felt a moral compunction to speak up, as did certain local gentlemen, there were no real legal implications for what Erzsébet and her husband were doing or permitting to happen to their servant girls. By this point, Ferenc Nádasdy had distinguished himself in battle, rising to the title of High Stable Master, and was lending enormous sums of money to the Hungarian Crown. At his death, the Crown owed him nearly 18,000 gulden, an amount which even King Mátyás II (1557-1619) could not afford to repay. So long as Ferenc Nádasdy bankrolled the Hungarian Crown and Hapsburg Empire, no one dared touch him or his wife.

In addition, victimization of the local people was quite common during that time. As discussed, the peasants who lived and worked on lands owned by nobility like the Báthorys or Nádasdys were considered property under the Act of 1517. The death of serving girls, by torture or otherwise, might raise an eye or the ire of the pulpit, but would cause no significant harm for the "Black Knight of Hungary"—the man who kept the continent safe from legions of invading Turks. Legally, the state prosecutor would not even bring an action against a noble on behalf of a low-born person; the "interested party" had to bring his own action against the noble—highly unlikely given the obvious risks.

For example, about that same time in 1588, a neighboring noble, Mihály Cseszeky, was actually kidnapping and ransoming not only Turkish prisoners but also his own peasantry in an attempt to raise money for the care and maintenance of his castle at Várpalota. Cseszeky, a lesser noble under the jurisdiction of Ferenc Nádasdy, was himself a royal hero, having fought off thousands of Turks with a few hundred Hungarian troops. He was given Castle Várpalota as a royal gift, but the Crown did not provide enough funding for its maintenance. Eventually, Cseszeky took matters into his own hands to secure the needed financing.

Although oppressed, the locals were unable to seek any sort of assistance from governmental authorities. As discussed, their only recourse was to bring an action against the noble himself. They finally petitioned Ferenc Nádasdy, Cseszeky's overlord, for relief from the constant raids and disappearance of loved ones. For Nadasdy, the matter was complicated: Mihály Cseszeky's relatives had fought with his father, Tamás, against the Turks, and Ferenc himself had, on more than one occasion, held prisoners for ransom in an effort to raise money. History does not record any significant punishment levied against Cseszeky; again, the peasantry had little standing to complain against the nobility—no matter what was done to them.

12

THE DEATH OF FERENC NÁDASDY

In March of 1601, when Count Nádasdy was in Bratislava, history records that he was hit by an illness that caused such severe pain in his legs that he was unable to stand. After a few weeks, he recovered and was able to return to public duty. From his letters, though, the condition appeared irreversible.

Meanwhile, Ferenc continued to loan the cash-strapped Crown and Hapsburgs money, despite their inability to repay him. His loyalty to them never waivered, either. In August of 1602, although ailing, he joined forces with Count György Thurzó to lead a new campaign against the Turks and shore up Hungarian garrisons in towns along the Danube. The two men, who already knew each other, became well acquainted during this time—rather ironic, since György Thurzó would later arrest Erzsébet and administer her trials.

In the year 1603, Ferenc fell gravely ill again, this time permanently disabled, and began to prepare his family and friends for the possibility of death. Ferenc Nádasdy was closest of all to his military comrade, Ferenc Batthyányi. As mentioned, the Nádasdy and Battyányi familes co-owned a palatial manor home in Vienna and, from correspondence, we know that Erzsébet kept in touch with them even after her husband's death.

Ferenc Nádasdy was not naïve: he knew what life for his widowed wife would likely become. In that time, a widow's fate depended on her protectors. In the case of Erzsébet, because of her influential family, she was entitled to live comfortably on the estates, cared for by her servants. However, it was nearly certain that she would become the target of attacks aimed at her massive fortune—whether from predatory nobles, disloyal staff, the Crown, the Church, or the Ottoman Turks.

The ailing Nádasdy entrusted two letters to messengers. The first went to Ferenc Batthyányi, asking him to protect his wife and children. The Nádasdy estates were already under constant threat from the Turks, the Crown appeared to have no intention of repaying its massive debts, and he feared for the worst for his family. We do know from correspondence that Erzsébet would later write to Batthyáni, and that he advised and helped her with a few economic and military issues.

The second letter went to György Thurzó.

On January 3, 1604, the day before he died, Ferenc wrote to Thurzó: "God has visited upon me this disease," and that, "should the unthinkable happen" and he not survive, "I formally entrust my heirs and widow under your generous protection."

The letter could have been an aristocratic convention between friends and a sign of the confidential relationship they shared when they fought together against the Turks. On the other hand, it could also have been a tactical maneuver to ensure that Thurzó, already one of the most powerful men in the kingdom, would feel shame if he in any way planned to discredit the family or commandeer its possessions.

Nádasdy was already too ill to actually sign it. He died in his bedroom at Sárvár on January 4th, shortly after the letter was sent. The funeral for Ferenc Nádasdy was typical of a national war hero: lavish, military-style, and filled with pomp. His open casket was surrounded by four large candles that burned throughout the night vigil before his burial. At seven a.m. the following morning, the attendant funeral service, pageant and procession began. Pastor István Magyari who, only two years prior had castigated both the count and his wife from the pulpit for cruelty and oppressing their subjects, now recalled in a stirring eulogy how Lord Nádasdy distributed food to the poor and provided scholarships for students, how he always ate and drank sparingly, and kept all indulgences in check. In fact, the more exalted his position, the pastor declared, the more modest he became, since pride had never been a part of his nature.

Ferenc had clearly reconciled with Pastor István Magyari before his death. If the aging pastor had any questions concerning Count's Nádasdy's own morality, one would have never known it from the words he delivered at the service:

> *His Grace fought the good fight against Satan, the world, temptations of the flesh, and sin. He carried forth the word of God with forethought and love. Happily is he now gone to the Lord's table. He did not spend his leisure time in idleness but was dedicated to the reading of the Bible. He was like a good father to his subjects. He distributed food and clothing to the poor and supported the young in their studies. He ate and drank sparingly and never overburdened his heart with excess. He ate only once on Saturdays and on all days before holidays, and then only sparingly. The more recognized and great he became, rising in the eyes of his king and countrymen, the more ever so humbly he conducted himself, because any such pretensions were far removed from his inner character.*

Apparently, Magyari's loyalty—and hatred for Jesuit Archbishop, Péter Pázmány—continued even after Lord Nádasdy's death. As mentioned, when Pázmány began to stir up theological arguments as to why the deceased war hero would not be going to heaven, Magyari quickly fired back with a series of ideological rebuttals.

INFAMOUS LADY

Two weeks after his death, Ferenc' cousin, Orsolya Nádasdy Pethö, sent a letter to Erzsébet Báthory. Mindful of Count Nádasdy's death, as well as the recent betrothal of Erzsébet's daughter, Anna, to Nicolaus Zrínyi, Orsolya wrote the following:

My beloved, gracious Lady, sweet sister,...

My dear, sweet Lady, Your Grace has completely forgotten me; perhaps you are angry with me that, my dear sweet Lady, I could not attend the funeral of my beloved Lord (Ferenc), who, acting in place of a father, was my protector! Had only God not allowed me to live to this day! I want to apologize to you, my beloved Lady, because when I received the letter from Your Grace, and I saw that the seal was black, I dropped it, my beloved Lady. I was sick for two weeks, I could not eat a bite. When I asked, when was he buried and wanted to send someone because I was very weak, I was told that it was over. The letter was sent too late.

My beloved mistress, since then I have suffered much, because hostile Pethő relatives anger me constantly. They complain: my star has fallen! Earlier, they threw my son before the penniless Lords. Oh, my dear, sweet Lady, for me he died, I am an orphan, I have no support, no hope left on this earth! No day goes by without me mourning for him. Indeed, my beloved Lady, all my sons and my whole family are dead! Now that I know I would not find them anymore, I no longer wish to live there.

I hear that my Gracious God has brought great

happiness to my beloved niece (Anna). Thank God, may she be blessed with a long life and much luck. My beloved Lady, to whom I write this, I have tearfully thanked God for you. As God is my witness, even though it hurt my Maria, I have not had greater joy to know of the happiness that my niece now enjoys. God grant that my dear brother-in-law (Nicholas Zrínyi) will be a similar protector to me and my niece, like her father (Ferenc) was....

My beloved Lady, now I bring you my services: I beg you, command and order me about. Do not treat me like a stranger or as the other relatives-- only as a guest, but let me serve and help you. I will gladly go a month earlier, because I am obligated, until my death, to serve your children, because of their father, who for me in joy and sorrow was like a father. Believe me, Your Grace, that I no longer wish as much good for my own children as I do for your dear children. Consider me as such a relative, forget me not, your orphaned relative, command me and let me serve you.

About my condition, I can write you that my relatives cause me all sorts of trouble. In the castle, I could not live with them, my servants were beaten; they occupied my house. God alone knows my miserable state, there is no one left to whom I could tell this that would pity me or who would give me good advice and that I could trust. My God, my beloved Lady, I have no more comforter, God took away my support and my strong confidence in this world. My wish is to see you, my beloved beautiful Lady, as long as I'm still

*alive. After all, etc. Written in Sztropko, accord-
ing to the new (calendar) on Saint Margaret's
Day (January 18), 1604.*

*Your gracious servant,
Orsolya Nádasdy*

*P.S. I can assure you of no other news to report,
except that the Christian (i.e., Protestant) predi-
cate was pursued. In Kosice, there is no more.
His Majesty has now sent out the same article
(law) to the counties, saying that those who are
not Catholic will lose all of their goods. They
send us however, as I hear, more and inform his
Majesty, that if he does not leave us to our belief
(faith), then the warden of the Assembly (the parliament probably) will no longer visit, and they
will not even pay the taxes anymore. What God
sends us next, I do not know.*

Orsolya Nádasdy Pethö's letter described not only her
own plight as a widow but also the impending tension felt by
Protestant nobles whose property was increasingly the subject of
hostile Catholic interests. Her correspondence is, interestingly, a
foreshadowing of a similar struggle that the newly widowed—
and Protesant—Countess Báthory would herself soon face.

Meanwhile, it was customary at that time for a widow to
remove herself from society and formal life for at least one year
to mourn. If we have any indication of what Erzsébet truly felt
for Ferenc by then—or perhaps the urgency in which she felt to
maintain certain appointments—it can be summed up in the fact
that only four weeks after his death, she was already devoting
herself to business in Vienna. She also made a personal appearance at Court that, apparently, shocked even the Emperor. In
addition, deceased nobility were typically not interred until two
to three months after death; thus, the speed at which both funeral

and burial had taken place, including the fact that notice of the event failed to reach even close relatives like Orsolya Nádasdy Pethö, raises something of a question.

Eight months later, in September 1604, Lady Widow Nádasdy went on a lavish shopping spree, purchasing for herself and her personal attendants an exorbitant array of clothing for a lump sum of 2,942 gold and 11 denar. Both her signature and that of the Viennese merchant, Georg Pech (György or Juraj Pechy) are present on the sales document. The amount is absolutely enormous: at that time, the annual income of a senior officer of high rank, or any doctor with a good reputation, was approximately 150 silver. The amount today would be in the millions. Like all of her many transactions, the Countess always paid early or within the month, and in cash.

Erzsébet paid all remaining obligations owed by her husband and continued to support his charitable endeavors, such as providing scholarships for students and money to support Lutheran efforts at Wittenberg. She also continued litigation with his debtors, including the Royal Treasury. She assumed control over all asset management now, as illustrated by a variety of letters in her own hand from 1604, including her signature on the annual tax bill for her various properties. Despite their previous harassment, she also protected the local clergy. One of the unfortunate consequences of the Reformation was that the properties and wages of Protestant clerics, now disenfranchised from the Catholic Church, were frequently subjected to the predatory practices of local nobility. However, on January 31, 1605, Countess Báthory issued a letter ordering the protection of the clergy's wages and property, to be held in escrow by the bailiff and available on public record to the town and village judges and citizens, so as to answer all questions and maintain integrity. Whether she made this gesture because she wanted to or had to is not known.

From correspondence, we also learn that Erzsébet traded costly and rare jewelry with a few business partners, including the same German merchant, Pech, and that she occasionally lent out cash or goods, both to servants and nobility. The list of servants from Sárvár who owed her, whether in the form of currency or raw goods, included: Sárvár Paymaster, Benedek Zalay; Paymaster, Squire János Zambothny (Zamabory); Court Master Benedikt Deseö; and Castellan Benedek Bicsérdy, all of whom would later be called to testify against her.

Yet, during the same time, it is said that the monks who lived across the street from her Viennese manor were so disturbed by the screaming of tortured girls coming from her residence that they hurled their pots at the walls in anguish. The woman who spent her free time torturing servant girls in private was a complete paradox in public, providing scholarships, supporting the clergy, making helpful loans to needy staff, paying all of her bills promptly, and appearing at high-society affairs.

We cannot say exactly what triggered the escalation of torture and murder after Ferenc' death in 1604. The couple was obviously not close by then, and Erzsébet was certainly used to running the estates by herself. By all accounts, her daily life did not change very much. She did, however, rely on certain things for her support; namely, the steady stream of income that Ferenc had provided while alive, and the military as well as social protection that his office brought to her. Although her vast properties generated great wealth, the estates were enormously expensive to operate, and the tax bill increasingly heavy. In addition, much of this wealth consisted of real estate holdings, crops, and livestock—not always quickly or easily convertible to cash. Erzsébet had come to rely on the quick cash provided when Ferenc and his troops plundered the treasuries of Turks as well as the occasional, offending European noble or merchant. When the money dried up and the protection evaporated, it appears that her mental state deteriorated just as quickly. She was vulnerable now and knew it. By this time, she was also in her mid forties and aging fast in an era when few people lived past fifty.

13

ESCALATION (1604-1610)

Sometime before the year 1605, Erzsébet Báthory surrounded herself with an intimate cohort of servants. In addition to Anna Darvolya, four others—an unusual mix of three old women and a disfigured boy—would come to serve as her chief torturers and even execution squad. The four included: a boy named János Újváry, known simply as Ficzkó; her children's wet nurse, the elderly widow Ilona (Helena) Jó Nagy; an elderly friend of Ilona Jó, named Dorottya (Dorothea) Szentes; and an elderly washerwoman named Katalin (Katarina or Kata) Beneczky.

Ficzkó was brought into the Countess' service, allegedly by force, some time between 1590 and 1595, likely 1593 or 1594. We are not sure exactly how old Ficzkó was; however, the trial documents, as well as letters of the period, refer to him as a "young lad." Witnesses called him a "boy" or "kid," and later on, when convicted in 1611 for torturing and murdering servants, his sentence would be reduced, in part, due to his "youthful age."

During this time period, the age of majority, or adulthood, varied based on country and circumstance. For most of Europe, one could inherit property at the age of 21, considered majority. However, under Roman law, which was still being applied throughout Europe, including countries such as Hapsburg-controlled Austria, one was not considered a full "adult" for purposes of criminal conviction until the age of 25. Depending on the legal standard used during the proceedings, Ficzkó thus could not have been more than mid-twenties, and was probably younger than that. This also indicates that he was no more than eight or ten years old when first brought to Erzsébet's court.

Some commentators believe that Erzsébet called Ficzkó by the name of "Thorko," and that he taught her various magical spells. Given Ficzkó's young age, however, this would have been highly unlikely. In addition, we know from Rev. Ponikenusz' letter of January 1, 1611 that Thorko (or Torkoss) was actually a woman who lived "miles beyond Sárvár." The name first appears in a letter dated some time around 1594, when Erzsébet supposedly wrote to Ferenc: "Thorko has taught me a lovely new one. Catch a black hen and beat it to death with a white cane. Keep the blood and smear a little of it on your enemy. If you get no chance to smear it on his body, then get one of his articles of clothing and smear the hen's blood on it."

Chronicles from the time indicate that Ficzkó was disfigured, something akin to the "Igor" character known today. It may be that he was sold into slavery as a child or, perhaps, had been part of a sideshow act before being taken to the Lady's court. One wonders why the Countess accepted him into her service at all: like the other young people that came into her employ, Erzsébet would have paid the parents or guardians, often poor people, a sum of money in exchange for the child. Márton Deak's wife, allegedly the person who brought him to the Countess' court by force, might have kidnapped or taken on Ficzkó as an abandoned baby, looking for an opportunity to sell him off. It also may be that the Countess felt sorry for this unusual, disfigured child; it is unlikely that he had any sort of gainful skills at the time.

ESCALATION (1604-1610)

However, Ficzkó appears to have done anything that the Countess desired, and this may have been what ultimately made him so useful. He apparently also ran around the estates as he pleased, getting into fights and running off his mouth regarding the bodies hidden or people he had killed. At least one witness, a judge, confronted the Countess about him; she apparently did nothing to discipline him.

Ilona Jó Nagy, referred to as the widow of the "bald coachman," served as the wet nurse to Erzsébet's children, including the Nádasdy girls and Pál. She stated that she had lived in the Countess' house since 1600. By the time of trial in 1611, the surviving Nádasdy girls, Anna and Katalin, were adults in their twenties, with Pál just reaching the teen years. Thus, Ilona Jó would have worked for the Nádasdys at Sárvár during the children's early years. The trial documents, in fact, state that Ilona Jó was the cruelest of the accomplices and that, because of this, she was later brought from Sárvár to Csejthe by Erzsébet.

At about the time when the youngest child, Pál, was entrusted to the care of his tutor and governor, Ilona's services were no longer needed. It may be that the Countess felt sorry for her. By then, Erzsébet was spending increasing amounts of time away from Sárvár and setting up her nearly permanent residence at Csejthe. When Ilona Jó says that she lived in the Countess' house, she was referring to the residence at Csejthe. Since her actual service with the Nádasdy family likely spanned a period of decades, the Countess cared for her in her retirement, setting her up at Csejthe after the death of her husband and the end of her usefulness as a nanny at Sárvár.

Another accomplice, Dorottya Szentes, also known as Dorka or Dorothea, stated under oath that she had been living at the Countess' house in Csejthe since 1605. She was summoned to the castle by Ilona Jó on the best of promises (or "beautiful words") that she would be chosen to serve the Countess' daughter, Mrs. Katalin Drugeth de Homonnay. This never happened. One wonders if there was some disappointment on the part of this old woman at how differently things turned out.

INFAMOUS LADY

The final accomplice, Katalin (Katarina or Kata) Beneczky, had also been living at the Countess' house (Csejthe) since roughly 1600. She was brought to the castle by the wife of ValentinVarga, the mother of Sárvár preacher Michael Zvonaric (Hung.: Mihály Varga Zvonarics), to be a washerwoman— somewhat ironic since preacher Zvonaric was the same man who wrote the letter of inquiry regarding possible excommunication of the Countess' other henchman, Anna Darvolya.

Anna, Ilona Jó, Dorottya, Katalin and Ficzkó would collectively torture and kill dozens of children—almost exclusively servant girls between the ages of 10-14—in their administrative and supervisory roles over the Lady's Staff of young seamstresses, washerwomen, and kitchen maids. Physically, little girls were easy targets for the old women and boy to harass. All of the accomplices agreed that Anna taught them how to torture and kill these children, and all agreed that Countess Báthory took a whip, cudgel, dagger, fire iron, needle, or cutting sheers to them, as well.

It is said that Countess Báthory obsessed about her age and appearance. It was said that she could sit or stand in front of a mirror for hours and, once, in a rage, went on a rampage smashing mirrors throughout the house. Those she missed were ordered either destroyed or covered (in the case of special heirlooms or property on loan). Stories of Erzsébet's remarkable beauty still persist today. We do know that a portrait was rendered in 1585 when the Countess was 25 and that subsequent copies were made from this single original. It is thought that at least one of the copies was commissioned by her son, Pál Nádasdy. One portrait, argued to be the original by historian Raymond T. McNally, has been lost to us, unfortunately, stolen some years ago from a museum. Scholars, however, continue to debate which portrait among the remaining pieces is the original.

The fact that such a wealthy woman would have only one original portrait rendered, especially someone as supposedly vain as Countess Báthory, seems a bit odd. It may be that other works were commissioned but, given the shame later brought upon the family and contempt felt for her by those of her time, they were destroyed. It may also have been a matter of security: Ferenc Nádasdy was no friend of the Turks, and numerous images identifying his wife might not have been particularly wise at the time.

In any case, the few portraits we do have is of a young woman with dark hair pulled back, high forehead (wealthy women of the time plucked, cut and shaved away the hair line so as to make the forehead appear higher and more pronounced), wearing what appears to be a lighter-weight, summer gown (perhaps the portrait was taken around her birthday in August?).

Much has been said that Erzsébet maintained her beauty through sorcery; specifically, she drained her victims of blood so as to bathe in it and thereby restore youthfulness and vitality to her appearance. Supposedly, she discovered the remarkable properties of blood as a "skin cream" after striking a servant so hard that the girl's blood splattered onto Erzsébet's face. Initially, the blood baths worked well. Over time, however, as the Countess continued to age, peasant blood began to lack sufficient anti-aging properties. Only the blood of nobles would work now. Upon the advice of the local forest witch, so the story goes, Erszébet began to seek out high-born girls in order to prepare a stronger remedy.

It is interesting, however, that of all the allegations lodged by over three hundred witnesses—including the Countess' four accomplices who confessed under torture—none specifically mentioned her bathing in the blood of victims. This is likely because the blood-bathing story actually began two hundred years after Erzsébet's death.

In the 1720's, a Jesuit priest named László Turóczi (Turóczy) discovered the sealed trial documents relating to the Báthory case in the attic of Bytča Castle, where the court proceedings had taken place. Intrigued, Father Turóczi used portions of this original source information for his book, *Un-*

garia suis cum Regibus Compendio Data ("Hungary, a Dated Compendium with its Kings"), along with stories he collected from locals living in the villages surrounding Castle Csejthe.

At a time when "vampire mania" was sweeping Europe, the villagers shared their fascinating legends with him about the vampire countess who had bathed in blood to look beautiful. If true, Erzsébet must have been taking her blood treatments when Ferenc was alive and, no doubt early in the marriage when she still cared for him, for she is reputed to have said, "It is my duty to be good to my husband and make myself beautiful for him. God has shown me how to do this, so I would be unwise not to take advantage of this opportunity."

Fr. Turóczi's story was then adapted by Matej Bel in his encyclopedia on Hungarian history and geography, *Notitia Hungariae Novae Historico Geographica*. Because Matej Bel was an academic and his work considered credible, the story went unchallenged. In the latter part of the 18th century, German writer, Michael Wegener, continued to spread the blood bathing legend in his work, *Beitrage zur Philosophischen Anthropologie* ("Atricles on Philosophical Anthropology"). He also contributed new details about a maiden whose blood supposedly splattered on the Countess' face, thus creating the first anti-aging treatment. Hungarians, meanwhile, continued to embellish stories about the Countess. At the time of her death, locals referred to Erzsébet Báthory as the "Infamous Lady" or "Notorious Lady." Two hundred years later, she had become the "Vampire Lady."

Accomplice Ilona Jó stated that Erzsébet beat and murdered the girls such that it drenched her clothes in blood; she often had to change her shirt after administering a beating. If henchman Dorottya (Dorka) Szentes beat the girls, Erzsébet stood alongside, ordering the girls to be stripped, thrown to the ground, and lashed or beaten so hard that a person could scoop up their blood by the handful. Trial testimony seems to indicate that, although she drew a great deal of it, the Countess actually cared very little about the blood from her victims.

ESCALATION (1604-1610)

Specifically, if Erzsébet truly prized her victims' blood for purposes of bathing in it, then one would assume she would have deliberately drained and collected enough of it to fill her bathtub. In fact, given the cubic volume of an ordinary tub, it would have required the blood of nearly thirty victims to do so. According to Ilona Jó, however, the Countess threw off her blood-sodden clothing, let blood wastefully sop into the beds, and even ordered it washed off the stone pavement and floors—hardly the actions of someone who desperately needed it for anti-aging baths. Blood that soaked into the beds and floor was supposedly "enough to scoop up by the handful," but nothing says that anyone actually collected it.

The vampire legend may have begun when witnesses testified that, in her rage, the countess bit her victims. Ilona Jó stated that the Countess bit out pieces of flesh from the girls, but she also attacked them with knives and tortured them in various other ways. Dorka agreed that Erzsébet bit the girls' faces and shoulders when she was indisposed and couldn't actually get out of bed to beat them. We also learn how she stuck needles under their fingernails before cutting off the digits of those who tried to remove the needles. Murderous, sadistic, or psychopathic rage? Yes. Vampire? Hardly, even by the standards of vampire lore itself.

While history has embroidered portions of the Countess' infamy, she was still, however, torturing and killing servant girls (or permitting her overseers to do so), without doubt. Ferenc' reputation and standing could no longer see her through her misdeeds anymore. The Turks were still at large, threatening her properties, and she no longer held any strings over the Emperor, Crown, and Church without him. Worse, her debtors knew that, with Erzsébet out of the way, they would not have to repay their enormous loans. Indeed, Erzsébet is said to have referred to herself now as the "relicta Nadasdyana" (the Nádasdy relic).

Clearly this is why Ferenc sought the protection of his powerful friends, including György Thurzó, to see to his widow and children's welfare. What actual help they provided, however, is questionable. We do know that in 1606, two years after Lord Nádasdy's death, she wrote a letter to Thurzó who, unbeknownst to the Countess, was away in Vienna at the time. Her tone appears urgent, as if she has been trying repeatedly to contact him; the nature of the matter is, unfortunately, unknown to us:

> *Beckov, April 28, 1606: I would like Your Grace to look at these letters and bring to your attention that I have arrived, with the help of God, and am currently here in Beckov (Beczkó) now. I would gladly like to know from Your Grace your current whereabouts. I would like to call your attention to my situation. I urge you, my trusted benevolent Lord, to inform me as to where I can find you and how I might get there in order to speak with you and hear your opinion.*

By November of that same year, she wrote again to Thurzó regarding a political/religious appointment within her lands. Thurzó apparently had a candidate in mind. The Countess, however, demonstrated in an artful and diplomatic way that she was not about to take orders from him:

> *Keresztur, November 11, 1606: I received the letter from Your Grace and took from that which you wrote regarding our close friend, Peter Calli, such that I might give him the Csornaer provost/diocese. I can only write that I would like to do this with great joy and, in fact, have already visited earlier with some close nobles, such as Lord Octavio, to discuss this situation, although I still have not decided the matter. However, today*

I will write to these trusted lords and ask them to convene with me to discuss the matter further and offer what advice they have to give. What action these gentlemen decide to take, I will follow. I will immediately give Your Grace an answer, because you are also involved in the situation, so that our close friends can say what he should be promised.

It appears that if advice or assistance were offered, the Countess probably refused much of it, anyway. She probably did not trust anyone now; everyone had an eye on her property. In any case, she typically fought her own battles.

For instance, when some of her lands were invaded by the troops of Count Banffy, she did not run to Thurzó or Batthyányi for help. Rather, she wrote a warning directly to her assailant: "So, my good sir, you have done this thing. You have occupied my small possessions because you are poor, but I do not think that we will leave you to enjoy them in peace. You will find in me a man."

Indeed, if the Emperor raised an eye over her appearance at Court while still in mourning, even more eyes would be raised. In the coming years, the Countess made frequent trips back and forth to Court, each time demanding that the King himself repay the debts owed to her deceased husband. The Crown refused each time, although always promising to make good. Without Ferenc' steady supply of plundered goods or ransom fees, Erzsébet's funding started to dry up quickly, and she was becoming desperate. The Countess began selling off items in an attempt to raise cash. At first, this was not very hard to do: the manor homes and castles of the Nádasdy estates were like museums or treasure troves, filled with rare and costly items plundered from the Turks over the years.

Finding a buyer, however, was harder. The German merchant, Pech, along with a few others, dealt with the Countess when she wished to sell off her smaller, personal items. Larger items, however, required someone with significant assets. Eventually, as finances grew tighter, Erzsébet Báthory began eying her real estate. She put her castle at Theben up for sale; ironically, the Crown that could not afford to repay any of its debts managed to come up with the money to buy it from her in 1607. Later, in 1610, she would sell Beckov Castle (Blindoc, in Hungarian) for another 2,000 gulden.

We do know that the stress of being alone and vulnerable was catching up with the Countess. Although until the very end she continued to play the *grande dame*, behaving confidently in outward appearance, it does seem as though she suffered from a mental breakdown. Outside of the public eye, she no longer cared what happened to her, simply living for the moment, seeking to indulge herself in any way possible and lashing out with a murderous rage when worried about money or imposed upon by outsiders and obligations.

She may also have suffered from a theological crisis. We know that the Countess was very religious, even mystical perhaps, particularly in her early years. She had grown up in the company of great religious philosophers. The tenets of Calvinism and Catholicism were taught in her own home and, at Sárvár, she became even better acquainted with Lutheranism. Ferenc was raised in the Lutheran faith, as were the Nádasdy children. Erzsébet had been raised a Calvinist, however, and she likely took its theology to heart. For a Calvinist, only the "elect" would go to heaven; although the atonement was sufficient for all, it was efficient only for some. In other words, not everyone would go to heaven: unless he or she was one of the pre-ordained elect or chosen, no amount of prayer, fasting, good deeds, confession or otherwise could change that fate. In this sense, Calvinism departed radically from Catholicism. Calvinism also departed radically from Lutheranism, which taught that the atonement was sufficient, as well as efficient, for everyone; one had only to receive the gift of Christ's atonement in order to secure a spot in heaven.

ESCALATION (1604-1610)

When the Lutheran pastorship at Sárvár threatened to ex-communicate her servant, Anna, with veiled threats to include her as well, and later, when Cardinal Peter Pázmány postulated, rather cleverly, why her deceased Lutheran husband would not be going to heaven whether he was "saved" or not, it probably disturbed Erzsébet more than a little. She may have decided then and there that she was not one of the elect; thus, why bother engaging in any further pretenses. If she was destined for hell, then she might as well do as she pleased in life.

A year after her husband's death, in July of 1605, Erzsé-bet received news of yet another death: this time, her older brother, István Báthory. She put together a retinue to make the journey back to the Ecsed family home for the funeral. A num-ber of young girls attended her. The strain of another funeral was too much for her; according to witnesses, three of the girls were tormented so severely during the trip that they later died. The Countess ordered the bodies to be buried at Branisk, near Sirok, close to the Polish border. A girl of high lineage by the name of Zichy had also been taken to Ecsed and was later killed at Keresztúr. When the girls' relatives came to Erzsébet to ask how the children had died, they received the usual excuse that all had passed away from cholera.

Squire Adam Szelesthey, from the village of Denesfalva, testified regarding this particular trip. He confirmed that, he, too, had heard the two daughters of Gábor Sittkey were cruelly tortured and put to death, as well as the daughter of István Szol-tay. Furthermore, he had learned from a coachman named Petrus, that when the Lady traveled from Ecsed, she tortured the young daughter of a nobleman at length. When the girl died, she was buried midway on the same trip.

Witness Frantisek Török also recounted the terrible tor-ture inflicted on the girls during the Countess' trip to Ecsed. Elaborating on Adam Szelesthey's account, he added that before being buried somewhere between Branyicsa and Sirok, the bod-ies of at least two dead girls were carried in the freight car for three days.

INFAMOUS LADY

During this time, the tension at Sárvár began to mount uncontrollably. It appears that the Lady Widow Nádasdy, now free of her husband's restraints, went on a killing spree. This time, however, without Ferenc' protection, increasing pressure was put on her both by the pastorship as well as her son's tutor, Imre Megyeri. Servants in her household at Sárvár would later testify that within a few years of Ferenc' death, the death toll had risen to nearly 200 murdered victims.

"Only God," one former servant declared, "knows an account of all of her crimes."

Although she had a right to spend the remainder of her life at Sárvár, Erzsébet essentially moved out around this time. With the exception of routine visits to inspect the various properties and winter holidays spent at Sárvár, she took up a nearly permanent residence now at her favorite country retreat, Castle Csejthe.

As discussed, Erzsébet had authority from which to judge local disputes and disagreements personally, much of the time devoted to addressing cases of injustice, revenge, family feuds, and various misunderstandings that occurred at her court. And again, the usual court officials assisted her with this, as we know from documents provided during the investigations. Benedek Bicsérdy, in fact, may actually have been using his power and influence as Castellan at Sárvár to steal from the Countess during her prolonged absences. We know that by 1607, she was becoming increasingly removed from administrative functions. In addition, she was spending less time at Sárvár, preferring the quiet solitude of Csejthe. During this period, Bicsérdy was preparing paperwork, managing the estate, and settling disputes in her name. Documents were prepared, for instance, to resolve a three-year misunderstanding between Benedek Zalay and Michael Tulok, and signed on Erzsebet's behalf by Bicsérdy and local juror, Adam Szelesthey.

88

ESCALATION (1604-1610)

This may shed new light on the recording of a rather unusual gift from Erzsébet and her then nine-year-old son, Pál, (who allegedy requested to sign off on the document, as well) in April of 1607 to Bicsérdy:

> *We, Countess Erzsébet Báthory, in connection herewith to all that it may concern, do hereby declare that the land which, until now, has had no owner and located at the village of Hegyfal, worth an amount of 100 gold, be herewith gifted to Benedek Bicsérdy in acknowledgement of his loyal service of employment to me and my illustrious warrior husband. We give this land to him and his wife Orsika Mesterhazy and their children, namely Jan Bicsérdy, Ferenc Bicsérdy, and those called Anna, Kata, and Erzsébet, and any other future lives under the following terms, so long as in the future he continues to provide us with his loyal service. Should he ever live elsewhere and we or our survivors or heirs desire to acquire the land back, in any event, we shall reimburse Benedek Bicsérdy or his heirs 100 gold.*

One might wonder if the Countess ever made the gift at all and if Bicsérdy, in collusion with the child Pál's tutor, Imre Megyeri, used the boy's signature to line his own pockets. In her weakened state, it is possible that her other high-ranking servants, particularly those at Sárvár, were also robbing her of both cash and property. If that were the case, the later betrayal of the Countess by Bicsérdy and other Sárvár officials would not be so surprising or ironic due to any apparent ingratitude.

Meanwhile, the accounts of torturing continued. In late 1607, György Thurzó prepared to celebrate the marriage of his 22-year-old daughter, Judit, to Baron András Jakusith de Orbova. Erzsébet, of course, was invited to the lavish gala held at the magnificent new Wedding Pavilion at Bytča. On November 16th, she communicated her reply through one of her scribes:

> *Csejthe, November 16, 1607: Erzsébet Báthory relates that she safely reached Csejthe, last Tuesday (13th of November). If God grants her good health, she will comply with Thurzó's wish to attend the wedding of his child. It is her pleasure to serve him.*

That same day, she also sent a personal letter to Thurzó's wife, Erzsébet Czobor. Apparently, the palatine's wife had knowledge that the Countess sent a letter to a certain Lord Derssfy. Athough the contents or purpose of this letter are unknown, the Lady Widow Nádasdy apparently wanted to guarantee its safe passage:

> *Csejthe, November 16, 1607: [You have knowledge] that I wrote a letter to Lord Derssfy. I request you lovingly, as my benevolent Lady Cousin and Relative, to allow the letter to be carried to Sohl by a trusted man. In several and similar cases, may you be convinced that it would cause me joy to show you a service in return....*

As was typical, the stress of another social engagement proved too much for her. The trip home with the Countess through the frigid countryside must have been unbearable for, according to a witness, one of her attending maids tried to escape along the way. This, of course, could not be tolerated. Enraging the Countess, the girl essentially sentenced herself to death. Witnesses recounted that the young servant was taken to the nearby village of Predmier where she was stripped naked in the bitter cold. She was then made to stand up to her neck in water and repeatedly doused until she froze to death.

ESCALATION (1604-1610)

One wonders what might have provoked such retribution. We know that the Countess tended to mete out punishments that, in a dark sort of way, fit the crime. (For example, when a servant girl was accused of stealing a coin, Erzsébet had it heated red hot and then pressed into her hand.) One can almost imagine the scene in the coach: irritable and peevish directly after the wedding, drumming her fingers angrily as she thought about how much cash had been laid out on gifts for Thurzó's daughter, the Countess was already in a foul mood.

Meanwhile, pressed uncomfortably in the carriage amidst her attending maids and their piles of gowns, tresses, and furs, one of the newer, younger girls started to complain—she was cold, thirsty, and had to relieve herself. The Countess' hand turned white as she gripped the handrail. The girl continued to prattle on, chatting and complaining, ignorant of how black Erzsébet's eyes were becoming and how the more senior attendants were now looking away nervously.

Suddenly, the Countess lashed out, grabbing the stupid girl's wrist and twisting it violently. As she cried out in pain, Erzsébet screamed at her, "So you're cold? You're thirsty, you miserable little whore? I'll give you something to drink!"

As she began crying, the Countess struck her violently, pulling her by the hair and clawing at her face. The carriage, which had just started to depart, began to slow as the girl's cries were heard by the coachmen.

"You need to piss, do you?" the Countess continued to twist her arm as the girl writhed and tried to wriggle away. Grabbing for the door, she suddenly managed to break free, nearly falling on her face as she fell from the coach.

The driver wheeled the carriage to a halt as the sobbing girl frantically collected up her garments and struggled to run from the road.

"Go after her!" Erzsébet demanded.

Her coachmen and attendants immediately jumped to the ground, giving chase. As they dragged the crying and kicking girl back, the Countess looked on, livid.

"You will pay for this," she hissed at the girl, "I promise you that."

The girl was bound and gagged, and Erzsébet gave brief instructions to her driver. The carriage set off again, and the moody silence that followed made the senior attendants even more nervous. Meanwhile, the younger girl, still bound and gagged, hoped briefly that the Countess' anger had abated.

Just outside of the nearby town of Predmier, the coach slowed and then stopped near the river. The Countess turned to her young attendant.

"So you're thirsty," she mused, looking out the window. "You're cold. You have to piss."

She reached out and took the girl's chin in her hand.

"Are you still thirsty, dear?"

Tears began to well up in the child's eyes, and she shook her head.

"No?" Erzsébet raised on eye. "Oh, I think you are."

We know from witness testimony that the girl was then stripped naked in the December cold and forced into the river, made to stand up to her neck in water. She was doused repeatedly with water. Taken back to Csejthe, she later died of exposure.

Some months later in 1608, Countess Báthory attended the coronation of King Mátyás. It is interesting that, less than three years before her arrest and trial, Erzsébet Báthory was still making significant public appearances. For the most part, her staff either remained discreet, or the nobility took little notice of lower class gossip (and murder). In any case, some ugly rumors apparently did not bar her from being invited to one of the most prestigious events of the year.

The trip, however, was not without its costs: during the return journey home, Erzsébet's attendants were burned with molten iron and nearly tortured to death. According to witnesses, they were sent barely alive from Presporka to the estate at Keresztúr, where some died shortly thereafter.

A pattern clearly emerges: while Erzsébet made high-profile, public appearances typical of the nobility, they were unusually taxing on her psychologically, particularly in her later years. Accounts of her torturing and murdering are frequently linked to the times when either she had to make a trip or receive visitors socially; the more uncomfortable the visit or social engagement, the worse the fate inflicted upon her victims.

14

CSEJTHE (1604-1610)

When Countess Erzsébet spent time away from Sárvár and Vienna, out of public life, one would have imagined that things quieted down. In fact, they did not. With the exception of the winter months spent at Sárvár and routine visits to the other estates such as Beckov and Keresztúr, the Countess established her new permanent residence at Csejthe. A reign of terror began for the inhabitants of the small, nearby villages such as Újhely, Verbó and Trenčín. In addition to rumors of torture and murder, talk of witchcraft began to surface, as well.

Csejthe (or Cacthice, in Slovak) lies in the Carpathians in what is today western Slovakia, near Trencsény Trenčín. In those days, the region was a part of Hungary. The castle was surrounded by a village and farmland bordered by outcrops of the Carpathian Mountains. Turks plundered the village in 1599, and in 1606, a flood washed away bridges, homes, and scarecrows in the field but, by the time Erzsébet set up her new court there, things had quieted again.

The court at Csejthe was considerably smaller and less distinguished than that of Sárvár or Kerezstúr. Approximately twenty to thirty people cared for the fields and vineyards, and records indicate that matters related to agriculture and livestock were exceptionally well-organized. For the local families, raising their daughters to hold a position as a court seamstress, maid, or household assistant was a great honor. Each applicant had to be personally recommended for her skill.

The household staff at Castle Csejthe was considerably smaller than that of Sárvár, as well. History records the names of the Countess' administrative staff there: her court master who oversaw all of the estates was a man named Benedikt Deseö (or Benedek Deszo). The Countess knew Deseö from Castle Sárvár and brought him with her to head up Csejthe. In addition to the staff at the other properties, Deseö oversaw a number of assistants at Csejthe: Castellans Michael Horwath and János Andachy; Dániel Vas, the stable master; Provisor, Michael Herwoyth; Cellar Master, Mátyás Sakathyartho; and Steward Jakob Szilvassy, who also administered castles Leka and Keresztúr. István Vagy also assisted the main staff, as did Balthizar (Baldisar) Poby, both from Sárvár, and another man by the name of Kozma.

Deseö supervised what is known as the "Lord's Staff" of men who maintained castle security, ran the house and stables, and provided accounting and administrative services for the Countess. Meanwhile, the Countess maintained her small, personal retinue of accomplices that headed up the "Lady's Staff" of female servants, including kitchen staff, seamstresses, maids, washerwomen and female attendants. Of course, the majority of tortured and murdered servants would be taken from this female staff. Anna Darvolya and Dorottya Szentes supervised the Lady's Staff, in addition to János Újváry (Ficzkó), Ilona Jó Nagy; and Katalin Beneczky. In time, all but the deceased Anna Darvolya would be brought in chains to Bytča to defend themselves on criminal charges of torture and murder, while the Countess remained under house arrest awaiting her own fate.

Court Master Benedikt Deseö is an interesting character. Of the 306 depositions gathered during the proceedings against Countess Báthory, we learn that only eight people had access to actually witness her torturing sessions: her accomplices (Anna,

Fizckó, Dorottya, Ilona Jó, and Katalin) certainly, a lady-in-waiting named Ilona Zalay, and then Benedikt Deseö and Jakob Szilvassy. Deseö had an additional connection to the Countess: he was one of eleven trusted men who witnessed and signed her Will in 1610. Janós Ficzkó claimed that Deseö knew the most of anyone regarding what went on behind closed doors; and yet, he never spoke of it to anyone.

Years later, when Benedikt Deseö finally admitted to what he knew, it must have shocked the court.

. . . . .

Having entered the Lady's private chamber to report on castle business, Deseö was somewhat startled to see the Countess with one of her young maids in hand. He knew the girl, a child named Ilonka, who was the daughter of the local shoemaker. The child was crying, evidently terrified. Somewhat embarrassed, he immediately turned back toward the door, when the Countess called out to him.

"Don't leave us, Benedikt. I want you to watch this."

He stopped and turned back around slowly.

"This girl," the Countess said testily, "needs a lesson in discipline."

The Lady suddenly began tearing the clothing from the girl until she was stripped completely naked. Screaming now, the child huddled on her knees, begging and crying, while the Countess retrieved a dagger.

"She is so clumsy with her hands," the Countess went on. "She can't do anything right at all."

The Lady grabbed first the right hand of the girl and then stuck the blade into each of her fingers, one at a time: "She can't seem—to use—her—fingers—properly!"

As the girl continued screaming and crying, the Countess grabbed her other hand and again began stabbing each finger in turn: "Maybe this—will—help—loosen—your fingers, dear."

CSEJTHE (1604-1610)

The girl fell to the floor, clutching her bleeding hands as the Countess slowly swirled around her. Deseö found himself inching back toward the door.

"Mmm," the Countess mused, "Maybe it's not your fingers, after all, is it, dear. Maybe it's your arms."

She appeared to study the sobbing girl for a moment, and then suddenly reached out and grabbed the child's right arm. She began plunging the knife in repeatedly, straight up the arm. Blood pooled around each wound as the girl struggled to get away. The Countess grabbed her hair, jerking her head back, and then began knifing her way up the other arm.

Huddled on the floor now, the girl struggled to rise on her bleeding hands.

"Maybe it's not your arms, after all," the Countess mused, again pretending to study her.

She then went and secured a long crop. She stood over the girl for a moment and suddenly began lashing her violently and repeatedly on the back.

"Maybe the problem is right here!" she screamed, "on the back of the lazy, good-for-nothing little whore that you are!"

Each time the girl tried to crawl away, the terrible pain in her arms and hands caused her to stumble forward. The Countess grabbed her by the hair and began thrashing her again, this time on her legs, thighs, belly and breasts—wherever the crop happened to land in the bloody assault. She also leveled the blows directly into the wounds on the girl's arms and hands, causing her to scream until she lost her voice. Blood, including chunks of flesh, splattered the floor and walls.

Hair disheveled, eyes flashing white behind black pupils, the Countess went and retrieved a burning candle next. The girl was lying on the floor moaning now and on the verge of passing out.

"Don't go into shock yet, dear," she said. "We're not done with you."

The Countess put the flaming candle directly into her hands, causing her to revive momentarily in a new wave of screams. When the eyes rolled back in the head, the Countess held the flame to the hands again until they were burned black.

Deseö watched the torturing continue in this manner until the girl finally died.

. . . . .

Deseö saw other incidents, as well. He also saw how a girl's lips were pierced on two sides with needles, thus fastening her mouth shut; when she moved her tongue between her lips to let it extend out, the tongue was also perforated with a needle. In fact, the Court Master said that he had seen "countless cases in which girls were made to stand naked before Lady Bathory as she beat them."

The scene repeated over and over, as follows:

The girl accused of sewing too slowly or making long or clumsy stitches was stripped naked and made to stand before the Countess. The Countess held either an iron bar or a heavy cudgel in her hands as she paraded past the shivering, sobbing servant.

"Hold out your hand," she commanded.

Wincing, the girl obeyed, only to have the hand struck hard.

If she screamed and pulled the hand back, the Countess would demand, "Hold out your hand and keep it out!"

If the girl shook her head or begged for mercy, the Countess would go into a rage and pummel her. In any case, the hands and fingernails would be smashed and beaten repeatedly until they became swollen, infected, and broken. The Lady then threw needle, thread and fabric at the girl.

"Sew, you whore!"

Unable to raise her hand or move the broken fingers, the sobbing girl cried for mercy.

The Countess now turned to Deseö and her attendants who were standing by.

CSEJTHE (1604-1610)

"What a useless, spoiled whore she is. She can't even sew!"

And then, in a rage, she began shoving the needle into the girl's arm repeatedly, straight up to her shoulder. When the girl tried to wriggle away, the Countess immediately went for her whip or crop, flogging her over and over.

.　.　.　.　.

"She withheld water from many of them until they became very thirsty," Deseö told the court reporter. "When she eventually and finally—on on my honor!—brought them water, each one standing naked before her, the hand was held underneath and then used to drink from."

When asked by the court officials what else he knew, Deseö said that he heard how the wide fire iron was heated; the girls' arms were "burned to smoke and ash."

"The smaller, round fire iron was also heated," he added, "until very hot and—on on my honor!--, shoved into their vaginas."

One can only imagine the look on the notary's face as he took down this information.

"On one occasion," Deseö continued, "while traveling in the direction of Bratislava [along with two female attendants in her coach], Ferenc Zemptey gave Lady Báthory two potato *pogácsa* (*Pogatsche* in German; a type of sweet appetizer) to take along. The mistress gave these to the German girl to hold. The girl ate one and could therefore no longer present it. As a result, the mistress heated the other until it was very hot, and then shoved it, nearly flaming, into the girl's mouth. She subjected these two girls to all sorts of different torments until they finally breathed their last."

.　.　.　.　.

It is no surprise that Benedikt Deseö gave the longest and most elaborate testimony of all the witnesses, and he expressed remorse over what had happened. Deseö was also close enough to the Countess to try to pursuade her away from her actions. He said that he had begged her to stop the killings for fear that she would be arrested; her reply, essentially, was that she was above the law. By late 1610, he had reached a breaking point. At fifty years of age, Deseö had seen enough and was ready to resign. It was Imre Megyeri, however, who urged him to stay on for just a few more weeks until the Countess was arrested. Megyeri evidently knew of the plan to apprehend her after some time after Christmas.

Countess Báthory also hired local tradesmen and practitioners, including carpenter Nicolaus Krestyan, craftsman Adam Pollio, doctor and plaster/paver craftsman Ambrosius Borbély, and the apothecary known as Martinus. Although well-educated and versed in the sciences of the time, Erzsébet Báthory had always been fascinated by the occult, often seeking out the services of local peasant women trained in folk medicine and the black arts. Some of these occult arts were quite legitimate: many of these Slovak peasant women, so-called "forest witches," were trained herbalists who could offer effective, healing medications in a time when doctoring, or barbering, consisted only of battlefield medicine, leeching, amputations, and extractions with iron tools. Other forest witches or town alchemists, however, provided drugs, poisons, magical spells, incantations, oracles and divining devices that fascinated the Countess.

Servant Janós Zluha was ordered to go into the town of Tirnau and visit the apothecary shop of Doctor Martinus, the local pharmacist. He was given orders from the administrator of Castle Csejthe, on behalf of the Countess, to pick up an order of antimony. In small doses, antimony was used to make cosmetics and also valued as a medicinal folk remedy; in large doses, however, it was highly poisonous.

CSEJTHE (1604-1610)

When Doctor Martinus learned of how much antimony was desired, he refused to fill the order. János Zluha now had to provide the letter of authority from the castle administrator, and only then would the pharmicist comply. He did so grudgingly, however: "Tell your mistress," he warned, "that one in possession of such a drug could kill a hundred people if he wanted to!"

Erzsébet believed in black magic as much as she did diplomacy. István Vagy (Waghy), on staff at her court at Csejthe and Sárvár, confirmed that the Lady "possessed a cake of gray color,[braided] like a pretzel, which she was obsessed with." A communion wafer was placed in the middle of the cake. The Lady looked into the wafer to see the image of a person whom she either wished to curse or bless. According to Vagy, "She prayed both against the Palatine, as well as against our King, and also against the judge of the county." She repeated the following incantation over and over: "Herein show me (the name against whom she prayed), so that I cannot be seen by you, so that you cannot cause any harm against me." This went on, according to Vagy, for up to an hour and, according to Janós Ficzko, over two.

Accordingly, Erzsébet Báthory used the cake and wafer to recite curses again the Palatine, the county judge (in some versions, naming Mózes Cziráky personally), and King Mátyás II. Vagy's description of this simple, ritual-magic ceremony is typical of the period. János Újváry, one of the lead suspects in the murder trial, also alleged witchcraft on the part of the Ladyship, including a plot to poison her enemies. According to him, the Countess would do her conjuring with the assistance of a small box, while seated before the braided mirror cake.

Rev. Ponikenusz, the pastor at Csejthe, wrote to his superior to advise him that the Countess engaged in the black arts. He claimed that she received assistance not only from a Slovak forest witch called the Mistress of Miava (Erzsi Majorova) but also from "a wicked woman named Torkoss (also Thorko) who

101

resides miles beyond Sárvár," who once gave her the following advice: "Find a black cat (or hen), kill it with a white stick, keep the blood, and smear it on your enemies. And if not their body, then at least the clothes—and not so stained with blood that your enemy can hurt you more."

As girls died and the clergy increasingly resisted or refused proper burials, the castle staff sought to hide the bodies by burying them in secret, and often at night—frequently in the local cemetery, but in other places as well, including gardens, drainage ditches, grain bins, and fruit pits. Of course, this caused even more rumors of witchcraft and black magic to circulate.

The witnesses, including clergymen, testified uniformly that Anna Darvulia (or Darvolya) was particularly evil. She, in fact, had taught the other servants how to torture girls. János Újváry claimed that she would bind the girls' arms and hands behind them so tightly that the hands would turn deathly pale. The victims would then be beaten repeatedly—up to 500 times, in some cases—until they died. Dorottya Szentes was also particularly cruel, cutting off girls' hands or fingers with scissors. It was also claimed that Ilona Jó was so cruel herself that she had specifically been brought from Sárvár to Csejthe to continue her "work" there.

Any misdeed of duty was an excuse to brutalize or murder the young servant girls. If brushwood was not bundled or the Countess' garments not properly ironed, if the fire was not set for the night or obligatory sewing and mending not completed by 10:00 p.m., if aprons were not set straight or head coverings out of place, the offending girl would immediately be taken out for torturing. In some cases, girls could be tortured ten times in one day. Benedek Bicsérdy spoke of torturing sessions that went on for over six hours.

It is clear that the domestic supervisors of female servants, including Anna Darvolya and Dorottya Szentes, performed a great deal of heavy disciplining and that Ilona Jó and János Újvary assisted in the later years. As for how much torturing Countess Erzsébet Báthory herself performed, the witnesses' responses are interesting. In their initial testimony, the primary accomplices tended to blame each other or, in some cases, Anna Darvolya (who, by then, had died). As they warmed up to the interrogation, however, they began to implicate the Countess directly. They stated that she either commanded them to perform the beatings or would perform them herself.

For example, Szentes and Ilona Jó stated that, when a girl was reported as having stolen a gold piece, the Countess had the piece heated until red hot and then had it pressed into the girl's hand. The Countess would stick pins and needles into the girls' lips or under their fingernails. If the girls cried from the pain, she allegedly said, "Well, if it hurts the whore, then she can pull it out," but if any of the girls dared remove the needle, the Countess would immediately beat them and cut off the fingers in a rage.

Once, when Katalin Beneczky had tired from administering an uninterrupted beating, Dorottya and Ilona Jó, who had been watching, started shouting, "Hit her! Hit her again! Harder! Hit her harder!" The victim, already half dead, was finished off when the Countess herself took up a cudgel, supposedly the width of an armchair, and continued with the beating herself. She would actually have to change her shirts, as they became too blood-soaked to wear.

Her accomplices stated that she would order János Újváry to strike the girls in the face over and over and would then order them locked up in the coalhouse to be starved for a week. Katalin Beneczky testified seeing Erzsébet take a candle to the private area of one of the girls. Although the majority of torturing took place in the washhouse or kitchen at Csejthe (no doubt, since the blood could be washed away more easily there), Szentes added that once, when the Countess was indisposed in bed, she ordered the offending girl to be brought directly to her bedchamber. There, she grabbed the girl from her bed, biting her on the face and shoulder.

As mentioned, the Countess also ordered girls to be submerged in freezing water or doused with water in the winter weather. Most died from this treatment.

Katalin Beneczky recounted another bizarre story that probably took place in October of 1610. When Erzsébet's daughter, Anna (now Mrs. Zrínyi), was visiting Csejthe, the entire female staff was sent upstairs and ordered to remain there. It may be that the Countess merely wanted them out of sight or out of the way, for the mistreatment that followed appeared to be the sole doing of Dorottya Szentes. Beneczky states that Szentes held the girls "in strict captivity like criminals." Those who objected received a cold-water dousing and were made to stand naked outside, overnight. Szentes then watched over them carefully, assuring that they be starved as further punishment. When the male servants became aware of this, they tried to sneak food to the girls. Szentes, however, prevented this, watching over the girls so carefully that no one could help: "May the thunder slay anyone who gives them something to eat!"

Some days later, when the Countess decided to take a trip to the nearby spa at Piešťány with her daughter, she sent Katalin Beneczky to retrieve one of the girls to accompany them. From the trial transcripts, we learn that Katalin herself sometimes refused to perform beatings, such that she herself was punished so severely that she once needed a month of bedrest to recover. It is clear that Anna Darvolya, Dorottya Szentes, and Ilona Jó were the most vicious. For some reason, however, the Countess retained the meaker Katalin Beneczky in her employ—and allowed her to remain alive—despite her refusal to participate fully. In fact, Beneczky was often given the task of hiding bodies or finding new girls. Evidently, the Countess had a soft side for her. It was also said that Beneczky would sneak food to the girls at great risk to herself. In any case, she found all of the girls in deplorable condition as a result of Szentes' actions; they had passed out from hunger, exposure and beatings.

Returning to the Countess, Katalin said nervously, "Not a single one is in a position to travel with Your Grace."

CSEJTHE (1604-1610)

Engraged with Szentes, the Countess clapped her hands together and declared that this should not have happened. The girls were then revived, only to be mercilessly beaten by the Countess and Szentes; they later died in a room of the castle.

15

THE *GYNAECAEUM* (1609-1610)

Anna Darvolya, who had been described as taking particular delight in torment and the one who taught the Countess and others how to torture servants, suffered a blinding stroke and become incapacitated, probably around the year 1609. At this point, the Countess turned more and more to Erzsi Majorova, the forest witch, for advice. In witness testimony, this woman was referred to as the Lady Steward or House Mistress of Miava, indicating that she held a close position to the Countess and, perhaps, had authority over even the four remaining accomplices who ran the Lady's staff of domestics. It does not appear, however, that she actually lived at the court of Csejthe but, rather, only made appearances when summoned.

Unfortunately, dealings with the forest witch may ultimately have contributed to the Countess' downfall. We know that she was becoming out of touch with reality, obsessing more and more over her advancing age and vulnerability. When politics and diplomacy let her down, she turned to black magic for assistance. Erzsi Majorova suggested that the Countess try more drastic measures: the blood of noble girls would have a more powerful influence than that of commoners. Erzsi began supplying her with spells, potions, and magical cakes, as well.

Countess' court. Rumors quickly circulated, however, that the girl was being beaten severely. He went first to one of Erzsébet's accomplices, asking her to see his niece and perhaps give her a little money. The following is his account of what happened.

According to Deseö, the old woman said, "If you value your head, you should not dare to try this without the knowledge of Her Grace."

Deseö learned that the Countess was planning an extended trip to Csejthe; she planned to take the niece with her for an unknown period of time, and he wished to intercept her traveling party before they left. As the horses were being fixed to the carriages, he met up with the Countess.

"Your Grace," he said, bowing to her, "Might I please see my niece before you take your leave? I hear you are going to take her along to Csejthe and no one knows when I might be able to see her again." He added breathlessly, "I also want to give her some money."

Avoiding eye contact, the Lady replied evenly, "You definitely cannot speak with her now."

As his face fell, she added, "But if you want to see her, you can see her when she climbs into the carriage."

She then turned in a rage and hurried to her coach. At this point, only two horses had been hitched, yet she still ascended the carriage, believing the entire team to be ready. Meanwhile, Deseö caught sight of his niece. She was freezing and in tears, and seeing her brought him to tears, as well. He ran after the Countess.

"Merciful Lady," he begged, "please do not take my niece with you! I implore you in the Name of God—not by me alone but on behalf of all my relatives."

The Countess pretended not to hear. Deseö persisted.

"We indeed see that she does not know how to serve the will of Your Grace."

Erzsébet turned to him now, furious.

"I certainly will not give her back, because she has already escaped from me three times. All the more will I kill her!" She cried to the coachman to hurry on now, while Janós Deseö grabbed onto the coach, weeping and begging. The horses secured, the coach lurched forward. Deseö recounted that his niece never returned and that she was later beaten to death.

. . . . .

We also know that by this time, the Countess was getting sloppy. She had managed to hide direct evidence of her torturing for years such that few knew more than rumors as to how the girls had actually died. But not any longer. The girls were now appearing in public with bandaged hands, welts, black and blue marks on their faces, and burn scars. And efforts to keep the beatings a complete secret were also slipping.

For example, when the Countess went to Trencsén in early 1610, György Pellio, a young man from town, saw one of her girls bound and violently beaten and lashed near the river. The girl was then forced into the icy water in her clothes and not permitted to remove them when taken out. Another local, Georgius Habdak, testified under oath that he had seen girls "who were cruelly shattered and covered in bleeding wounds," and kept shackled by the creek. Michael Pepliczky said that in the autumn of 1610, when the Countess came to Csejthe, he saw "two ladies from her entourage with bruises and black and blue marks, and their faces scratched as if by nails." Martin Gonda said that he himself "often saw virgins with swollen faces and hands covered with blue patches." Andreas Somogy, a city official in Újhely, saw two girls whose hands were burned so badly that they needed help ascending into their carriage, and Judge Tomás Jaworka had frequently seen the faces of the virgins in her retinue "disfigured and covered with blue spots from numerous blows." When craftsman Adam Pollio was called to the castle to do a job, he actually witnessed a "naked girl with her feet shackled to a table." Perhaps the worst slip occurred when a tortured servant girl managed to escape and make her way back to town, a knife still stuck in her foot.

In addition to townspeople, church officials and grave diggers also saw their fill. János Palenyk saw for himself the bodies of the girls who died during the wedding celebration of Katalin and György Homonnay, "covered with horrible wounds, their faces crushed, burned and full of blue spots." The sexton at the church in Kosztolány, György Mladych, added that they were "disfigured...shattered and covered with stains," and Michael Palenyk testified to the same.

Even the household staff was seeing direct evidence now: Sárvár servant, Ferenc Török, testified to seeing girls with their arms tied up "such that their hands were blue and blood came from the fingers," and the knight Ferenc Bornemissze said that, once, as he arrived into the house of the Lady, he witnessed girls "with their hands bound, wrapped with rein straps and hanging from the iron lattice at the window by their hair."

Sárvár Judge, Gergely Páztory (a man who would witness the Countess' Last Will and Testament) had an odd encounter with henchman, János Ficzkó, the boy kept on staff by the Countess to assist with torturing and burying girls. While in Csejthe, one of the judge's servants got into a fight with Ficzkó. When Ficzkó became enraged and began beating the servant mercilessly, the judge stepped in. Ficzkó immediately ran inside to the Lady to complain.

Countess Báthory came out. Calling to the judge, she demanded, "Why have you upset Ficzkó?"

The judge answered, "Because he is a bad person who hit my servant. If my servant does something wrong, I can punish him for it."

The judge did not stop there but, rather, levied an accusation against Her Ladyship: "I am rather surprised that Your Grace keeps such a bad man in your court. You should have a chat with him about the things he sees and hears around here. Just now he spoke of things, which, if Your Grace knew, would certainly not be good to publicize. He just told us that five dead girls would be hidden under the hemp!"

The Countess paused and then said, "Tomorrow I will ask him what he said."

According to the judge, the mistress summoned Ficzkó the next day, "but said not a single word and asked him nothing, but rather talked about other things."

The judge went on to say that, during the war, when they had fled to Sárvár, he saw an unsealed crate in the Lady's house, and it was said that the dead girls would be shut in there. Henchman Ilona Jó, who would later be executed for complicity, was actually taking the box out from the castle when a nobleman from Zopor, named Sebestyén Orbán, asked her, "What is really in that box, Ms. Ilona?"

She is said to have replied, "Ask not, on my soul, your Honor!"

The judge added that, once when he was traveling with the Countess as part of her entourage, they took overnight accommodations. There, he saw a bag packed with small chains and locks. When the loaded bag was taken from the carriage and brought into the house, he asked Ilona Jó, "For what do we need these chains and locks?"

Her reply was simple: "At night, all the girls are put in chains."

Members of the area nobility also made allegations. Lady Anna Welykey (who, herself, would be accused of procuring girls for the Countess) recounted that she had once asked Lady Widow Nádasdy to bring her girls around again so as to introduce them to the local aristocracy. Countess Báthory is said to have replied, "Ah, how could I trust or introduce these girls after so many bad and terrible things are told far and wide about them." She then turned to Lady Welykey and added, "Those whores lie."

But what was perhaps most shocking were allegations of exactly how these girls were being tortured and killed: washed with and made to roll on the floor in nettles; pins stuck into their lips and under the finger nails; needles jammed into their shoulders and arms; floggings on the breasts while held in chains; their hands, arms and abdomens scorched with burning irons; chunks of skin wrenched from their backs with pliers; noses, lips, tongues and fingers pierced with needles; mouths forced shut with clamps; flesh cut out of the buttocks and from between the shoulders, then cooked and served to them; flesh and private parts singed with candles; knives plunged into arms and feet; hands crushed and maimed; fingers cut off with scissors and sheers; red-hot pokers shoved up vaginas; bodies beaten to death with cudgels; lashings until flesh fell from the bones; and girls made to stand naked in the cold, doused with water, or submerged up to the neck in icy rivers.

In a matter of weeks, in fact, the entire "school" had been wiped out. Instead of using her usual excuse of an epidemic, this time Erzsébet concocted an elaborate explanation: one of the girls had murdered all the rest because of her greed for their jewelry. The child later committed suicide when Erzsébet's servants discovered what she had done.

This time, the Countess had gone too far. Nearly a dozen complaints from the families flooded both the Palatine's and King's Courts, specifically accusing the Countess of torturing and murdering young girls from the Hungarian aristocracy. When news reached the King that noble girls had been murdered, he had what he needed to push for a criminal conviction.

16

THE PROCEEDINGS AGAINST THE COUNTESS (1610)

By 1610, time was running out for Countess Báthory. Ironically, the man most responsible for whether she would live or die for her crimes was not the king or emperor but, rather, her family confidante, György Thurzó. Thurzó came from an old and distinguished line. Together with the Fuggers Dynasty of Augsburg, the Thurzós were one of the wealthiest families of the 15th century, controlling the vast mining industry of central Slovakia. Unfortunately, by the mid-16th century, the Thurzó lineage was on the verge of dying out. György Thurzó's father, who served as a Catholic bishop (although not ordained) in Nitra, eventually left the Church, converted to Lutheranism and married in order to preserve the line and consolidate the family fortune.

György Thurzó received a magnificent education in Vienna, studying, in fact, with companion, Prince Ernst Hapsburg. We know that Thurzó could read and write in Hungarian, Latin, German, and Slovak, was versed in the humanities, and studied law. Although raised a Lutheran, György Thurzó was politically savvy enough to know his interests would be well served by maintaining good relations with the Catholic Hapsburgs. He also believed that the Hapsburgs comprised the only force realistically capable of overpowering the invading Turks.

When Thurzó finally rose to the status of Palatine in 1609, the same post that Tamás Nádasdy had held, he became second in command to the king. The palatine functioned like a governor or prime minister, representing the king in all political matters and holding appropriate judicial as well as military rank. Amidst the political and religious turmoil of the time, Thurzó would become well known for his diplomacy and ability to draw compromise out of opposing parties. He would certainly need to bring all of his skill to bear in the coming months with Her Ladyship, the Widow Nádasdy.

By February of that year, anonymous complaints and rumors of Countess Erzsébet Báthory's torturing and killing, including the murder of noble girls, had reached both György Thurzó and King Mátyás himself. Of all the nobles and renowned clergy who knew of the Countess' activities, the parties who brought an actual written report to the authorities were probably the most unlikely of all: an elderly country priest, recently retired, and his relatively inexperienced replacement.

Like other clergymen in his situation, the elderly pastor at Csejthe, 90-year-old Rev. András Barosius (Berthoni), was concerned over the Countess' bizarre and repeated requests for funerals. When his questions went unanswered, he began to keep a record of the bodies, and this document eventually made its way into the hands of both Palatine and King. Erzsébet had dealt with this type of situation before at Sárvár, under Pastor Magyari. In those days, however, Ferenc Nádasdy was there to protect her. Whether through charm, reputation or bribery, the Count had always managed to extricate himself and his wife from harm, appeasing the clergy every time questions arose over mysterious deaths.

Now, however, the Countess was on her own. And this time, the clergy was beginning to speak out and stand up to her wherever the killings were taking place. At Keresztúr, for example, where girls had been killed at Erzsébet's estate, Pastor Pyrethräus (or Pythiräus or Piterius) flatly refused to bury the continuous stream of maidens who had died of "unknown and mysterious causes." Despite the Countess' threats, he stood his ground. In return, she ordered her servants to bury the girls secretly at night in the town cemetery.

At Csejthe, Pastor Barosius updated his in-coming successor, Reverend János Ponikenusz, on the strange events and rumors going on there, as well. Ponikenusz was also made aware of his predecessor's continuous arguments with the Countess over the death of so many young girls. Each time the elderly man tried to speak up, the Countess would snap, "Do not ask how they died. Just bury them!"

Intimidated, Pastor Barosius complied, but he began drawing up his report and documenting all of the bodies that had been buried in secret. In one entry that shocked even György Thurzó, the pastor wrote that on a single night he had buried no less than nine virgins, all of whom had died of the same "unknown and mysterious causes."

When Ponikenusz took over at Csejthe, he decided to see for himself what was happening. Following up on a rumor, he went down to explore a series of underground tunnels that connected the church and castle. The Countess and her staff used these tunnels for storage where they housed heirlooms, Ottoman treasures, wines, and documents. Along with the crypt of Count Kristóf Orságh, one-time owner of Csejthe Castle, Rev. Ponikenusz found something else far more ghastly. Amidst what he described as "an unbearable stench," he discovered nine unsealed boxes that contained the remains of recently mutilated girls.

Upon discovering the bodies in the tunnels, he hurried back to the church to write a letter to his superior, the Very Rev. Élias Lányi: "Oh such terrible deeds," he wrote, "such unheard of cruelties! In my opinion there has never existed a worse killer under the sun. But I must not go on, for my heart is bleeding and I cannot speak any more."

Ponikenusz attempted to send the letter, but it was promptly intercepted by the Countess' staff. Upon learning that the letter had been captured, he feared the worst for himself and tried to escape out of town. Castle staff went after him, however, and sent him back to the church with a stern warning. The bodies, meanwhile, were taken away to Leseticz for burial, according to witness, Tamás Zima.

It was at this point that Ponikenusz began plotting how to get his letters, as well as his own newly-found information from Pastor Barosius' disturbing report, to the authorities without being discovered. Ponikenusz evidently figured out how to do it, and the report was secretly delivered to Palatine György Thurzó. It is likely that a second copy was also delivered to King Mátyás II, for it is the King who specifically demanded an investigation into allegations that had reached his Court regarded certain "inhuman and ferocious acts" of Erszébet Báthory. The King was especially displeased that some of these acts had been committed against daughters of the nobility. As Palatine, György Thurzó had full authority to act in the King's name and was ordered to convene an investigation.

For Thurzó, this must have been delicate: he had been given Ferenc Nádasdy's deathbed request to care for the Lady Widow Nádasdy and her children. In addition to his friendship with the late Count, György Thurzó and Countess Báthory were also personally close. Correspondence indicates that they referred to each other as "cousin," attended their respective children's weddings and, in general, kept company together during the holidays. Countess Báthory was also cordial with Thurzó's young wife, Erzsébet Czobor. Given her high station, he knew that it would take a special act of Parliament even to bring formal charges against the Countess. György Thurzó probably hoped to appease the King, quiet things down and then let the matter die. Letters to Erzsébet's son-in-law, as well as public statements, indicate that Thurzó initially planned to put the Countess away in a convent. György Thurzó was not naïve, however; he also knew that the Crown had a personal interest in seeing Erzsébet Báthory convicted criminally. Should that happen, the King's debt to her could be cancelled and, possibly, her lands ceded to him.

It is difficult to truly understand Thurzó's relationship with the Countess: some commentators have vilified him as a man who sought only to betray and deprive her of her property. And yet, history does not bear this out: at all times, Thurzó conducted his coming dealings, albeit secret ones, with both Báthory and Nádasdy family members and, in fact, worked hard to make certain that neither King nor Church confiscated their properties. Other than protecting the interests of fellow Protestants, Thurzó does not appear to have benefited, at least financially, from his pending prosecution of the Countess.

Others have argued the opposite, claiming that Thurzó and the Countess shared a romantic relationship and that he did all in his power to protect her. Yet history does not demonstrate this fully, either: as Lord Palatine, Thurzó had a job to do, and both Monarchy and Parliament were watching him carefully. While, without question, he worked tirelessly to spare the Countess from the death penalty, Thurzó ultimately sentenced her to life imprisonment. He also testified in court as to having caught her in the act of torturing and murdering servants, declared publicly that she did not deserve to breathe air or see light, and referenced her with epithats such as, "wild animal," "bestial," "damned," "bloody," "godless," and "cursed"; hardly the words or actions of a lover.

We do know, however, that Thurzó placed his confidence in the Hapsburgs as the only force viable enough to conquer the marauding Turks. While the Transylvanians maintained a relative form of independence from both Hapsburgs and Turks, their loyalties swayed back and forth between the two opposing forces depending on their own self-interests. Erzsébet Báthory's relatives, Voivods of Transylvania, were now advocating a rebellion against the Hapsburgs and a new alliance with the Turks. This made Thurzó nervous. In 1608, Erzsébet began financing her cousin, Gábor, placing her in a dangerous position; her loyalty to the Crown was now at question. Prior to this, her brother István Báthory had educated and raised Gábor at his court and, upon Count Báthory's death, also left the young man with considerable wealth and weaponry.

Thurzó truly believed that Erzsébet's cousins, Gábor and Zsigmond, were stirring up a dangerous form of trouble that would ultimately threaten the interests of Hungarian landlords and nobles like himself; Gábor Báthory, in fact, would soon declare war on the Hapsburgs. And Erzsébet made it clear, on more than one occasion, that she supported her cousins against the King. That said, there was motivation on Thurzó's part, whether personally or as Palatine of Hungary, to curtail the power of the Báthory family in the interest of the nation.

The year 1610 began with a wedding. Erzsébet's daughter, Katalin, was set to marry Lord György Drugeth de Homonnay on January 6th. The wedding was to be held at Csejthe Castle, and Countess Báthory planned a lavish event. Despite the political intrigue beginning to swirl around her, the Countess temporarily put all out of mind.

Katalin was the youngest, and supposedly favorite, child of Erzsébet, and the one who would bring her mother food and supplies during her later incarceration. Apparently, Kata also participated in at least one torturing session with her mother. The soon-to-be Countess of Homonnay was spending time with Erzsébet at Csejthe just before her wedding day. It may be that mother was instructing daughter in the ways of being a good wife. In any case, the situation soon got out of control. Both Katalin and the Lady were reputed to have tortured and burned two servant girls in their chambers that night. A witness saw traces of torture, how the girls had been burned, and how he had heard the Lady actually put a hot iron into their vaginas. The two girls died while the wedding festivities were going on, and numerous servants and townspeople were aware of how their bodies were taken away to Kostolány for what was supposed to be a secret burial.

The church sextant at Kostolány, as well as two grave diggers, testified later under oath that the girls were covered in welts, their faces mangled. According to nursemaid, Ilona Jó, Katalin also provided her mother with a servant girl through the Countess' stable master, Dániel Vas. More likely than not, Katalin knew exactly what would happen to the child once in her mother's service.

The rumors continued to multiply, and the first legal steps taken against the Countess began in February of 1610. Under orders from the King, an investigation into the Countess' alleged activities was initiated. On March 5th, Györy Thurzó dispatched two letters: one to Chief Notary, András of Keresztúr, and the other to Deputy Notary and Judge, Mózes (Mojzis) Cziráky. Thurzó stated: "You know how, both in the past and present time, several serious complaints have come to us regarding the noble...Lady Erzsébet Báthory...; namely, that [she], through some sort of evil spirit, has set aside her reverence for God and man, and has killed in cruel and various ways many girls and virgins and other women who lived in her *Gynaecaeum*."

Thurzó then ordered the two men "to collect and make inquiries of witnesses, as the law of the Kingdom requires." No one was to be exempt: "...As soon as you receive this letter,...question every member of both the ecclesiastical state as well as the nobility and other honorable people of all classes and of both sexes." Thurzó ordered Cziráky to question residents of Györ, Sopron, Vas, Zala and Veszprém counties; András of Keresztúr was to interrogate witnesses from Bratislava, Nitra, Trenčín and Bars counties. To encourage honesty, a heavy financial penalty would be levied against anyone who lied under oath.

From March through July of that year, András of Keresztúr interrogated 34 witnesses, completing his report on

September 19, 1610. Many of the witnesses called were commoners, coming primarily from the nearby market town of Újhely. Fourteen of them were subjects of Dániel Pongrácz, the local lord who shared equitable holdings with the Nádasdys in the land surrounding Castle Beckov; seven were servants of Peter Rattkay; and five were vassals of Squire Ferenc Magochy who also also owned neighboring property. It is ironic that the servants who would never have been allowed entry onto the Countess' lands without permission were now being invited freely to testify as to what they knew about her. They behaved with discretion, however, admitting that they had seen nothing with their own eyes, having heard only rumors. It may be that they were afraid of the powerful Lady who was still at large. Nevertheless, they relayed what they had heard. For example, Miklós Kuzkleba, a servant of Pongrácz, testified that he had heard a rumor that the Countess murdered two noble girls from Liptov County. He had also heard from his son that a girl was bound and then very violently beaten and lashed before being submerged into the ice cold water of a river.

A number of witnesses, including György Premerská, Miklós Kochanovsky and György Blanár, said that they had heard Erzsébet Báthory killed two girls during the Homonnay wedding celebration and buried them in Kostolány. Other witnesses to step forward included Matthias Muraközy, and Rev. Stephen Raczyczenus. a noble and clergyman who testified to what they had heard regarding girls lost to the *Gynaecaeum*.

It is is interesting to note, however, that of the 34 witness accounts, nothing conclusive resulted. With the exception of a single witness, Andreas Somogy, a city clerk who claimed to have seen girls with badly burned hands, not a single deponent actually saw or heard anything personally. All admitted that they knew nothing other than what someone else had told them.

Meanwhile, things were not going much better for Deputy Notary, Mózes (Mojzis) Cziráky, who began his interrogatories on March 25th. While András of Keresztúr focused his efforts on the inhabitants of the town of Újhely,

Cziráky concentrated on the staff at Castle Sárvár. Most deponents were still in the Countess' employ at that time, however, and if they did know anything, they were reluctant to speak: Sárvár Vice Castellan (Warden), Gregor Paisjárto, knew only that a dead girl had been taken out for burial but had no idea how she died; Paymaster Benedict Zalay said that his only duty was to supply the castle—not to concern himself with rumors; doctor Ambrus Barbély saw only the faces of girls to whom he had administered medicines and knew of no ill effects on their bodies; Vice Warden Paul Beöd knew nothing more than hearsay and that some girls had been taken out for burial. As before, witnesses from town knew little more than rumors of cruelty, having seen nothing personally.

Only a handful of the 18 witnesses interrogated by Cziráky offered anything promising or useful to the court: Castellan Benedict Bicsérdy had seen a bloodstain on a wall, heard the sound of beatings from outside the castle, and knew of 175 dead girls and women taken out of the house; like the others, however, he never witnessed the torturing personally. Rev. Michael Zvonaric recounted the odd story of three girls packed into a single coffin; Ferenc Török claimed to have seen girls with arms tied so tightly that the hands were blue and blood came from the fingers; Castellan Balthasar Poby claimed to know of two or three hundred who had died; and István Vagy testified to magical practices against government officials.

In all, however, it was not the kind of case-closed evidence that the King or Palatine desired, particularly when trying to bring an action against a woman of such high stature as the Lady Widow Nádasdy.

By June, with the proceedings well underway and rumors against their mother-in-law nonetheless piling up, Barons Miklós Zrínyi and György Drugeth de Homonnay met with György Thurzó for a round of secret negotiations. How, they wanted to know, could they keep this scandal from getting out of control? Thurzó was already contemplating a plan and asked the younger men if he could count on their loyalty. They agreed.

THE PROCEEDINGS AGAINST THE COUNTESS (1610)

Meanwhile, Countess Báthory learned of the supposedly secret proceedings that were taking place against her. It would not have been difficult, however; by now, the inquests were public knowledge. In response, she launched a rather bold move by attempting to protest her innocence. Of the nearly dozen young noblewomen said to have died by her hands, one named Zsuszana Hernath stood out: either Zsuszana really did die of natural causes or her mother, a widow, was easily bribed. In any case, on August 24, 1610, the Countess personally appeared at the Court of Vasvár-Szombathely (Eisenburg), no doubt to the astonishment of the legal authority there, accompanied by the Widow Hernath. Mrs. Hernath proceeded to make a spontaneous declaration to the court that her daughter did not die of torture but rather from natural causes. We are not sure of the court's reaction; we know only that this statement was never taken into account either by the judicial system, King, or Palatine.

Evidently, the Countess realized that she had not gotten very far. That said, on September 3, 1610, she wrote her Last Will and Testament, declaring that all of her assets pass equally to her three children: son, Pál, and daughters, Anna and Kata. She asked only that they wait until the presently 12-year-old Pál reach the age of majority before dividing the property and, in the meantime, take care so that no harm came to it. It is nearly certain that she was now receiving legal advice and that a trusted advisor suggested she divest herself of her property; doing so would make her a less attractive target to the King. We do know that she began corresponding with her younger cousin, Gábor Báthory, Voivod of Transylvania, regarding the legal status of her holdings and, possibly, a political alliance with him.

One month later, she returned to Sárvár where she collected most of her jewelry and other personal valuables and then ordered it sent to Csejthe Castle, officially establishing Csejthe as her new court. She likely knew the walls were closing in on her.

The notaries' reports were submitted in the fall of 1610. After reviewing the documents, the matter was still not conclusive enough for Thurzó to make an arrest. However, he would have to act somehow, and soon—the King was becoming impatient. The Palatine was willing to stall at least through the Christmas holiday when Parliament was set to adjourn.

Meanwhile, relations between the Countess and Thurzó were rapidly breaking down. Fights, apparently, were even breaking out between their households. On October 20, 1610, Erzsébet Báthory fired off an angry letter to the Palatine, initiating a complaint against his servant, Kaspar Pattai. According to the Countess, this man was involved in a large controversy with her staff and also abused her entire house. "This cannot be tolerated," she concluded, "and therefore requires protection against such an insult."

By November, Miklós (Nicolaus) Zrínyi wrote to Thurzó, reaffirming his and Drugeth's loyalty. Thurzó was hatching a plot to either put the Countess away in a convent or imprison her for life in Csejthe Castle, and her sons-in-law promised not to interfere. In fact, they were preparing to take over the administration of her estates immediately upon her apprehension. Another letter from Zrínyi to Thurzó, written on December 12th, confirmed that the men had perpetual imprisonment at Csejthe Castle in mind. Whether or not they knew of the Countess' Last Will and Testament, they were already discussing how to divide her estate. One can even glimpse a bit into Zrínyi's personality by the concern he raises regarding his share of choice property:

> ....At your command, I sent my most loyal, main men and servants to Csejthe so that Mrs. Nádasdy can remain there in peace, as we have all agreed with you—also, so that no harm will come to the property and that the Royal Treasury cannot assess anything against it and, above all, so that no further injustice will be added to the family....

THE PROCEEDINGS AGAINST THE COUNTESS (1610)

*However, I would like to remind you that we have
not yet agreed concerning the allocation of property—indeed, it may not even happen quickly, and
I would object to that. I do not know in which
way Your Grace will decide; in any case, I am
convinced that I am to receive an equal share
along with the other relatives, and I also want the
same part of the property on this side as well as
the other side of the Danube. I am aware of Your
Grace's benevolence certainly and, in my heart, I
hope that you are pleased with my advantage....*

With Erzsébet's powerful sons-in-law in league, Thurzó
prepared to bring the matter to a conclusion. Before he took this
final step, however, he himself had to be absolutely certain of
the Countess' guilt. In December, his Castellan at Bytča, Gáspár
Bajáky (also spelled Nagy-Najáky, and even Casparus Echy))
recorded the testimonies of forty local villagers under oath who
claimed, in like fashion, that they had heard stories of torture and
murder at Countess Báthory's court. Sometime before Christmas, Thurzó went to Csejthe to meet personally with Erszébet
Báthory. He informed her of the numerous accusations lodged
against her and asked her to account for it. He particularly
wanted to know about the girls listed in Pastor Barosius' report
and the heavy denouncements that Rev. Ponikenusz was making
from the pulpit.

The one thing that we can say about Countess Báthory is
that she was an incredible actress who could lie with a smile and
turn on an almost hypnotic charm. In public, she portrayed an
image of noble bearing, calm stoicism, and enlightened intelligence. Everything about her *seemed* normal to her peers: her
letters, the way she entertained, her always-elegant demeanor.
In public, this was a noblewoman who simply raised a finger or
gave a slight nod of the head to summon servants. At least in
front of other aristocrats, she was not some disheveled lunatic or
shrill harpie. The accusations simply did not make sense when

one saw this well-spoken, level-headed woman. Thurzó, no doubt, wanted to see for himself if his distantly related kinswoman could account for the bizarre allegations.

In any case, the Countess replied with her usual charm and measured calm. While serving tea and cakes, she assured Thurzó that such accusations were pure nonsense and the mistake of Pastor Berthoni (Barosius), a very old man—many of the girls had simply died from an epidemic and had been buried hastily and in secret to avoid a panic. So it had been at Sárvár and the other estates. The Countess might also have retold the explanation given to the aristocratic parents, including the story of the girls' bloody fight over jewelry. Whatever she said, she managed again to delay the inevitable. Thurzó left her castle without deporting her to a convent, arresting her, or further incident.

Immediately afterwords, however, the Countess went into one of her rages, typical of stressful events. More girls died. As mentioned, whenever Erzsébet Báthory had to put on an act in public, whether through entertaining, attending a social function, or covering her tracks, it placed an absolutely enormous stress on her. Essentially, the pressure of playing the gracious host, submissive wife, or enlightened noble caused a murderous rage to well up within her. Whether this pathology was traced to brutalization she herself received, or some other imbalance, the rage was clearly psychotic. We know that when she suffered from illness or fretted about money, it also caused her to lose control. In some cases, she could not contain her murderous rage for even minutes after the conclusion of a stressful event.

Erszébet's servants were becoming noticeably careless, however. And it was getting harder for them to find ways in which to dispose of the bodies. Ficzkó recounted: "Beside the [bodies] referred to in Pozsony (Bratislava) already, five bodies were later tossed into a pit; two into the water canal in the Csejthe garden, one of which was dragged out by the dogs; two were brought at night to Leceticz (Lesticze) and buried in the church; these had been brought down from the castle where they had been murdered. The old women hid and buried the dead girls. Here at Csejthe, I myself helped to bury four: two at Leceticz, one at Keresztúr and one at Sárvár. Others were buried with chant (i.e., given ordinary funeral burials)."

The other accomplices testified in like manner. Dorottya Szentes and Katalin Beneczky described how five girls had died once within a ten-day period at Csejthe. Having no idea what to do with the bodies, the remains were simply stacked underneath beds, against walls, or put into storage areas. At Sárvár, Katalin Beneczky dragged bodies into a fruit pit, and once right through the courtyard amidst a crowd on onlookers; the pastor buried the corpses that could not be hidden. Dorottya Szentes, with János Újváry's help, buried another girl at Leseticz. At Sárvár, Katalin Beneczky was charged with the task of scraping out the floor of the house and burying bodies in there. With Dorottya Szentes's help, she also hid bodies in the canal—which, unfortunately, were later uncovered by Count Zrínyi's dogs and seen by his servant when he and Erzsébet's daughter, Anna, were visiting.

This time, the household staff stupidly dropped four dead girls over the walls of Castle Csejthe. Although they had hoped that the bodies would catch the attention of nearby wolves, it was the attention of nearby villagers that caused the real problem. These same villagers immediately reported what happened to the authorities.

On Christmas Eve, six days before her imprisonment, the local clergy paid her a visit: Pastor Nicolaus Barosius from the town of Verbó, as well as other clergymen, all exorting her to repent from her evil deeds. Thurzó was also summoned again: he announced that he would also be returning to Castle Csejthe on Christmas Eve, this time with King Mátyás himself, and Imre Magyeri, young Pál Nádasdy's guardian and tutor at Sárvár.

Although the clergymen were likely nothing more than an irritation to her, the Countess dreaded Thurzó and the King. In fear of their arrival, Erzsébet went immediately to the Slovak forest witch, Erzsi Majorova. It is here that she requested a means in which to render herself "invisible" from her attackers.

Though she probably did not expect a literal result, she would definitely have wanted the authorities to lose interest in her and go away. Around 4:00 p.m. on Christmas Eve, Majorova and the Lady prepared a special grey cake, braiding the dough like a pretzel and placing a communion wafer in the center of it. One supposedly could peer into the wafer to see the image of a person against whom the conjuring was performed. As servant István Vagy and Rev. Ponikenusz recounted, Erzsébet sat in front of the cake before the men's arrival, chanting a spell for over an hour to "render [herself] invisible from her enemies." Dough for two other cakes was made from the remaining ingredients, having been prepared from a special mixture of dirty bath water from a baking trough in which the Countess' is said to have sat, as well as creek water and certain other "special" ingredients. One cake was readied to be served after dinner that evening; dough for a second cake was held in reserve should another batch be required. Fizckó and other witnesses assumed that the cakes were made specifically to poison the three guests.

Whether Erzsébet actually intended to kill these men or merely use the cake as a magical means of driving them away from her, Fizckó stated in the original trial transcript that the King, Palatine and tutor all became ill after eating it, and even they themselves thought that she was trying to poison them. We know that they left shortly after this disastrous dinner party; the Countess' plan to drive the men away from her worked, but not in quite the way that she had hoped. Immediately thereafter, Imre Megyeri filed a formal charge against the Countess with the Hungarian Parliament, alleging the murder of servant girls at Sárvár. As for Thurzó's plan to settle the matter by sending Erzsébet off to a convent, all hope was now lost.

With no further options available and, under orders from the King delivered on December 27th, Thurzó set out from Bratislava on a two-day ride to Csejthe. He was accompanied by Megyeri; Erzsébet's sons-in-law, Counts Drugeth and Zrínyi; and an armed escort. He and his men arrived on the night of De-

cember 29, 1610, prepared to apprehend Countess Erzsébet
Báthory and her accomplices.

The same day that Thurzó set out from Bratislava, December 27th, his young wife, Countess Erzsébet Czobor, sent a
letter to him. The letter is fragmented and obviously picks up on
a prior dialogue between the two. It raises some interesting
questions, however:

> *My Lovely Soul, Dearest,*
>
> *As you requested, I sent a kitchen maid. They say
> that she (or he - Hungarian doesn't indicate
> which) is still the same, but whether it's true or
> not, only God knows. Well, whatever command-
> ment has been broken, then it is very likely that
> after this it will be easily done (or "to act even
> against the others") and it is possible that these
> people provide false testimony against them. Who
> knows what is at the castle. They say that she
> does the beating (flogging/whipping) herself, with
> her hand, and if she had to meddle and if she
> were surely, then it would have to be thoroughly
> investigated, as Your Grace commanded. I will be
> taking care of matters here with all my might, my
> lovely soul, my beloved, and my lord.*

Erzsébet Czobor's letter is, in many ways, a mystery as well as a
key piece of evidence. We know that Countess Czobor married
as a teen and was unable to read or write when she and György
Thurzó met. Her husband tutored her, however. While, by this
time, she could write, her style is nonetheless fragmented and
unsophisticated. We know from correspondence that Countess
Báthory and Countess Czobor had a cordial relationship and
that, in some ways, Erzsébet might have even taken the much

younger woman under her wing. We also know that Thurzó trusted his wife and confided intimate details regarding the case to her.

Even two days before the raid, however, there still appears to be some uncertainty as to whether Countess Báthory, Thurzó's long-time family friend and distant relative, was a monster or herself the victim of dreadful rumors. "Whether it's true or not," Countess Czobor mused, "only God knows." There are also unanswered questions: when Countess Czobor says that she sent a maid as her husband requested, one has to wonder if that person was a spy who infiltrated the Báthory court, a guide who would lead Thurzó's men to the victims, or someone completely unrelated to the present case.

Also, when she says, "it is possible that these people provide false testimony against them," one wonders if she was referring to servants who were spreading untruths against Countess Báthory or to the accused who might attempt to deceive the court. Finally, she concludes her letter with a promise to carry out mandates from her husband to the best of her abilities. We wonder whether that meant the ordinary care of the estate in his absence or something more directly related to the case.

Shortly before Thurzó and his men arrived, Countess Báthory and the Mistress of Miava (Erzsi Majorova) spent an evening engaged in the magical arts. According to Rev. Ponikenusz in a letter to Éliás Lányi, the Mistress gave Erzsébet a spell. The two women went outside, watching the stars and clouds that night, accompanied by a scribe. The scribe was then ordered to take down the following utterance (he later revealed this writing to judicial authorities, apparently under pain of death were he to falsify it):

> *Help, oh help, you clouds! Help, clouds, give*
> *health, give Erzsébet Báthory health! Send, oh,*
> *send forth, you clouds, 90 cats! I command you,*
> *Leader of the Cats, that you hear my command*

and assemble them together, from wherever they may be, whether they are on the other side of the mountain, beyond the water, beyond the sea—that these 90 cats come to you and, from you, should go straight into the heart of King Mátyás and also the heart of the Palatine! In the same way should they chew to pieces the heart of the Red Megyeri and the heart of Mózes Cziráky, so that Erzsébet Báthory shall not suffer any grief. Holy Trinity, so it is done!

17

THE TRIAL OF ERZSÉBET'S ACCOMPLICES

In eary 1623, some 13 years after the Countess was arrested and nine years after her death, a servant of her son, Pál Nádasdy, wrote a piece called, *Chronicle of Castle Csejthe*, listing "some memorable events, which in this century (17th) have taken place in the dominion of Csejthe." Under the entry for December 29, 1610, he simply wrote: "Lady Erzsébet Báthory was captured during dinner and next day brought into the castle."

As György Thurzó's letter details, when his men entered Csjethe Manor that night, they found the bodies of dead or dying girls strewn about, all having suffered from torture: beaten, flogged, burned, and stabbed. Within a few hours, additional bodies and victims would be found within the castle itself.

At least 30 known witnesses—townspeople and servants of Thurzó—arrived to take part in what was clearly a long-awaited spectacle. The manor house located in town was thoroughly searched, and then the Countess was escorted up the hill to Castle Csejthe, accompanied by the crowd and party of armed men. Witness testimony from those present reveals what happened next: the procession went directly to the castle keep, the central fortification containing both main tower as well as prison (dungeon). A search for bodies began, and the group immediately found what they were looking for. While the Countess stood by watching in silence, the men came upon the body of a dead girl. According to Csejthe Castle Provisor, Michael Herwoyth, a coat was placed over the body and it was taken out on a cart, "before the eyes of even this Lady Widow." The Lady departed soon after, and upon doing so, the men gathered about to inspect "the dead bodies down there more closely." Herwoyth reported seeing "cruel injuries" to the victims' cheeks, shoulder blades, and hands, inflicted with large wounds and severely burned. The flesh, he alleged, had been torn out with pliers.

Martin Vychko, another witness present that night, also saw how "before the eyes of the Lady Widow, a dead girl lying in a box, who had been killed by cruel blows, was put into a cart." Vychko also found another girl who had been tortured but was still alive, with wounds between her shoulders where the flesh had been cut out and her right hand and arm permanently mangled.

"Who cut you?" he asked her.

"The woman named Katalin cut me with pliers," she replied. "She ripped out the black and blue marks and the festering flesh. However, the Lady Widow Nádasdy hit and beat me with her hand."

The victim was later taken to and treated by a doctor in Újhely, where she stated that the Lady Widow Nádasdy herself destroyed the right arm and hand.

Nobleman András Pryderowyth testified like the others and added that he was able to see numerous slash marks on the body of the dead girl taken out on the cart, along with shackle marks on her neck. Another witness claimed that this girl had been strangled execution-style. The wounds found on still another girl were so deep from the flesh being cut out, "that one could easily stick a fist through them." Pryderowyth found an older woman amongst the group, still alive, whose feet were bound together. After freeing her, the woman recounted that she had been "so tied because she had refused to hand over her daughter to the Lady Widow Nádasdy."

The Countess returned to her manor house where she spent the night, while the men continued searching and cleaning out the castle. She gave a statement in which she maintained her innocence: any wrongdoing was the sole activity of her servants. The four servants apprehended with her—the three old women and Ficzkó—were held overnight (the women in town and Ficzkó within the castle) before being taken in chains to Bytča for formal proceedings. The next day, on December 30th, Lady Widow Nádasdy was taken back up to Castle Csejthe and formally imprisoned there, while her accomplices, now held in the prison of Bytča castle, had their confessions tortured out of them before the trial began.

According to deposition testimony, the local witnesses agreed that, at this point, the Countess was being held in the underground castle prison or dungeon—the same place from which the bodies of her victims were brought out the previous night. Members of the clergy, including Rev. Janós Ponikenusz from Csejthe, Rev. Nicolaus Barosius from Verbo, and Rev. Zacharias from Leszetice, went to visit her in prison on the last day of December.

In a letter to Élias Lányi, written on January 1st, Rev. Ponikenusz recounted what happened that day. By this point, before any trials had even taken place, he already knew that a judgement against her had been rendered—that she would be taken to the tower (or keep) "and into eternal prison, walled in, locked up"—and that confessions had already been extracted from her accomplices through torture.

Ponikenusz stated that they called on the Countess to "comfort her with prayers and support" so that she would not fall into temptation. Immediately upon seeing the priests, however, she flew into a rage: "You priests are the cause of my captivity!"

She spoke furiously in Hungarian. Rev. Zacharias, Pastor of Leszetice, knew the language, but Ponikenusz spoke only Slovak and turned helplessly to his interpreter. Rev. Zacharias immediately apologized to her in Hungarian. His apology calmed her down momentarily, to which she then said to him, "You might not be at fault, but the pastor of Csejthe is!"

Rev. Zacharias had obviously dealt with her before. He spoke softly, as if to calm a lunatic or wild animal: "Your Grace should not believe this."

"I can prove with witnesses that it is so."

At this point, Rev. Ponikenusz, who had managed to catch up with the conversation through his interpreter, declared, "I have preached God's word, and if it caused Your Grace to examine your conscience once, I have nothing to do with it, because I never named you."

The Countess replied testily in her native Hungarian, "Then you—you will die first—and then Mr. Megyeri! You two have brought all this trouble upon me and are the cause of my arrest. What," she said," don't you believe me that, because of this situation, a revolt will soon take place? The Hajduk (Transylvanian farmer soldiers), who have already gathered beyond the Theiss (river), have written to me yesterday that even the Prince of Transylvania will avenge my wrong!"

Ponikenusz remained silent as this was spoken; according to him, his interpreter did not tell him everything that she said in Hungarian. However, the pastor noted that the Countess now wished to send off letters and that she called for a knight. She said nothing outloud, and no one questioned her as to what she was doing. Ponikenusz thought the man whom she called was someone from her entourage. The fact that she could still summon servants, send secret messages, and make threats made him very nervous.

Meanwhile, the Countess continued to accuse the priests as the sole and unjustified cause of her imprisonment, maintaining her innocence. Rev. Zacharias attempted to change the subject: "Do you believe that Christ was born for you, died and rose for the forgiveness of sins?"

She shot back, "I also know Peter Faber." (Faber was a Catholic priest and co-founder of the Jesuit order who worked to bring Protestants, such as these ministers, back to the Church. What she said would have been insulting to them.)

Immediately Rev. Zacharias gave her the Holy Bible and asked her to read it in prison, to which she retorted, "I need it not."

Meanwhile, still stewing over her past remark, Ponikenusz demanded, "I want to know who has caused Your Grace to have so much contempt for me by claiming that I am the cause of your detention."

She turned to him and said flatly, "I will not tell you."

Her temper suddenly flared. "Now you have angered me—" she leveled her gaze at Rev. Zacharias, as well—"and soon both of you will have angered me!"

"I do not wish to anger you," Ponikenusz persisted. "I only wish to clear myself of the accusation of having been the reason for your detention."

"I have been a mistress and mother to all my staff," she snapped back. "I have never been treated right, neither in the small nor the large—by either of you."

Ponikenusz immediately insisted that she think well of him because he "prayed to God for forgiveness of [her] sins."

She looked at him for a moment and then said in her most patronizing way, "To ask God for the salvation of someone else—especially in a special case—is a good work."

Meanwhile, Pastor Nicolaus Barosius, who had been present on the night of the raid, who had seen the dead or dying girls for himself and had heard from the still-living that they had been forced to eat their own cut-out flesh, stood by in silence while she went into another rage.

"You nefarious and wicked priests are the cause of my captivity, but I gave my brother Gábor Báthory a message, and you'll soon have realized that you and your children will regret my fate!"

"Your Grace," Barosius suddenly spoke up, "Please do not despair but, rather, kindly accept this call to repentance and partake of Holy Communion."

THE TRIAL OF ERZSÉBET'S ACCOMPLICES

Her face fell for a moment. It looked almost like a pout.
"How could I do this when all of you are my enemies?"

Barosius said gently, "Your Grace is surely aware of what all has already been discovered here and what terribleness has been confessed under torture by your old women and the servant Ficzkó."

Her expression suddenly hardened again.

"I will not admit to anything," she flared, "even if they torture me by fire!"

"So then," Barosius said, somewhat confused, "After considering all of this, you still stand by your statement that you are innocent and that only the old women committed these horrendous deeds?"

"Yes," she declared. "I stand firmly by it and nothing else."

"Then why," he wanted to know, "did you allow your old women to do such things?"

Her answer shocked all of the priests: "I did it," she said, "because even I myself was afraid of them."

In those days, Bytča (Hungarian: Nagybiccse) was a part of Hungary and, today, is located in northwestern Slovakia at the Vah River near the cities of Žilina and Považská Bystrica. For all intents and purposes, Bytča was György Thurzó's hometown: dominated by a 13th century water castle, Thurzó's father, Ferenc, commissioned Giovanni Kilian of Milan to restore the medieval castle in the new, Renaissance style during the years 1571-74. György Thurzó himself continued the project and also had a ceremonial Wedding Palace constructed next to the castle in 1601. At that time, the castle contained a school, libraries, archives, a prison, and a pharmacy. Bytča Castle, like Sárvár Castle, was a center of prosperity and enlightenment, known for its pomp and circumstance.

In those days, testimonies from the criminally accused were gotten by means of torture in advance of depositions and trials. Beginning in the Middle Ages, torture accompanied all cases involving matters of faith. While early Roman common law opposed the use of torture and presumed that the accused was innocent until proven guilty, the Church reversed this position particularly during the Crusades and, later, during the Inquisition. In the following centuries, civil authorities also relied on the practice: guilt was presumed; innocence had to be proven.

During the Inquisition, the use of torture to extract confessions from prisoners was taken to an art form and would later be used throughout both Protestant as well as Catholic Europe and the New World, not only for ordinary criminal cases but during the witch trials of coming years. Historian, John Gibbon, wrote, "No power under heaven could save the prisoner. He was doomed." And Johann Weyer (1515-88), an eyewitness to the methods employed during the Inquisition, claimed that the victims were "slaughtered with the most refined tortures that tyrants could invent, beyond human endurance. And this cruelty is continued until the most innocent are forced to confess themselves guilty."

Although we do not know exactly what methods were used on Erzsébet's four accomplices to extract their confessions, we do know what means were commonly used during the period: starvation, darkness, beatings, attempted drowning, burning, stretching and pulling, pressing with heavy weights, pinching, throttling, and the twisting and screwing of fingers, toes, and limbs.

After being tortured, Ficzkó was summoned first to testify as both defendant and lead witness. His testimony, like that of the others, is recorded in Hungarian in the third person in the form, "he said," as well as *he*, *she*, and *it*, alike. When the words *lady*, *wife*, *head lady*, *Mrs.*, or *madam* are used, it is not always clear whether these salutations refer specifically to Erzsébet Báthory or to her female accomplices. The odd gaps or illogical connections in the text can perhaps be attributed to inaccurate witness testimony, later editing, or perhaps scribal error. In the case of inquisitorial proceedings, however, the quantity of evidence provided and used in the process, the commentary of those who verified the indictment, and relevance to their character took precedence over any conflicting facts. Indeed, it is often evident that shameless lying went on throughout the process with little notice or comment by the judicial authorities.

The original transcripts, long-since sealed and forgotten, were found over two hundred years later in the attic at Bytča and published in 1817. In the original document of the proceeding, it is recognized that there existed still another version of the trial testimonies that was kept at a different location. Indeed, today a copy is preserved at the Thurzó archive in Bytča, one at the Erdödy archive in Galgóc (Hlohovec, in Slovak), and another at the National Archive in Budapest. Each transcript has fundamental differences in detail, which are highlighted below.

During the trials of Lady Báthory Nádasdy, two separate proceedings were conducted: one taking place on January 2, 1611 in which the four servants apprehended at Castle Csejthe were interrogated on criminal charges for their own misconduct, and a companion investigation which ran almost simultaneously in which eye witnesses were called to testify against the Countess herself. Two separate writings memorialized the proceedings, and both are given below in their entirety.

Of the first of the two trials held at Bytča, Thurzó ordered various officials to validate the proceedings. They included Bytča Castellan, Casparus Echy (also spelled Gáspár Nagy-Najáky or Bajáky) and Gáspár Kardos. The trial was conducted in Hungarian and transcripts recorded in Hungarian and Latin by notary (magister) Dániel Eördeögh. Rev. Élias Lányi served as the sworn member of the Chancery.

In the first document, titled, *Transcript of the Witness Interrogation Regarding the Cruel Deeds which Erzsébet Báthory, Wife of Count Ferenc Nádasdy, is Accused. 1611*, the four defendants (Ilona Jó Nagy, Dorottya Szentes, Katalin

Beneczky, and János Újváry), testified. From this document, we learn more details concerning the activities of the Countess' four servants whom she, herself, accused of being responsible for torturing and murdering so many.

The four accused servants made frequent reference to deceased accomplice, Anna Darvolya. It may be that the accused defendants were playing the "empty chair defense" game by placing as much blame as possible on a defendant who was not, and could never be, present, thus relieving themselves of some guilt. Their testimony was fairly consistent, though, suggesting that Anna was influential, unbelievably cruel, and deadly. They placed blame equally on one another, however, as well as conceding individual wrongdoing and accusing locals of collaboration.

According to Ficzkó, he went out six different times with Dorka in search of girls, promising the young ladies future employment as assistants and maids. He also rattled off a list of women who, likely in exchange for substantial "finder's fees," assisted with the procurement of girls. These "finder's fees" must have been enormous: some of the people mentioned even brought their own daughters to the Countess, knowing full well what would likely happen to them.

Ficzkó testified that Mrs. János Bársony, who lived near Gyöngyös near the town of Teplanfalva, had gone with Dorka searching for girls; Mrs. Matej, the Croatian who lived at Sárvár across from Lady János Zalay, participated; Mrs. Ján Szabo procured girls and even brought her own daughter—although this daughter was later killed and the mother knew about it, she still brought in more; the wife of Juraj (György) Szabo brought her daughter to Csejthe where she later died; Mrs. István Szabo brought girls; and Ilona Jó did so, as well. Accoring to Ficzkó, Katalin never brought in any but merely buried those whom Dorka had killed.

Dorka contributed to the list, adding the name of János Szilay's wife. Katalin Beneczky testified that two women, Mrs. Liptai (or Liptov) and Mrs. Kardos, also assisted, sometimes even traveling as far as the Jewish quarter in Vienna to find girls. Ilona Jó said that György Jánosy, a nobleman, brought in his young sister to Csejthe, in addition to two other girls of noble birth, including one from Bytča and two from Czegled. Mrs. Bársony apparently brought in a big and beautiful noble girl herself.

During their times of service, the four defendants placed the number of murdered girls in the range of thirty to fifty: Ficzkó estimated 37; Ilona Jó guessed 51, perhaps more; Dorka said 36; and Katalin put the number at 50.

The responses to questions here are the same as those found in the original document. Some commentary has been provided to assist the reader, as well as indicators where the transcript versions differ. Variations in the transcripts, as well as commentary, appear in parentheses, with variations italicized. For English speakers who are familiar with the deposition testimony translated by Raymond T. McNally, significant as well as subtle differences can be found here. We find that this particular version, however, provides a number of interesting details that cannot be found elsewhere.

In the forward "protocol" or summary of the questions posed to them, it states:

"These are questions posed to persons of low (menial) birth against Lady Nádasdy, Erzsébet Báthory, on January 2, 1611 at the market town of Bytča where an assembly was held. First. János Újváry, otherwise called Ficzkó, was interviewed on the following points and answers under his own admission":

First: *How long had he been in the service of that Lady and how did he come to her court.*

Answer: Sixteen years, if not longer, he lived with the Lady, having been brought there to Csejthe by the wife of the teacher, Márton Deak, taken there by force.

Second: *From that time until now, how many girls and women has she (have been) killed.*

Answer: He doesn't know about any women, but girls, he knows 37, while he was with her. In addition, when the Palatine traveled to Bratislava, he (or she) buried 5 in a pit, two in a small garden, and one beneath the eaves/gutter. (*A girl whom they found there and she placed before them and) [t]wo (others) were taken at night into Leceticz* (a small village, known today as Podolie) to the church where they buried the same; they brought down the same from the castle, because Mrs. Dorka killed them.

Third: *Who were those whom they killed, and where (did it take place)?*

Answer: He did not know whose daughters they were (*to whom the girls belonged*).

Fourth: *In what ways were these same women and girls enticed (lured) and brought to the castle, (what was their lineage, and who brought them over)?*

Answer: Six times, the declarant went looking for girls with Mrs. Dorka; they attracted them with the promise that they would either marry a merchant or that they would be brought somewhere (to work) as a chambermaid. The now-deceased girl was brought from a Croatian village beyond (*somewhere in the neighborhood of*) Rednek, (*hence her trust*); the girl worked for (the Lady) for a month, and then they killed her (she (likely Dorka) had been there with her and later killed her (or was "involved with her death"; the Hungarian causative verb is also unclear)). Others who looked for girls, along with Mrs. Dorka were: Mrs. (the wife of) János Bársony, who lives near (*next to the*) Gyöngyös in the town of Teplanfalva, except for once at Sárvár; they found a Croatian woman living with Matthias Otvos, who lives at Sárvár, Mrs. Matej, who lived across from Ján

Szalay. Also, Mrs. (the wife of) Ján Szabo procured girls and even brought her own (*a daughter to her* (either Dorka or Báthory)), who was also killed, and though she certainly knew it, she still brought more and turned them over. Also, the wife of György Szabo gave (the Lady) her own (*their*) daughter at Csejthe, who was also murdered (*where she died*), but she did not bring anymore. In addition, Mrs. (the wife of) István Szabo also brought in many. Mrs. Ilona also brought enough. Kata never brought any but merely buried those whom Dorka had killed.

Fifth: *By what torture and what manner did they kill these poor (unfortunates) (How were they treated/handled, in what fashion were they tortured, and how were they killed)?*

Answer: They were tortured thus: their arms were bound with Viennese cord (woven cotton?). When she lived at Sárvár, (*the one called*) Mrs. Anna Darvolia tied their hands backwards (*behind their backs*). The hands turned deathly pale (*the color of death*), and they were whipped until their bodies burst (*covered in gaping wounds*). They were beaten on the flat of the hands and the soles of feet, as many as 500 strikes in a row (*wounds*). They learned this torturing style first from Darvolia, how to beat the same so long until they died. Dorka cut off their hands with sheers (*scissors*), which at Csejthe is no different (*also killing them at Csejthe*).

Sixth: *Who else assisted with (who were the instruments of) the torture and murder?*

Answer: In addition to these three women at Csejthe, is a lady, who is known as Mrs. Ilona, the wife of the bald coachman, who also tortured maids (*martyred girls*). She herself stabbed them with needles if their needlework wasn't done well. If they didn't take off their hair covering, if they did not start the fire, if they did not lay the apron straight: they were immediately taken to the torture chamber by the old women and tortured to death.

The old women burned them with the fire iron and she herself stuck pins into the mouth, the nose, and the chin of the girls. She stuck her fingers in the mouth and tore it apart. (*By this means they were tortured and starved.*) If their needlework was not completed by 10:00 p.m., so they were also brought into the torture chamber. They were taken to be tortured even ten times in a day; (*they were delivered*) like sheep. Sometimes four or even five girls stood naked there (*before them*), and in this way they had to sew or knit, accused, always suddenly, and would then have to embroider or knit lace and complete their labor or be punished later. The Sittkey girl (*Sittkey's daughter*) was killed because she stole a pear; in the same way, she was tortured and murdered in Piešťány with an emaciated old woman, by Ilona. (*They tortured her in the town called Piešťány, along with the old woman, and later on, murdered the two*). The milliner Modli from Vienna was killed at Keresztúr (*they also murdered the Viennese girl, Miss Modl (or Modli), at a location called Keresztúr*).

Seventh: *Where were the dead bodies buried or where were they taken? Who hid the same corpses and where were they buried (where were the dead buried and how were they hidden)?*

Answer: The old woman hid and buried the girls (*tended to hiding and burying girls here at Csejthe*). He, the accused (Confessant), helped bury (*hide*) four here and in Csejthe (*of the dead*), two at a location called Leceticz (Lesticze), one at Keresztúr, and one at Sárvár. The others were buried with singing at the three last-named places (*All the rest were buried at Sárvár with singing, also at Keresztúr and Leceticz*). When the old women murdered a girl, they were given gifts by the Lady (*When the baby of one of the girls was murdered by the women, the Lady rewarded them (paid their wage)*). She herself even tore the girl's face and scratched it all over (*girls' cheeks and stabbed them below the fingernails*). Then, the tortured girl was made to stand in the frost and splashed with water by the old women; also the Lady herself poured water on her until she froze and died. (*Later on, all of the murdered girls were doused with water. Even she herself doused them until they froze to death.*) When she was here at Bytča, she was ready to depart when one of her girls escaped to Ilava, but was brought back, put up to her neck in water and doused; she died afterward at Csejthe. (*Now once, when leaving from Bytča and driving across Predmier, a girl had been put into water up to her neck and then had water poured over her. This happened when she was captured, after having escaped. She later died at Csejthe.*)

Eighth: *The Lady herself also tortured and murdered? And how did she torture the poor (ones) and kill them? (Did her Ladyship torture them herself, and what exactly did she do and how did they die?)* (In still another version, the question read: *"How did they torture and murder those poor creatures?"* This could mean that the writer loosely recorded the questions, or the sequence of questions aligned for the final version).

Answer: When she herself did not torture them, she transferred them to the old women who tortured the girls, whom they put in the coal storage for a week without food, and whoever gave them something to eat in secret was immediately punished. (*When the girls shamed themselves, they were made to stand naked. The girls were locked in the laundry for a week and allowed to starve. Anyone who brought them food in secret was immediately punished.*)

Ninth: *In what sort of places at Csejthe, Sárvár, Keresztúr, Beckov and elsewhere were the poor (ones) tortured and killed? (In addition to Csejthe, Sárvár, Keresztúr, and Beckov, where there any other places where these miserable beings were tortured and murdered?)*

Answer: At Beckov, the same were tortured in the chamber next to the wash-kitchen (*at Beckov and Komna, they were tortured in the laundry*); at Sárvár in the interior of the castle where not everyone (*no one*) was allowed; at Keresztúr, in the latrine (*they were dragged into a secret room*); and at Csejthe, in the kitchen (*torturing took place at the laundry*). Even while we were traveling (*when on a trip*), her Ladyship tortured them herself in the coach. She hit them, (*would bite them*), and stick them in the mouth with needles.

Tenth: *Who, of important people, knew or saw the deeds of the Lady? (What other well-known persons were present or who knew about the acts of the Lady?)*

Answer: The Court Master Benedikt Dezso (commonly spelled Benedikt or Benedek Deseö) knew best over the others (*knew about it the most, was into everything, and knowledgeable more than the rest*); however, no one ever heard him say anything about the Lady (*But he* (apparently the accused) *never heard the gentleman say anything about it.*) Also, the other servants knew about it in general, even the riff-raff. A certain "Obstinate" (*Iron Headed*) Stefan," now beyond the Danube, who recently left the Lady's service, knows everything better than even the witness. He also talked freely with the Lady, and carried several dead bodies away but, where? The witness does not know. (*There was here another fellow who called himself Stefan Iron Head who recently left the Lady's service and headed out for Zadunajska* (the Transylvanian Danube). *The same knew about everything much better since he witnessed and even freely made jokes/played games with the Lady. He buried several girls, but the witness was unaware of where.*)

(Regarding the mysterious character Istaka (István or Stefan) called "Iron Head," it may be that Ficzkó tried to pass off some of the guilt on him or, perhaps out of fear, even invented him. According to the court records, "Stefan Iron Head" disappeared into Transylvania. Oddly, no one else seemed to know anything about or mention him, unless he is the man referred to simply as "Kozma," by the other defendants.)

Eleventh: *For how long have they known or learned that the Lady began committing these cruel deeds (How long did anyone know about the horrible deeds of this woman and did anyone do anything to prevent the murders)?*

Answer: She had tortured the girls even during the lifetime of the late Lord, but not so often murdered them as now. The poor Lord spoke to her about it, but did not forbid it. (*Even the lord knew about the murders. The lord himself prohibited and disapproved of it; however, she ignored his complaints.*) Anna Darvolia came to her, and she (Anna) killed the girls, and also the Lady became more cruel. (*Later on, Mrs. Anna Darvulia arrived and, after that, she (Darvulia) began murdering girls. The lady herself became crueler and crueler and things got worse.*) Something like a pretzel was kept in a box, with a mirror in the middle, before which she prayed for two hours. (*She would conjure with the assistance of a small box and a braided mirror at which she sat.*) Item: the Mistress of Miava made some sort of water in the morning, and at approximately 4:00 p.m., the Lady bathed in a baking trough; then she poured the water in the creek. (*Majernicka of Myjavy* (Erzsi Majorova*) prepared some water and brought it around four in order for the lady to bathe herself in it. The water was discharged into the creek and, along with other mixtures, was blended in a washtub where something was put into it.*) She wanted to bake two cakes in the trough, of which she wanted to poison both the King, the Lord Palatine and Imre Megyeri. (*The mix from this was given at the table to the king, the palatine, and also to Imre Megyery in order to poison them.*) But these gentlemen became aware of it and bested the Lady with the physical; because once they had eaten the first baked item, they all got stomach aches, and so she dared not permit the second baked item to be prepared/served. (*They must have realized the lady was trying to poison them because they*

*said so. It struck them badly and they complained about a foul
stomach after eating the prepared baked items.)*

. . . .

The second defendant heard was Ilona Jó, widow of István Nagy. The woman whom the Countess trusted to serve as
nursemaid for and raise her own children was now on trial for
butchering young girls not much older than her noble charges.
Like her accomplices, Ilona Jó attempted to place as much blame
on others whenever possible, particularly on the deceased Anna
Darvolia. Also like the other defendants, she was asked the
same questions as Ficzkó. Her answers followed immediately
after his in the following, abbreviated format:

*Second: Ilona Jó, widow of István Nagy, testified on the above
points in order, as follows:*

Regarding No. 1: She lived ten years with the Lady and was the
nursemaid for the three girls and also Pál Nádasdy.

2: She does not know the number of victims, but she has killed
enough.

3. She does not know of which families they were; but she
knows two Sittkey women; then a sister of Gregor Jánosi; also,
two noble girls were brought to her from Vécsei, also two from
Cheglét: the one she killed, the other is still alive. Also, the Lady
Szell had brought a girl, and one was also brought from Poland.
The (wife of) János Bársony also brought a large, tall girl, the
daughter of a nobleman, from where János Poliani lived; she was
also killed. In, she know fifty or more who were murdered.

4. The (wife of) János Szalay, then (brought) a Jewish and a
Slovak woman to live at Sárvár. The (wife of) János Szalay also

brought two or three girls, although she knew that the same would be killed, but the one named Chiglei is still alive. She went away with Janós Bársony and remained there, but the (wife of) Janós Barsony herself brought a noble girl from south of Poland. Stablemaster Dániel Vas brought many around; the Lady Homonnay looked for girls but found none, except for a little one from Vécsey.

5. Also she herself brought girls when the Lady ordered it, but Darvolia in particular murdered the same; she put them in cold water all night, bathed and beat them. The Lady herself heated a key, and then burned the hand of a girl. She also did the same with coins when the same were found with them and did not give them to the Lady. In addition, she herself murdered the Lady Zichi, along with an old woman, at Ecsed. At Sárvár, she killed the Lord's sister (translation mistake: it was a sister of Helen Jó) - which he saw with his own eyes - in the summer stripped naked, covered with honey, and made to stand the whole day and night in great pain until she fell sick and dropped to the ground. The Lord punished her, lighting oiled papers between the toes, which would make her stand up even if she was half dead. István Szabó brought enough girls from the Verpén area for gifts, the rest for payment. One (girl) was given a petticoat, the other a little winter skirt. Also, the (wife of) Balthasar Horváth, who lives in a village near the monastery, has brought many girls. Szilvásy, as well as the Court Master, have seen that the Lady herself tortured the girls, stripped naked, and made to stand before them. Dorkó cut the swollen bodies of the girls with a pair of scissors, and once, when the Lady allowed it, the servants here gave the girls mouthclamps. She threw the girls to the ground naked and beat them so violently that one could scoop handfuls of blood from her bed, and ashes had to be strewn. In a village near Varannó she also killed one of them, and left the Declarant behind in order to bury her. She herself stuck a knife into the girls, and beat them and tortured them in many ways.

6. After Darvolia went blind, the women Dorkó and Kata beat the girls, as well as the Declarant, so long as she was healthy (i.e., able to do so).

7. She does not know where the corpses are now buried, but they were first carried to a wheat shaft. The women Dorkó and Kata took five corpses to Sárvár during the day with singing and also buried them at Keresztúr accompanied by (ministry) students.

8. She herself, the Lady, beat and tortured the girls so much so that she was covered in blood, even having to change her shirt, and the bloody wall had to be washed. When Dorkó beat the girls, the Lady herself stood nearby.

9. Overall, anywhere she went, she looked immediately for a place where they could torture the girls. In Vienna, the monks even threw pots at the window when they heard the frightened cries. Also at Bratislava, Mrs. Dorkó beat the girls.

10. Namely, Balthasar Poki (Poby), Stephan Vaghi (Vagy), the Court Master (Benedikt Deseö), and all officials and servants knew of the atrocities; also Kozma (Stephen "Iron Head" perhaps?) knew about it.

11. She does not know when the Lady began committing these cruelties, because by the time the Declarant had come to her, she had already begun the same: but Darvolia had instructed her in cruelty and was her confidante. The Declarant knew and saw that she burned the genitals of the naked girls with a burning candle.

. . . .

Dorottya Szentes, also called Dorka or Dorkó, the widow of Benedikt Szucsov (also spelled Benedek Szeoch or Szócs), was the third member of Erszebet's retinue to be interrogated. She testified that she brought Ilona Jó to Erzsébet Báthory's court and that she (Ilona Jó) was there only five years. She did not know when her Ladyship began to participate in the criminal acts—only that there were about 36 dead girls. She did not know exactly where they came from, only that they were hired as seamstresses and maids and that they came from the local area. Szentes was interrogated on her statement that she assisted her Lady with the torture because it was so ordered. If she failed to act, the Lady would do it herself.

She stuck them with needles, burned them in the foot and legs with red hot spoons and iron bars, and pried pieces of their bodies off with tongs. Once, when the Lady suffered from a lengthy illness, in order to punish the girls, she ordered that they be brought to her sickbed. There, she pulled off chunks of their flesh with her teeth. At one time, five girls died over the course of ten days from the effects of torture. Szentes further accused Katalin Beneczky of having locked them away at Leccticz.

Szentes' remarks are occasionally abbreviated with scribal commentary such as, "Same as the others stated," or "consistent with prior testimony." This could be the result of avoiding the rewrite of a lengthy, repetitious testimony, or it can simply denote the fact that the accused testified in accordance with the others. It is also indicative of the curative (abbreviated) style of the time. By now, it had been established that the local people cooperated with Erzsébet Báthory and her retinue, that they sent many girls to her court, that girls were tortured and killed there over the course of many years, and that the members of the domestic staff were well aware of what went on, including: Court Master Benedikt Deseö; Stable Master Dániel Vas; and Steward (Provisor) Jakob Szilvassy. There were other staff members, as well, such as Baltazar Poby and István Vagy (both of whom had made statements in secret hearings conducted back in April 1610) who knew what was happening there. All identified Anna Darvolya (Darvulia), the servant of Erzsébet and Ferenc Nádasdy at their court at Sárvár, as the origin and prime inflictor of cruelty. Her testimony is given as follows:

INFAMOUS LADY

The third, Dorottya Széntes, the widow of Benedikt Szócs, confessed on the following, above-asked questions in order:

Regarding No. 1. It has been five years since she has been with the Lady. Mrs. Ilona lured her to the castle with beautiful words that she would be taken on by Lady Homonnay.

2. She knew of approximately 36 young women and sewing girls killed by the Lady.

3. From which families they came and to whom they belonged, she does not know but, rather, said the same as the above, that they came from many places.

4. The (wife of) János Szalay, the (wife of) János Bársony, and the Widow Keöcsé living in Dömölk. The (wife of) János Liptay brought some to Csejthe. She confessed the same way in all matters as the previous two Declarants.

5. Consistently she admits what the two previous Declarants had confessed, with the addition that the Lady also tortured the girls.... and that if the Declarant would not beat the same, then (the Lady) would do it herself with a club, like a chair leg. She stuck the lips of the girls together with needles and also tortured them in this way. When the Lady was sick and could not beat anyone, she ordered the Confessant over to her (the Confessant had dragged the victim onto the bed) and bit a piece out of the face and the shoulder. She pricked the girls through their fingers with pins, and said: if it hurts the whore, then she can pull it out; if she did so, the Lady would beat her again and cut off the finger.

6. Soon, they were all helping the Lady with torturing, first one and then the other, along with the Declarant herself, because she forced them to do it.

7. Within a week and a half, five girls died at Csejthe, which they stacked one on top of the other in the storage room. She then went to Sárvár, and Kata dragged the same, right past the house staff, into the wheat pit. Confessant was with the Lady at Sárvár at the time. The remaining corpses, which they could not hide, were often publicly buried through the Preacher. The servants, along with Kata, carried one to Leceticz and buried it there.

8. The Lady herself beat the girls -- in general, the Confessant testified the same as the previous two.

9. In regard to the places of torture, she said that the Lady tortured wherever she was.

10. She said the same as the others.

11. She does not know when the Lady began her cruelties, because she was only with her for five years.

. . . .

The last accomplice to testify was Katalin Beneczky, considered by most to be the least cruel of the four and the only one to avoid execution. Her interrogatories resulted in the following:

The fourth: Katalin Beneczky, the widow of Janós Boda, confessed on the previously-asked questions as follows:

1. It has been ten years since she has been with the Lady; the (wife of) Valentin Varga, mother of the current pastor at Sárvár, had appointed her to be a washerwoman at the palace.

2. Since she was a washerwoman, she doesn't know how many were murdered; she believes, however, that during her time with the Lady, it could be fifty that the Lady killed.

3. She does not know from which families or from where they came, because she did not bring any; she knew only the Sittkey women.

4. In all matters, she said the same as the others. The (wife of) János Liptay brought a girl, and she adds: that (the wife) of Miklós Kardos also brought two, such that she dared not even go into the village; however, the woman, Dorkó, brought in the most, and she brought in all of the ones that are now dead.

5. Continues identically with the foregoing, with the addition: that after Darvolia became blind and the two previous female Confessants had fully learned how to torture, the same forced this Declarant to perform beatings; indeed, the woman, Ilona, had them carry on with beatings until they were tired. Also, the women forced her into the beatings, constantly yelling at her and screaming: Hit her! Hit her! Harder! The girl who has now been found dead was so terribly beaten that, when she was already half-dead, Lady Nádasdy went inside and also started beating her, so that by 11:00 p.m., she had given up the ghost.

6. Mrs. Ilona was the most wicked in her bragging; even though she could do nothing by her own hand, she received permission from the Lady to control Sárvár. The Lady Nádasdy even married two daughters of the same and gave them 14 beautiful gowns. She was above all others an advisor (to the Lady). Mrs. Dorkó beat the girls and also the Declarant when she was forced to do so; she herself was beaten when she refused to do it and once spent the entire month in bed because of the beating suffered. Once, when the Lady Zrínyi came to Csejthe, she sent her entire staff of housegirls, along with Dorkó, up into the castle, where Dorkó kept the girls in strict captivity like criminals,

washing and making them bathe in cold water and then forcing them to stay outside, naked, for entire nights. May the thunder, she said, slay anyone who gives them something to eat. She guarded the same so strictly that neither the castle steward nor anyone else could feed them. But when the Lady wanted to travel to Piastány with Mrs. Zrínyi, she sent the Declarant up to see if one of them could go with her; she found all of them having fainted from lack of food, and said to the Lady, when she returned: "Not a single one is in a position to travel with Your Grace." The Lady clapped her hands together; she was very angry with Dorkó and said that this should not have happened. The girls were brought out and died in a room of the castle. Because both the Lady and Dorkó beat them, and now that they had gone without food, they had to give up the spirit. A young lady from Dömölk, who was with the Declarant in a coach, died on the journey from Piastány to Csejthe. This girl had already collapsed at Piastány, but was propped up again and beaten by the Lady.

7. Two of the dead girls were buried in Leceticz. The rest was as the previous. Regarding five girls, of whom Dorkó knows are dead because she was with them, she stacked them one on top of the other under the bed and threw oakum (a kind of tar) on them. Nevertheless, they brought food every day as if they were still alive, no matter how long things were different. Then the Lady went to Sárvár and ordered that the Declarant should break up the floor and bury them there; she did not do it, however, because she was too weak. The poor corpses remained in this way such that a foulness was given off, and it caused such a stench in the manor that one also felt the same. Now the Declarant did not know what she should do, so she buried all of the bodies, by God's will, in a wheat pit with the aid of Bulia, (and) the servantwomen Barbara and Käte, who were together with Dorkó daily and when they died. At night they buried the same. Dorkó herself even had a corpse buried under the eaves, which the dogs dug up, and which was seen by the servant of Lord Zrínyi. This one was then buried in the wheat pit, which was now filled with

these five bodies. At Csejthe, where she had been only a short time, eight were killed.

8. Same as the previous.

9. The same, with the addition, that she had tortured her girl, Ilona Harczi, in Vienna.

10. The same as the others.

11. She learned torturing and the other forms of cruelty from Darvolia.

. . . .

These voluntary confessions were given before us on the day and year above.

Magister Daniel Eördeögh, m.p., Caparus Echy, Castellan at Bytča, m.p., Kaspar Kardos, Élias Lányi, sworn clergyman, m.p.

The content of the second writing is as follows:

We, Theodosius Szirmay of Szulio, Royal Presider; Kaspar Ordody of Trencsén, and Janós David of St. Peter; Georg Lehotzky, Janós Záturetzky, Nikolaus Hrábovszky, Janós Borsitzky, judicial chair; Gabriel St. Mariai, also known as Hlinitzky, Trencsén court presider; Michael Prusinszky, (30th member of the committee), Raphael Kvasovszky, Benedikt Kozár, Stephan Mársovszky, Georg Záluszky, Janós and Michael Hlinitzky, Apollo Milicius, Janós Draskovszky, Nikolaus Mársovszky, Stephan Akay and Janós Medveczky, decree through all here present: that we, on the 7th day of this month in the Year of the Lord 1611, at the request of His Grace, the Lord György Thurzó of Bethlenfalva, Palatine of the Kingdom of

THE TRIAL OF ERZSÉBET'S ACCOMPLICES

Hungary, Judge of Kumans, Count of Árva and everlasting presider of the legal committee, senior confidential advisor to His Royal Majesty and governor of the Kingdom of Hungary, in the distinguished market town referred to as Bytča, for the investigation and trial of certain subjects who were assembled there in the name and under the authority of his Lordship, the beneficent György Závodszky, against János Ficzkó and against Ilona, Dorottya and Katalin, women from Sárvár, do hereby issue the following oder:

It is evident that the supreme God, through His Royal Majesty, with the determined wishes and elections of the national occupants and estates of our homeland Hungary, His Grace, through the honor and dignity of the palatinal office, called this summit, so that in the furtherance of the requirements of His office, without regard for the person, to protect the good and innocent, should punish the guilty: so we, the above, who desire to sufficiently accomplish His order have made, among other things, so far a salutary undertaking and fortunately finished this public matter, having heard about and questioned regarding the one who, unheard of from the beginning of the world by the female sex, committed outrageous, inhuman rage and satanic cruelty against Christian blood, the high noble, Lady Erzsébet Báthory, widow of the high-born and high noble Lord Ferenc Nádasdy who, to this kingdom and fatherland, was otherwise a much-deserved man, which she perpetrated, for many years now in a nefarious, inhuman way against her female servants, other women, and other innocent young souls, wretchedly killing an unbelievable number of many of the same. Given such a huge, unspeakable atrocity, this committee in no way wanted to (as one may care to say) see through the finger (i.e., make a rash decision). They set up a much more rigorous investigation, from which evidence could be shown that the Lady Widow Nádasdy had really committed the crimes of which she was accused, according to the confessions of her own servants. After His Grace heard of it, the committee applied His directive from Bratislava

to the legal proceedings, and the designated high nobles and gentlemen, Count Nicholas Zrínyi and György Drugeth of
Homonnay, relatives of the said Lady Widow, and Mr. Imre
Magyeri, guardian of the orphaned Pál Nádasdy, and also a not
insignificant number of troops, accompanied him to overtake the
castle at Csejthe. Right at the entrance to the manor was the
truth of what the witnesses had offered. There, a young lady was
found, maiden name of Doricza, miserably killed from beatings
and torture, and two others, also tortured to death in different
ways in the said manor at Csejthe, by the aforementioned Lady
Widow Nádasdy. This inhuman, more than tiger-like ferocity
and anger moved His Grace, with the well-mannered advice of
the above-mentioned, to hand over the blood-thirsty, highly nefarious Widow Nádasdy, caught in fresh atrocity (i.e., red
handed) and to condemn this woman to eternal imprisonment in
Castle Csejthe. János Ficzkó, however, as well as Ilona, Dorottya, and Katalin, as assistants and murderers of innocent people,
knowledgable and participants in such Godless deeds, henchmen
in this terrible execution and butcher shop, are set against their
Lord Judge and in need of fair punishment for their horrible and
nefarious crimes. Specifically, we the Committee, both because
it is the sacred course of justice and fairness, as such entails, as
well as to send a warning and example to those who have acted,
or plan to act, in a similar way; for these, however, who have
perpetrated such monstrous deeds, they shall receive the sharpest
punishment and eternal shame, based on the document submitted
by us, including the legal writings and copies, both of which
have been brought against the Widow Nádasdy, as well as the
voluntary confessions given by the defendants. After such was
publicly read, the defendants individually interviewed on all
points of the confessions and, in turn, heard, all being in agreement and nothing from the same confession omitted or modified,
but set down just as they had been taken, regarding all that they
had commited, in everything they violently perpetrated and
forced by threats by their mistress; has the Committee finally
determined from the aforementioned testimonies and confes-

sions and also established from witnesses who appeared before us in the following order.

. . . .

As mentioned, a second judicial proceeding was convened, this one on January 7th, involving a ceremonial panel of 18 judges and 13 sworn witnesses. Recorded in Latin, this trial began with a reading of the accomplices' confessions. It then proceeded to the eye-witness testimonies of the men who were present at the Csejthe raid.

The judges and jury listened in awe as the men described what they had seen the night they entered the manorhouse and castle at Csejthe. The witnesses identified a young servant girl, Doricza, *ex flagris et torturis miserabiliter extinctam* (burned and tortured), including two other girls who died in similar fashion. György Kubanovich claimed witnessing *existens cadaver puellae* (corpses of girls), confirmed by witnesses János Krapmann and András Butora. Upon conclusion of such testimonies, Church authorities waived their right to interrogate (i.e., torture) the four criminal defendants further on charges of occult practices. The document reads as follows:

Transcript of the Witness Interrogatories regarding the cruel deeds which Elizabeth Bathory, wife of Count Ferenc Nádasdy, is accused. 1611. (Decision of No. 31)

The first witness, the honorable György Kubanovich, resident of Csejthe has acknowledged under oath: he was in attendance at Csejthe Castle when he saw the corpse of the last murdered girl, full of blue welts and burn marks and strangled execution-style, carried out in a trough, while the Lady Nádasdy was being taken into custody.

INFAMOUS LADY

The second witness, Janós Valkó; the third, Martin Jankovich; the fourth, Martin Krsskó; the fifth, Andreas Ukrovich; all residents of Csejthe, have been sworn and testified the same as the first witness.

The sixth, Ladislas Centalovich, residing also in Csejthe, was also been sworn and testified like the others, with the addition: he had seen the girls when they were still alive, and had also seen the welts and burn marks on the shoulders of the same.

The seventh, Tomás Zima of Csejthe testified as the others, and also stated that two female servants of the Lady were buried in the cemetery at Csejthe, while the third was buried at Leszetice, specifically because the preacher at Csejthe challenged the murder.

The eighth, Johann (Janós) Krappmann, church servant at Csejthe, testified as the previous sworn witnesses, and added that, regarding the girl martyred execution-style, he had spoken with one of the assistants while still alive and received this answer: the Lady herself had perpetrated such, with the aid of a certain woman in a green dress which, however, she did not identify.

The ninth, András Butora of Csejthe, in general testified in all things the same as the rest.

.   .   .   .

Throughout history, both prosecutors and defense attorneys alike have enjoyed staging a remarkable surprise near the end of a trial—the so-called "smoking gun"—that one remarkable piece of evidence or witness testimony that virtually assures a verdict and case-closed conclusion. Particularly for show trials, witnesses have often been bribed and evidence forged to assure such a desired outcome. Although we cannot say with certainty that such is the situation here, just such a remarkable event did indeed take place here.

Near the end of the proceedings, one of the biggest sensations of the entire trial occurred when a young servant girl, a maiden named Szuzanna, was called to testify. While the Csejthe witnesses believed the number of dead to be around 50 or less, and the staff at Sárvár offered numbers of 175 to 200, an amazing testimony followed. It was Szuzanna's sole declaration that an astounding 650 girls had been killed. These numbers, she claimed, were based on figures written in the Countess' own hand and kept in a kind of log or register. Steward Jakob Szilvassy had seen this supposed registry in a box in the Countess' possession. (In the original translation, the word used for this document is equivalent to "register" or "list," contrary to popular belief today that a diary was used.)

While a figure of 100 or 200 dead was in line with what prior witnesses had said, Szuzanna somehow had to account for her incredible allegation of over 650 dead. Without the Countess present to cross-examine, more was needed to defeat a claim of hearsay. Thus, the girl had to say that steward Jakob Szilvassy from Cjethe had discovered actual written proof of these murders. Of interest, however, Szilvassy was never called during those proceedings to validate what the girl said and, nearly a year later when he was finally summoned to testify, never mentioned a word, nor was questioned directly, about something as significant as the supposed list of 650 dead. Based on later comments by the king and court, it appears that the authorities ultimately did not give this young girl's account very much credibility.

We do not know if Szuzanna or Szilvassy really saw such a list, and it seems unlikely that the document was ever offered into evidence. Some have claimed that the document actually does exist and that it can be found in the National Archives in Budapest; however, given its age and poor condition, it is very difficult to read today. Unfortunately, these commentators do not provide any sort of identification for this document and, to this writer's knowledge, no one has yet attempted a translation. For this reason, we shall hold our opinion as to whether the document is real or a fabrication created by servants who had either been bribed, desired revenge against the Countess, or were looking for some way to advance themselves personally by this testimony. One even has to wonder if Szusanna was the mysterious "maid" who had been sent by Thurzó's wife, referenced in the letter shortly before the castle raid.

The testimonies continued as follows:

. . . .

The tenth, Szuzanna, a young girl, was sworn and testified that the executions, which the Widow Nádasdy perpetrated against her handmaidens, was horrifying, and that her execution henchmen were: Ilona, Dorottya, Anna with the surname Darvolya, and János Ficzkó, who was also sent out to steal girls and bring them back. Katalin was milder and gentler, but while alive had thrashed the girls enough, but was so merciful that she brought food in secret to the martyred dead. She remembered also that she had heard that Jacob Szilvásy had found a list of the dead girls in a box of the imprisoned Lady, numbered at six hundred and fifty, which number the Widow Lady Nádasdy signed with her own hand.

The eleventh witness, Sara Baranyai, widow of Peter Mártiny, testified the same as the previous girl, Szuzanna, with the addition: she knew for certain that in the previous four years (namely, during her entire time of service), while she was with Lady Nádasdy, over eighty girls in the women's quarters were killed, which is confirmed by the testimony of a certain Bichierdi (Bichérdy), Warden of Sárvár, which agrees with the number, and that this is completely true, with her claiming conscientiously to repeat several times. Finally, it also strengthens the admissions of the defendants.

Twelfth, Ilona, Widow Kotsis, said under oath: she could comment on so many things over the past three years, namely during her time of service; over 30 girls were killed from multiple torture executions by Lady Nádasdy and her assistants. The Lady Nádasdy was very knowledgeable in magic and the art of poisoning, of which there are many examples but, in particular that, through magic and poisoning, she wanted to take the lives of His Royal Majesty, and the Lord Palatine, and also Imre Megyeri and others, too, against whom she prayed a certain wishing formula/spell. In all ways, she confirmed the confessions of the defendants.

The last witness, Anna, widow of Stephan Geonczy, recounted generally as the previous witnesses regarding the butchery perpetrated by the Lady Nádasdy and her female helpers, and also confesses: among the number of slain victims, was also her ten-year-old daughter, cruelly tortured to death, whom she wanted to visit but, to her greatest pain, was not permitted inside. The rest was the same as the previous.

. . . .

The testimonies concluded, the sentence upon the four defendants was read openly in public and judgment carried out immediately. The document was signed and sealed by the eighteen tribunal magistrates and delivered "to His Excellency, the Palatine, dated 7 January 1611." The document concluded as follows:

After all that we have heard and considered, we have set forth the following recommendation.

As apparent from the defendants, and also the strong evidence before the present Tribunal, as well as repeated testimonies, but especially the confession of Dorottya, as the one guiltiest of so many cruelties against the innocent blood of the female sex, through her Lady and mistress clearly perpetrating crimes in which she and Ilona, as well as János Ficzkó, the secret helper, were not only knowledgable, but also participating in and hushing up such cruel deeds; because of such an obvious suspect and from the defendants themselves who made clear and apparent declarations on suspicious matters, including the overall secret and cruel deeds shown, first and before all others this Dorottya, then Ilona, and finally János Ficzkó were taken in for interrogation. The interrogations here are unlike anything contained in the indictment, and the interrogated ones themselves previously acknowledged, including said witnesses who also claimed and strengthened, abbreviated and withdrawn, even more so in view of the ways of the often-named Widow Nádasdy through which was perpetrated terrible slaughter and maltreatment; thus, the following judgment is passed upon the defendants, through us, and publicly pronounced: After the confessions of the defendants, which were given either voluntarily or after torture, as well as the revelations from the witness interrogations regarding the defendants' crimes and, indeed, crimes which exceed all notions of inhumanity and cruelty consisting of multiple murders, butchery, and sophisticated execution-style torture -- such atrocities require horrible penalties: thus, first, Ilona and Dorottya, as primary participants in so many misdeeds and as tools of such serious, ongoing atrocities perpetrated against Christian blood, shall have the fingers of both hands torn out by the executioner, and shall then be executed and burned.

Regarding János Ficzkó, his age and fewer crimes somewhat lessen his punishment: he shall be beheaded, the corpse placed on the pyre, and burned together with the other two criminals. Regarding the last, Katalin, the statements of both of these two defendants, as well as some witnesses will be excused, and the statement of János Ficzkó alone cannot convict her: it seems to us that she should be returned to the dungeon and remain there for some time until perhaps other more clear evidence is given against her. This is our verdict on the accused, publicly pronounced and soon thereafter to be duly completed.

Given in the aforementioned market town of Bytča on the 7th of January in the year of the Lord 1611.

Theodosius Szirmay, Georg Lehotzky, Kaspar Ordody, Janós Záturetzky, Nikolaus Hrábovszky, Janós Borsitzky, judicial chair; Gabriel Hlinitzky, Assessor; Michael Prusinszky, Stephan Társovszky, Benedikt Kozár, Nikolaus Társovszky, Stephan Akay and Janós Medveczky, Janós St. Mariay, István Akay, Janós Draskovszky, György Záluszky, and Michael St. Mariay, also known as Hlinitzky.

. . . .

The three condemned were led that same day to the place of execution, where a crowd gathered to watch. A huge, flaming pyre was prepared near the river, while the public executioner sharpened his axe and heated his iron tongs before the crowd and the condemned. Ilona Jó was taken first. She was restrained while the executioner clamped the iron tongs onto her first finger. He wrenched it out amidst screams, not only from the condemned but from Dorka and members of the crowd. It is alleged that after her fourth finger was torn out, Ilona Jó fainted. At this point, she was probably given a fatal blow or strike and then thrown into the bonfire. Dorota apparently fainted, as well, having seen Ilona Jó's sentence carried out; her fingers removed and the death blow delivered, she, too, was then thrown into the fire. Ficzkó went last. When the executioner's axe came down onto his neck, severing the head, his dead body was thrown into the fire on top of the women. After sentencing was carried out, a gibbet was erected outside of Csejthe Castle to indicate that justice had been done.

During that same month of January, on the 24th , the residents of Bytča witnessed yet another satisfaction of justice. In probably what was not a very long ceremony, and no doubt lacking in formal process, the blind spinster and forest witch, the same person who made the magical cake for the Countess, was lcd to the place of execution. Erszi "Majorova" (also translated as "Beta, Slovak woman," "Busorka of Myjava" or the "Mistress of Miava") was then burned alive as a witch.

We know nothing more regarding the fate of Katalin Beneczky, the accomplice who managed to escape immediate execution. It seems that no further evidence was ever brought against her, nor a sentence carried out. Likely, after a period of time, she was quietly released.

THE FATE OF COUNTESS
BÁTHORY (1611-1614)

What was perhaps most interesting was György Thurzó's allegation, during the proceedings, that he had caught Countess
Báthory *in flagrante delicto*—in other words, red-handed or in
the act of commiting the crime. However, when King Mátyás'
representative insisted that Erzsébet be brought in personally for
interrogation, Thurzó refused:

*As long as I am Lord Palatine in Hungary, this will not come to
pass. The family that has won such high honors on the battlefield
shall not be disgraced in the eyes of the nation by the murky
shadow of this bestial female. In the interest of future generations of the Nádasdys, everything is to be done in secret for, if a
court were to try her, all of Hungary would learn of her murders
and it would contravene our laws to spare her life. However,
having seen her crimes with my own eyes, I have had to abandon
my plan to place her in a convent for the rest of her life.*

For the panel of sitting judges, as well as the King's representative, this must have seemed highly unusual: the Palatine

had just accused the Countess personally, yet refused the court permission to question her? Nádasdy honor or not, the pressure on Thurzó from the King to bring Erzsébet to justice was enormous; despite this, however, he held fast, and one has to wonder why. Because of her high station, the court could not convict or sentence the Countess without confirmation from both King and Parliament. On the other hand, the justices certainly had a right to question her. Thurzó's assertion of power here as prime minister was a bold and certainly risky move: he was essentially telling the King that, for now, he alone would control the proceedings. As we shall later see, this move was not without its complications.

One has to wonder if, indeed, Thurzó was telling the complete truth about what he had seen at Csejthe Manor and Castle. Perhaps this is what caused him to waiver here. Specifically, Thurzó, as well as the other eyewitnesses in the castle raid, all agreed to having seen dead girls and girls suffering imprisonment and torture upon their arrival. There is no doubt that Erzsébet's four accomplices were present and participating in one way or another in the torturing and killing. Thurzó's letter to his wife, written the following day, states: "Now, *those who tortured and murdered the innocent*—those evil women in league with that young lad who in silent cruelty assisted with their atrocities—were sent to Bytča." This implies that only the four accomplices were caught in the act. It is interesting that Thurzó does not specify the Countess' direct participation here, particularly when we know that he and his wife were wondering, just a few days prior, whether she personally harmed her servants or not. One would think that Thurzó would have finally answered that burning question without hesitation. Instead, all he said is that he had imprisoned the Widow Nádasdy in her castle tower and that: "There was another girl who'd been tortured and even others whom this cursed, bloody lady had imprisoned and went about torturing." From the verb tense, we still cannot tell for certain if the imprisonment and torturing occurred in the present or the past—in other words, on the day in question or

prior to that—or if Thurzó was yet certain, through actual obser-
vation or merely by implication, as to whether the Countess
herself performed the deeds.

However, Thurzó could still allege her guilt, one way or
another, with a clever legal loophole: the doctrine of *respondeat
superior*. This legal doctrine which, in Latin, means "let the
master answer" (and is sometimes called the "Master-Servant
Rule"), states that the master is responsible for the actions of his
or her servants. In Erzsébet's time, if a servant harmed another's
person or property, the lord or lady could be held personally responsible and have to make good on any claims. Thus, if the
Countess' servants were caught in the act of torturing or murdering, even if Thurzó did not actually see Lady Widow Nádasdy
personally involved, he could still allege her guilt vicariously
through them. It may be, too, that he found an article of her
clothing, still stained with blood. Of course, he might actually
have caught her red-handed but, unfortunately, we cannot be
sure. Thus, we speculate that Thurzó's lingering doubt caused
him to hesitate.

Indeed, throughout this time, we know that he and the
Countess corresponded and that she continued to maintain her
innocence. She also accused him of failing to protect her honor,
claims she could hardly make had he actually caught her red-
handed. While judgment against her four servants was swift and
their guilt clear beyond a shadow of doubt, there appeared to be
continued hesitation regarding the Countess.

Back at Castle Csejthe, still under house arrest, Countess
Erzsébet Báthory embarked on a letter writing campaign to free
herself. She sought both the assistance of her relative, Gábor
Báthory, as well as the opportunity to put on the greatest per-
formance of her life: namely, testifying to her own innocence.
György Thurzó repeatedly denied her petitions to appear on her
own behalf. Such testimony, he argued, would only further

damage the family's reputation. She, in turn, accused him of not defending her honor.

Meanwhile, Rev. Ponikenusz was so disturbed by the threats made by the Countess when he last visited her in prison, that he immediately wrote a letter to his superior, Reverend Élias Lányi. Lanyí had just served as an official in the last proceeding against the Countess' four accomplices and held the ear of the Palatine. Ponikenusz informed him of his conversation with the Countess and asked for intercession on his behalf from Palatine György Thurzó as well as Counts Zrínyi and Homonnay: "Soon I will have many enemies," he wrote, "so I commend your venerable jurisdiction immediately and ask that His Highness deign to support me, unworthy as I am, including the Lord Homonnay as well as the mighty (Nádasdy) son or daughters, and not to refuse the protection of his power."

When Erszébet spoke of the Hajdukes and Gábor Báthory, her cousin and Voivod of Transylvania, she was not making idle threats. He, indeed, had been gathering troops across the river—but not necessarily to rescue her. By 1610, Gábor, along with others, was inciting rebellion against King Mátyás, and it may be that Erzsébet was encouraging him to link up with those in her own lands that were displeased with the King; as mentioned, she had been financing his campaign since 1608. Staging her rescue would be a convenient flourish. Meanwhile, she continued to accuse György Thurzó of acting illegally by holding her under house arrest.

We are not exactly certain of Erzsébet's living conditions while under house arrest or whether she spent the entire time in the underground dungeon where she was originally brought. We do know that she was kept apprised of the proceedings and that she had access to parchment, ink, and messengers so as to send and receive letters. She also had at least a few remaining loyal (or fearful) staff members in place and, as the story goes, was staging an escape plan to reach her younger cousin Gábor in Transylvania. We are not certain of how far she got with her plans. We do know, however, that György Thurzó, along with her relatives, arrived soon after the trial for a showdown with the Countess.

The Palatine was definitely not pleased with her threats to Ponikenusz or her attempted collaboration with Gábor Báthory. In addition, she had also been threatening him with the "dire consequences of his illegal actions."

In any case, in front of her relatives, György Thurzó lost his temper. On his own authority, he pronounced sentence: "You, Erzsébet, are like a wild animal. You are in the last months of your life. You do not deserve to breathe the air on earth or see the light of the Lord. You shall disappear from this world and shall never reappear in it again. As the shadows envelop you, may you find time to repent your bestial life. I hereby condemn you, Lady of Csejthe, to lifelong imprisonment in your own castle."

We can be sure that this did not go over well with the Countess. Thurzó had pronounced life imprisonment; all that remained now was a confirmation of the sentence. Countess Báthory immediately petitioned for an appeal and chance to defend herself. Meanwhile, Thurzó and the family hoped that with justice done to her four accomplices and the Countess sentenced, the matter would finally end. It did not. King Mátyás had no intention of letting the matter rest—or letting Countess Báthory avoid the executioner's axe while his debt to her remained outstanding. His representative insisted on bringing yet another judicial hearing—this one directed against the Countess personally—on behalf of His Majesty the King.

The legalities were complicated; the King firmly believed that if Erzsébet received the death penalty, her property would cede to the Crown and his debts to her be cancelled. Thus, he would do everything in his power to see her dead. He was angered, in fact, that nothing had brought the death penalty upon the Countess during the two proceedings and demanded that the Lady Widow Nádasdy be interrogated immediately so as to mete out proper justice.

In a letter dated January 14, 1611, King Mátyás spoke of experiencing "serious displeasure, paralyzing fear and internal shuddering" upon learning that Widow Nádasdy killed "more than 300 innocent virgins and women, of both noble and lower levels, who served her as maids, and of whom no such action was deserved, without any involvement of the judiciary, in a most monstrous and cruel manner, their bodies mutilated, burned with hot irons, their flesh ripped out, roasted on the fire and this roasted flesh then allowed to be served."

After declaring the need for justice, the King then demanded that the Countess be interrogated at Castle Csejthe. He issued the following order to Thurzó:

We instruct you earnestly and we give you the emergency order as soon as your receive this letter, that you immediately summon this woman Erzsébet Báthory on the said date or through dates of letters to your bondsmen and by warrant of the honorable Chapter of the Metropolitan Church of Esztergom to appear at Castle Csejthe with leave to discover and discuss her aforementioned immense and outrageous deeds and that the judgment proceed and be carried out in fulfillment of the law, whether she appears personally or sends someone or not, and warn at the front where you set the date and place that she personally or by legal representation appear before you. Your handling of the matter, however, given the insistence of the parties involved, has to be done in accordance with the law. Anything else shall not proceed.

In a postal script, the King added that he had ordered Mózes Cziráky and András of Keresztúr to "stay on to collect testimonies from all of the Nádasdy places of residence on both sides of the Danube as soon as possible...." He added that the testimony "gathered by the torture of the old women should not be neglected." In conclusion, he ordered Thurzó to send the authenticated information to the King's own representative.

THE FATE OF COUNTESS BÁTHORY (1611-1614)

We realize from this letter that King Mátyás no longer has complete trust in Thurzó: he independently appointed a president over a special legal council and ordered the Countess' interrogation with no regard to the life sentence which Thurzó pronounced.

The Church was also weighing in on the matter. Catholic nobles lobbied the Hungarian Parliament in support of King Mátyás, expressing displeasure over the leniency shown by the Protestant Lord Palatine. Although some might have felt genuine moral outrage, a political agenda was also at work. The Thirty Years War (1618-1648) between Catholics and Protestants was looming. This struggle would eventually turn the region into a bloody wasteland, particularly in Germany, and signs of it were mounting. King Mátyás was a Catholic, and the Church desired a reunification of Catholic-held lands in western Hungary with those northern and eastern lands held mostly by Protestants, under Mátyás' control. The Catholic Hapsburgs were putting down Protestant rebellions ruthlessly and taking away Protestant lands all across Austria. If the King played his cards right, he was next in line to become Emperor. Pleasing the Church meant a great deal to him—and that included securing Erzsébet Báthory's vast holdings for the Catholic Hapsburgs.

Thurzó's replies to the King indicated a rather awkward attempt to quibble over the legalities and complexities of the case; he was buying time, of course, and he knew it. The King was determined to get his way, however, and Thurzó needed a better strategy: life imprisonment for Lady Nádasdy would not satisfy His Majesty. But Thurzó, along with the Báthory and Nádasdy families, also realized that this was now becoming a showdown between Catholic and Protestant interests: if the King could commandeer the Báthory-Nádasdy estates, then the holdings of a Protestant like Thurzó could be next.

On a personal level, the necessary interrogation of Countess Báthory would also result in her being tortured to extract a confession. The precedent of publicly humiliating a high noble—a woman, no less—and her illustrious family could not be set. Immediately, the powerful families embarked on a letter writing campaign, aided by Thurzó, to explain to His Majesty that the interrogation and death of Lady Widow Nádasdy would not necessarily accomplish the King's purpose; rather, Thurzó's life sentence should remain in place.

Probably all of Erszébet's family members, including her children and sons-in- law, by now realized that their own property rights were also at stake, so closely tied to hers. Should the King confiscate her estate, they could lose their own holdings, including inheritances and currently held lands. In addition, a public trial and execution, including disclosure of such horrific deeds, would bring unprecedented disgrace upon both families.

In a letter to György Thurzó dated February 12, 1611, Erzsébet's son-in-law, Miklós Zrínyi, thanked him for his "kinsman-like goodwill" and wrote:

....I have received and understood your sincere letter along with the copy of the letter from His Royal Majesty to you and the copy of your answer to it. And although with sad heart and suffering I heard the news of the shameful and miserable situation of my wife's mother, Mrs. Nádasdy - in view of her immense, shameful deeds, I must confess that, regarding a penalty, you have chosen the lesser of two evils. The judgment of Your Grace served us for the better, because it has preserved our honor and shielded us from too great a shame. When, in your letters, you made known to us the will of His Royal Majesty, including punishment by horrible, judicial torture, we, her relatives, felt that we must all die of shame and disgrace. But Your Grace, as our benign, truly beloved cousin and Lord, has prevented our shame, having imposed the best kind of punishment in perpetuo carceri inclusa delineatur *and not public punishment, which would shame all of us, including her children and the memory of her pious, blessed and good, knightly husband. We want to thank Your Grace for the rest of our lives and repay you with all our available strength; we wish to offer you a humble token of our mortal existence. We ask that you, therefore, implore His Majesty to*

reconsider his decision so that it is in accord with your previous verdict and to be content with your judgment and not to litigate against her in public. This would, as you can imagine, cause much shame and harm to us. By God have we placed our hope in you that you and His Majesty will decide this case in our favor, as we trust you will govern. For a more detailed discussion of this matter, I send my devout servant, Mr. András Milley, to you. I ask you as my benevolent, beloved Lord and brother, to believe his words and allow him to return to me with the desired answer. Lifelong will I repay you. May God grant Your Grace long life.

Shortly thereafter, on February 23rd, 13-year-old Pál Nádasdy also wrote a letter to Thurzó from his winter residence at Castle Kuresztúr, crafted with a brilliant legal argument that, undoubtedly, was influenced by his guardian, Megyeri (who might also have been having a change of heart now). In it, young Pál asked Thurzó for a favor on the basis of their kinship, to do all that was possible to prevent the King from punishing his mother as intended. He argued that Thurzó had already conducted sufficient discovery in the case, such that no additional interrogations were required and that any further summons would be inappropriate in lieu of the sentence. Most important, he argued, the King would stand to gain nothing: all of Erzsébet Báthory's properties had already been distributed to her three children before the trial, thus putting it out of the King's reach:

....I took from your letter what His Majesty has ordered you to do to my miserable mother. I have your response to His Majesty, and realize how often you are well disposed toward me and my sisters. God grant that we, I and my sisters and brothers-in-law, can reward your kindness by obedience from a pure heart throughout our entire lives. It is true, as you wrote to His Majesty, that the Citatio *(court summons) should have been issued sooner and that it is now inappropriate, because Your Grace, as the country's Chief Justice, has already done enough* extentio. *It is no longer necessary to continue, since the present punishment*

of my poor mother is worse than death, and not necessary to proceed according to the command of His Majesty since a judgment on her life has already been made. Turning now to her property, there is no need to fear, because before her arrest, she turned it all over to the three of us. Nevertheless, we the relatives and humble subjects of His Majesty, wish to ask that your use of legal force against my mother not impose eternal shame on our family. However, we do not want to act without the knowledge and advice of Your Grace; it is not fitting. I therefore implore you, please, write us your opinion on how my sisters and I should proceed with our intercession to His Majesty so as not to cause Your Grace any grief; indeed, as we learned from your letter, which we have kept secret. I await a favorable response from you, as my beloved father and Lord. God grant you many years in good health. Castle Keresztúr, 23 February, 1611.

Thurzó must have been intrigued; until this letter, he may not have even realized that a will was already in existence. The Palatine immediately engaged in a round of politics with legal advisors to the King and his own Protestant friends in the Hungarian Parliament. Finally, on March 30th, Thurzó sent a reply letter to the King, who, meanwhile, had been pressuring him repeatedly to move forward with the interrogation of Countess Báthory. Thurzó wrote:

...I, as Chief Judge next to Your Majesty, arranged her imprisonment after careful deliberation with the common consent of her relatives and her sons-in-law. The same Council of Lords and sitting judge confirmed for me today that I have taken the correct approach. The difficulty in this case, when weighing justice, is that it very rarely happens that highly regarded women of our time, as a result of their way of life, find themselves in such a highly alarming situation that the death penalty should be imposed on them, as well as to ask, what benefit would the government (treasury) receive in this case. Your Majesty will receive a full report on everything contained in this message

176

THE FATE OF COUNTESS BÁTHORY (1611-1614)

*upon the return of the sublime and dignified (*Magnificus ac generosus*) noble directors and their associated Council of Lords of the Court Chamber of Pressburg)*....

In support, Parliament issued a formal reply to the Catholic nobility that Thurzó had conducted the proceedings against Countess Báthory in a proper manner. On March 31, 1611, Judges Tamás Vizkelety and Ferenc Leranth composed a letter to the King, co-signed by the Learned Secretaries of the Royal House and Legal Council to the King (Council of the Hungarian Chamber). They advised His Majesty that nothing would be gained from another trial: first, it would be difficult to prove, under the law, that the Countess killed noble girls in a premeditated way; second, even if proven, by law the Crown was entitled to receive a maximum of only one-third of the estate of the decapitated; and third, in the case of simple murders (i.e., of low-born people), the interested parties themselves had to make the allegations against the Countess—not the prosecutor (i.e., suggesting that it would be highly unlikely, given the local people's fear of the Countess, that they would actually step forward to make accusations against her). In addition, certain procedural errors were mentioned to the King, such as the continued taking of preliminary interrogatories—which were supposed to be kept confidential—even after they had become public knowledge.

The lawyers of the Royal Curia concluded:

....However, since nearly all of the judges of the Kingdom and Assessor of the Royal Court are so inclined and, thus, since we hardly have to do anything to secure a ruling, [we] recommend a mild verdict on the part of Your Majesty in consideration of the gracious, faithful and useful services of the deceased husband of this woman and her minor son and daughters, one of whom is married to the illustrious and glorious Lord Count Nikolaus Zrínyi, the other to Lord György Homonnay, both important nobles and Your Holy Majesty's faithful servants and useful and good citizens of your country, who are against the

extreme punishment of putting this woman to death, but rather beseech you to decide her punishment so as to effectively remain at life-long imprisonment, respectively....

All of this must have only infuriated King Mátyás more; his bid at becoming Emperor could have depended on winning the matter. Possibly, he had also learned of Erzsébet's attempts behind the scenes to depose him in collusion with her cousin, Gábor Báthory. Thus, he refused to certify Thurzó's sentence of life imprisonment, ignored the advice of his legal counsel and, instead, reopened the case by fiat. The King ordered a new investigation, summoning Notary András of Keresztúr to call up more witnesses against the Countess, including her court officials and those from all of the areas under her administrative control, including Beckóv, Kostolány, Csejthe, and Vrobvé (Hung. Verbó).

When completed, András of Keresztúr would submit his report in July of 1611 after questioning an incredible number of people—224 in total. The results, however, were not at all what the King desired.

19

FINAL SENTENCING

In a document dated July 28, 1611, Notary András of Keresztúr dutifully recorded the testimonies of 224 people—court officials, servants, administrators, townspeople, clergy and nobles—from all throughout Erzsébet's vast holdings. The King also received a report of the testimonies given under torture by the Countess' four accomplices. In sum, the results, unfortunately, were not what anyone wanted to hear—including King Mátyás.

In a shocking turn of events, these witnesses laid bare the putrid "dirty laundry" of not only the Countess, but also the outwardly illustrious Báthory-Nádasdy families and neighboring nobility, in no uncertain terms. Hungary's beloved war hero, Ferenc Nádasdy, was exposed as a villain who brutalized servants, taught his wife bizarre torturing games, and covered up her murders; personnel from Erzsébet's court and towns, respected squires and nobles, were accused of assisting in the murders by procuring girls (in some cases, their own relatives), engaging in a cover up, or turning a blind eye. As the allegations continued to pour out, suddenly Imre Megyeri was on the defensive: he and young Pál Nádasdy had to lobby intensively now to protect their own staff against accusations of complicity or cover up.

The King was astonished. As much as he wanted to implicate Erzsébet Báthory, he could not risk such terrible evidence against Hungary's national hero—or against so many other nobles. That would raise the ire of too many. Desperate, he called another tribunal of witnesses to be certain of the testimony. Besides Csejthe, the worst offenses seemed to have occurred at the Báthory-Nádasdy holdings at Sárvár, Keresztúr and Lockenhaus (Leka): Mátyás next ordered Deputy Notary Mózes Cziráky to summon witnesses from those particular holdings: twelve were called, and the report completed on December 14, 1611. Those testifying came from the nobility and supposedly held the "highest credibility"; among them were star witnesses, including court officials Benedikt Deseö (no longer in the Countess' employ) and Jakob Szilvassy, the two men who had rare permission to witness the Countess and her assistants in action.

However, the witnesses repeated exactly what had been said about the shameful goings on. No mistake had been made. At Thurzo's repeated urgings, the King finally conceded: Countess Báthory would not be brought to public trial. Relieved, Thurzó immediately brokered a clever deal. In light of the evidence, he recommended his original sentence of *perpetuis carceribus* (perpetual/life imprisonment) rather than the death penalty. This time, however, he included a caveat to please Mátyás: legally, it would be as though Countess Erzsébet Báthory never existed. Mátyás' debt to her was immediately cancelled, and a small portion of her lands would cede to him. Any documentation regarding the Countess, including all legal records of the incriminating proceedings, would be sealed. By order of Parliament, the name of Erzsébet Báthory would never again be spoken in polite society.

King Mátyás agreed to the terms. As a result, the Báthory and Nádasdy reputations, including Ferenc' national honors, remained intact; Sárvár passed to Pál Nádasdy, and Erzsébet's sons-in-law were appointed permanent administrators of her estates until Pál came of age; the lands of other Hungarian nobles were temporarily preserved against undue Catholic advances; and in 1612, the following year, King Mátyás was crowned Holy Roman Emperor.

For everyone, the news was good—except for Countess Erzsébet. Stonemasons arrived shortly thereafter to carry out her final sentence: she was never to be let out of confinement. Legend says that she spent her final confinement in the private apartments within the tower of Castle Csejthe, although some commentators insist that she remained below in the dungeon of the keep. In any case, she was allegedly walled in with only a single space left between the bricks large enough for the passage of food, supplies, and excrement.

Some have argued that Erzsébet's final confinement was not literally to her tower apartment or dungeon (i.e., she was never actually bricked up inside) but, rather, that she was sentenced to perpetual house arrest where she could roam freely throughout her castle estate. We believe that during the course of the various trials and tribunals, Erzsébet was indeed subject to a much looser form of house arrest in which she had some latitude to come and go within the estate or, at least, was not yet walled into a particular space. After the December 1611 tribunal, however, Thurzó's sentence of *perpetuis carceribus* (life/perpetual imprisonment), confirmed by both King and Parliament, was actually enforced by means of walling her up.

One wonders what daily life was now like for Countess Báthory. Likely, during the first few months after imposition of her final sentence, she received visitors—her daughter, Katalin, for instance, who brought supplies such as candles, parchment, ink, and favorite food items. As her sons-in-law, Counts Drugeth de Homonnay and Zrínyi, assumed full responsibility for administering her estates, there must have been at least a few visits in which they or their representatives inquired after details.

We also know that György Thurzó's wife, Erzsébet Czobor, paid more than a few visits in January of 1612. Each time that Countess Czobor visited, however, she left with more than she came: she was systematically raiding Countess Báthory's coffers, including her jewelry. The Thurzos'daughter,

Borbála, was engaged to marry Count Kristóf Erdődy in September of that year, and substantial finances were required for the wedding. The plundering was so bad, in fact, that Count Zsigmond Forgách, writing on behalf of the Supreme Court of Hungary, ordered György Thurzó to put a stop to his wife's activities.

Slowly, however, the visits diminished, and people began to forget about the Countess. No longer in charge of the estates, her importance faded. Of course, she continued to write letters, protesting her innocence and demanding an appeal, but no one answered. It is said that when supplies of parchment ended, she began writing on the walls.

While by no means an ideal living condition, the Countess did have enough food, water, and air to survive: in her fifties now, she would still live another two-and-a-half years behind the wall, at an already advanced age for the time. How she spent those last years is hard to say. Eventually, however, Erzsébet herself knew the end was coming. We know that she had no great affection for her sons-in-law. As matters currently stood, upon her death both men planned to assume permanent control over the sizable properties they were administering on behalf of her two daughters.

Thus, on July 31, 1614, three weeks before she died, two priests from the Esztergom bishopric, Imre Agriensy (Emericus Agriens) and András Kerpelich, arrived at Castle Csejthe by her request to witness and notarize an addendum to her Last Will and Testament. In this document, she reiterated that all of her property had previously been given to her three children. In particular, she wished to make clear that György Drugeth de Homonnay was not to receive anything further. Apparently, ownership of the City of Keresztúr was at issue: the Countess wanted to reiterate that her daughter, Katalin, should receive this property—not her husband, György Drugeth de Homonnay— and that appropriate legal action had been taken toward this end:

FINAL SENTENCING

We, the Cathedral Capital of Eszertgom, commemorate the following: that we, on the amiable request of the noble lady, Countess Erzsébet Báthory, the widow of the former illustrious and noble gentleman, Count Nádasdy, who, because of her captivity is not personally able to come to us, sent two of our Venerables, namely Messrs. Andreas Kerpelich and Emericus Agiens, our brothers and fellow clerics, who took the following confession that the lady gave to us; this, in turn, made it appropriate for them to serve witness to what this finally reported, after they were returned to us, under oath, as set forth in a general decree:

That in the current year of the Lord, 1614, on the 31st day of July in the castle called Csejthe, having been built in County Neutra, where the aforementioned Lady Countess Erzsébet Báthory, in the personal presence of our brothers voluntarily and on her own initiative stated the following and in this way expressed: that she bequeathed the City of Keresztúr in the County of Abauj to her daughter Katalin Nádasdy, the wife of the illustrious and venerable György Drugeth of Homonnay; and that this bequest had already been transferred and assigned during her captivity but in such a way that, up to this point, had merely released it and that she was not yet in her full and permanent possession. Also, she bequeathed nothing more to Lord György Homonnay; rather, after they put her in prison, she made her assignments only to her heirs and passed along nothing further.

Therefore, if she desired, and even if she still wanted to exclude someone from her property, nor could she have so wished in the least; her intention therefore continues to be that the entire property will be divided among them (her heirs). Finally, had she established in documents of the aforementioned Lord György Homonnay, in the journal of 1610, what property she had assigned, which is why we have kept for ourselves these writings on these dispositions aforementioned by Lady Erzsébet Báthory to the knowledge of our trusted brothers, in writing referred to under the seal of our chapter and entrusted to them. Given on Sunday after the Feast of St. Peter in Chains (in vinculi), in 1614.

Erzsébet's attempts to keep property away from György Drugeth de Homonnay were likely in vain, however; a little less than three weeks later, on Thursday, August 18, 1614, 16-year-old Pál Nádasdy transferred one-third of the dominion of Csejthe and Beckov over to him.

Two days later, on the night of Sunday, August 21, 1614, Countess Erzsébet Báthory was concerned about her poor circulation. She told her bodyguard, "Look, how cold my hands are!" Her attendant told her that it was nothing and that she should simply lie down. With that, she put her pillow under her legs and then began singing with a beautiful voice. Commentators say that she passed away at two hours after midnight (2:00 a.m.), but a letter from Slanislav Thurzó to his cousin, György, states that she was found dead in the morning.

Three days later, on August 25, 1614, Stanislav Thurzó wrote to György Thurzó, in which he reported that Countess Báthory had died:

....The death of Mrs. Nádasdy may already be known to you and how she unexpectedly resigned from this life. In the evening, said she to her bodyguard: "Look, how cold my hands are!" The bodyguard told her: "It's nothing, Mistress. Just go and lie down." She then went to sleep. She took the pillow that was under her head and put it under her feet. As such, she lied down and, in the same night, she died. In the morning, she was found dead. They say, however, she prayed imploringly and praised God with beautiful singing. Regarding her funeral, we still have no information. I commend myself and my services, along with my wife, to Your Grace, your wife, and your beloved children. God grant Your Grace a long and healthy life. Pöstyén, 25 August, Anno Domini 1615.

According to a servant of Pál Nádasdy who wrote a historical chronicle of Csejthe, Erzsébet was buried at the church in Csejthe (some say in a crypt beneath the church, while others claim the local cemetery), on November 25th. It is said, however, that the residents soon began to complain that the "Infamous Lady" was lying under holy ground and demanded that she be removed. Erzsébet's remains were supposedly taken back to the Báthory family estate in 1617. Where she lies today, however, is something of a mystery: in his book, *Trencin, Trnava*, J. Branecky reported that on July 7, 1938, the crypt at the Csejthe church was opened but that the Countess' grave was not found. It is also claimed that in 1995, the Báthory family crypts at Nyírbátor were also opened. No remains of the Countess were found at that site, either. Other commentators claim that she is buried in the Lamosz Cemetery in Budapest, although there does not yet appear to be any credibility to this assertion or the existence of the site itself.

20

A GLIMPSE INTO THE COUNTESS' PERSONALITY

As a result of Hungary's decision to declare Countess Báthory "legally dead," as though she had never existed, no archives exist for the Báthory family, and it is likely that significant correspondence, personal items, portraits, and information regarding intimate details have been lost forever, whether forgotten, pilfered, or destroyed. Experts have nonetheless attempted to piece together more information on her character and personality, particularly from analyses of her handwriting.

We do have her signature on the Last Will and Testament. Graphologist Klára Ácsová rendered the following opinion on it: "Partially due to her decadent nature, but also as a result of sexual dissatisfaction, sadism overcame her more and more. Her sadism might have originated in unfulfilled love because she was forced to marry somebody other than whom she loved. This broke her and initiated increasing cravings for revenge in her. She was mischievous, dangerous and harmful to her surroundings. We can equate her with Lucrezia Borgia, but Erzsébet Báthory was more realistic and deliberate. According to her handwriting, she was not schizophrenic or mad, as some of her biographers say."

It is possible, however, the Ácsová's opinion was skewed. She was given only a rather poor reproduction of the original signature to study and did not have access to the entire document. Also, she knew to whom the signature belonged, and this might have clouded her objectivity. Of interest, Ácsová would be asked to render a second opinion, this time under more controlled circumstances, and her opinion changed as a result.

Specifically, Hungarian judge Irma Szádeczky-Kardos ordered a second graphological test done for a comprehensive study. This time, the entire will document was used. To ensure impartiality, all names, dates and significant data were blacked out of the text so that the expert had no idea whose handwriting was under analysis. Ácsová was called a second time to render an opinion. Unaware that the will belonged to Erzsébet Báthory, Ácsová's study revealed this time that the writer had a "strong, determined and self-confident personality, with a logical mind and manly character." These qualities resulted from a strict and cold upbringing. The writer was realistic, critical, hated resistance, and stood high above others. She was not so much loved as respected – not due to her cruelty but rather for her uncompromising attitudes, strictness and frequent humiliation of others. She required order in everything. The handwriting does not reveal any signs of sadism or sexual deviation, and does not reveal any signs of pathology except for occasional bouts of hysteria. However, the signature, coming right before she died and during her internment, bears signs of schizophrenia.

The graphologist was repeatedly asked whether she found indicators of sadism or other sexual deviation, since her second report conflicted with the first. Of interest, Ácsová consistently replied in the negative.

Tomáš Gugenberger carried out another graphological analysis on two of the Countess' personal letters. However, he was told beforehand that he would be analyzing the characteristics of a serial killer. This may have influenced his opinion, unfortunately. In any case, his findings on the personality and character of Erzsébet Báthory differ from Ácsová's.

According to Gugenberger, the Countess did have some good qualities: she was religious, generous and dignified. Dignity, in fact, seemed to be very important for her. She could also be optimistic, on occasion. However, she had a number of weaknesses: "self-contented, impatient, emotional, egocentric, distrustful, insensate, irritable, impulsive, unpredictable, indecisive and guileful. Her intellectual abilities were poor and she was controlled by strong sexual desire, cruelty and self-indulgence."

Gugenberger based his findings on a letter written in 1606 by the Countess to György Thurzó's wife, Erzsébet Czobor. Gugenberger also analyzed a second letter written in 1610. By that time, he identified "a tendency for criminality, cruelty, whimsicality, unstableness and perversity joined, and all these features determined her sadism. Also a mental disorder appeared."

21

POSTSCRIPT

In the end, as with every sensational murder trial, we are often left with the questions, 'Did they really do it?, and, 'Why did they do it?'

We know that, were Countess Báthory to be tried under the existing criminal legal system in the United States, she would undoubtedly be acquitted for the simple fact that she was denied various Constitutional rights—most especially, the right to representation and the chance to face her accusers in court. In her own time, however, such was not the case: no such rights were guaranteed, even for the nobility.

There were, however, various inconsistencies, even in her own time, that merited attention. The King's legal advisors admitted to certain procedural errors that occurred, including the premature public knowledge generated by the inquest before its completion. And even the royal notaries conceded that much of the testimony against the Countess included little more than hearsay.

We are still not absolutely certain that she was caught in the act: along with the sitting judicial council of the time, two hundred years after the trial, Fr. László Turóczi made the claim that Countess Báthory was caught red-handed, thus immortalizing the tradition. However, we have yet to find actual documentation from the period to verify this. Thurzó and the men who followed him into Csejthe Manor on the evening of the raid never testified to having caught the Countess in the act; Thurzó never made that assertion in answer to his wife's question as to whether or not the Countess was personally guilty; and even the King's Chamber cryptically wrote that the Countess had been caught in the act only *"so to speak."*

This author believes that it would have been impossible for the Countess to continue protesting her innocence or making the kind of bold statements to the clergy and nobility that she did, after the raid, had she actually been caught red-handed that night.

On the other hand, this author does not believe that she was innocent, either. The testimony from her accomplices and most trusted staff is too clear and consistent to deny. Hundreds died—whether by her hand or through her staff—and she most certainly knew what her accomplices were doing even if she did not commit all of the deeds herself. It is doubtful, however, that she killed over 600—even the King, Palatine and court system of her own time gave no credence to this incredible number submitted by a mere child. Likely, the numbers submitted by her accomplices were most accurate: they had nothing to lose at that point and knew her secret activities best.

In the end, we wonder why she did it—how someone as brilliant, poised, and wealthy as Countess Báthory could spend her free time tormenting and murdering the small and innocent. And yet, we wonder that about all serial killers. Many seem to start out the same: inflicting small acts of cruelty upon those weaker than themselves—animals, perhaps, or young children—gradually increasing in intensity until the killer can no longer control the urge. Like an addiction, the desire for power, or the murderous rage that explodes, simply cannot be helped—or stopped—no matter the consequences.

POSTSCRIPT

We know that Countess Báthory was receiving advice, warnings, and even urgings from her personal staff to stop what she was doing—yet she still refused, fully assured that she was above the law of her day. In that sense, she must have believed that she *was* the law. And yet, a pathology clearly existed. Likely, she was brutalized as a child and as a young wife: it is common that one who victimizes others was frequently a victim, as well. Witnesses claimed that the Countess could not eat or drink if she did not kill a victim first, and that she even wrapped herself in nettles, allowing her maidens to look upon her and touch her in that state. The fact that her girls—victims who, for the most part, ranged in age from 10 to 14—were repeatedly stripped naked, made to tend to her in a state of undress, and then forced to suffer heinous punishments for the least infraction indicates an extreme sexual disorder.

In the end, the Countess had convinced even herself that, somehow, she was innocent of any wrongdoing and insisted on this with a fervent, almost righteous indignation. At the same time she was making charitable donations to help the poor and needy, she was also torturing and murdering children—perhaps the most needy of all. Yet she had no hesitation blaming this brutality on her hand-picked servants, going so far as to say that she herself was afraid of what they were doing and, in essence, somehow helpless to stop them. Again, the complexity of her case—and the depths of her disorder—make her a figure of fascinating study. Over time, hopefully, we will come to better understand her personality—and her disorder—or history will inevitably repeat itself.

As for the people who figured prominently in the Countess' life, we can say the following:

Her cousin Gabór Báthory, Prince of Transylvania and the man whom she hoped would rescue her from prison, was murdered on October 18, 1613, by his own men, roughly one year before she died.

Daughter Anna died on August 13, 1615. She had no children.

In December 1615, Palatine György Thurzó died. His wife, Erzsébet Czobor, famous for pilfering Countess Báthory's jewelry, would later die in poverty.

On March 9, 1616, 18-year-old son Pál Nadasdy divided the goods at Csejthe and Beckov between himself and György Drugeth de Homonnay. On August 3, 1620, Pál Nádasdy was betrothed to Judith Revay. On December 15, 1621, their first son, György, was born. On January 14, 1623, their second son, Ferenc, was born, followed by numerous other children. In 1671, Ferenc would be executed for treason by the Hapsburgs.

There was a survivor from Castle Csejthe, a young girl named Anna who was rescued on the night of the raid. She was taken to the nearby town of Újhely and treated there by the town barber (surgeon), Thomas. Anna was then taken back to the home of her widowed mother. Anna's hand had been cut into pieces; on her back, pieces had been cut out on both sides of her shoulders; on her buttocks, flesh had also been cut out on both sides. She was bedridden for over two months. The local records indicate that, "Because of this treatment, she received 56 guilders and 15 pounds of wheat, guaranteed by the Újhely measure, from the Administrator of Csejthe by command of the illustrious Lord Palatine. After her recovery, she and her mother were given a small farm in Csejthe as free property."

APPENDIX

LETTERS, TRIAL TRANSCRIPTS, DEPOSITIONS, AND DOCUMENTS (LISTED CHRONOLOGICALLY), INCLUDING PORTRAITS AND BIBLIOGRAPHY

EMPEROR'S LETTER TO THE HUNGARIAN COURT CHAMBER IN VIENNA APRIL 26, 1575

We have respectfully asked Ferenc Nádasdy, after he proposed marriage to the late Count Gyorgy Bathory's daughter Elizabeth Bathory--to be joyfully celebrated on Sunday the 8th, in the coming month of May at Varanno—to know that it is our delight and desire to send our wedding envoy delegation. And (we) graciously granted, in accord with his obedient request, an order for a master craftsman to build a decorative credenza. We commend their mercy that they receive a silver-overlaid goblet or a picher and basin valued at 200 Thaler to be brought to them instead of our appearance at their wedding, the delivery of which is to be ordered. In addition, we graciously want you to know that the Roman Empress, our amiable, beloved spouse, thought Nádasdy should also receive a goblet worth 100 Thaler, and we desire to allocate the money for that. So we have also graciously granted that our amiable, beloved sons, Rudolph, King of Hungary, and Archduke Ernst of Austria, should also provide cups worth 150 Thaler, as well as have the credenza inscribed, and issue this gracious command: Your choice will certainly be honored,

whether they bring the serving cups with them and herewith order them, or you have the craftsman make them in a style similar
to our Spanish Court (as otherwise will not pay for it). This indicates our gracious will and opinion. Prague, 26 April 1575.

THURZÓ'S LETTER TO ANDRÁS OF KERESZTÚR
MARCH 5, 1610

Count György Thurzó of Bethlenfalva, Palatine of the Kingdom
of Hungary, Judge of Kumans and Arva, and also governor of
the same counties under His Majesty, Mátyás II, by the grace of
God King of Hungary, Dalmatia, Croatia, Slavonia, etc., Councilor and Governor of Hungary, etc.

To the laudable councilor, András of Keresztúr, Notary of the
aforementioned Holy Kingdom, hail and greetings. You know
that we have heard at various times credible and serious allegations regarding the generous and famous Lady Erzsébet Báthory,
widow of the late, illustrious and famous Lord Ferenc Nádasdy;
that, namely, this woman Erzsébet Báthory, disregarding her
reverence for God and the people, cruelly murdered one-knows-
not-how-many girls and virgins and other women in her *Gynaecaeum* in various ways, and that it was incumbent upon us
equally by the will of said Royal Majesty, as well as by virtue of
said laws and regulations of the Kingdom Hungary, as Palatine
of the same Kingdom of Hungary, appointed on the basis of our
office and our inherent authority as Palatine under the laws of
the Kingdom, against the aforementioned violence and unbeara-
bly severe crimes. However, according to law and to proceed

against said Lady Erzsébet Báthory, and to be able to speak of a proper judgment when it should be necessary and possibly obtained, we wish to proceed in the above manner according to the law of the Kingdom and ask you to make inquiries of reliable witnesses. We therefore send you with serious intent and by virtue of our authority as Palatine, and give you binding instructions and strict commands as soon as you receive this letter, over all and every individual, including ecclesiastical dignitaries and aristocrats as well as nobles and other people of both sexes, of whatever origin they may be, from the counties of Bratislava, Nitra, Trencén and Bars, all of which is covered by our commission, after their appointment and summons for questions on the above, regarding the killings perpetrated on girls and women by said Lady Erzsébet Báthory, to the fullest, most reliable and pure truth to be known and discovered: from the spiritual leaders in the purity of their conscience, and by those nobles and other ordinary, honest people of both sexes in their faith in God and, above all, the Royal Majesty and their sacred duty of fidelity to the Crown. (In addition, under the power of our authority as Palatine, with serious and strict intent, we add the following -- under threat of a strict penalty of 16 marks, the heavy weight of which shall be relentlessly pursued from the affected, as this shall be a general decree -- that they indeed may not have the nerve to deviate in any way from the pure truth in their responses to the questions.) And after a thorough investigation of this evidence, you should send to us our customary and necessary letter report, so that justice may be done. Given at Bratislava, on the 5th day of the month of March, the year of the Lord 1610.

\THURZÓ'S LETTER TO MÓZES CZIRÁKY MARCH 5, 1610

We, Count György Thurzó of Bethlenfalva, Palatine of the Kingdom of Hungary, Judge of Kumans and Arva, and perpetual governor of the same county (Arva), a confidential councilor of the holy Prince and Lord, Lord Mátyás, by the grace of God elected Roman Emperor, at all times and of several kingdoms the King of Germania, Hungary, Bohemia, etc., Archduke of Austria, Duke of Burgundy, etc., and governor of Hungary.

We give the following with this well-known text, so that all may benefit. By the good prompting of the Holy, Imperial and Royal Majesty, our lenient Lord, through special mandates and extensive writings containing interviews, confessions and statements about the cruel and outrageous acts of sacrilege apparently committed by the noble and illustrious Lady Erzsébet Báthory, the widow of the former Lord Ferenc Nádasdy, etc., issued under the seals and handwritten signatures of certain loyal nobleman who gave public notice and all of whom are known to you, having been reported equally, we desire to and must assign under our Palatinal Seal and Handwritten Signature:

That the first report of the honorable Mózes Cziráky, our Deputy Notary, in the form of a book, together with our judicial seal, reaffirms as follows:

We, Count György Thurzó of Bethlenfalva, Palatine of the Kingdom of Hungary, Judge of Kumans and Arva, and also governor of the same counties and Council to the Holy Prince and Lord, Lord Mátyás II, by the grace of God King of Hungary, appointed king of Bohemia, Archduke of Austria, Duke of Burgundy, and Governor of Hungary.

We submit and publish this, our report, for the advantage of all; that the honorable Master Mózes Cziráky, our Deputy Notary, under our orders summarized these reports and handed them over, which were written on unsealed paper and then attached at the inner edge with our secret and valid seal, with our Deputy Notary adding the following text to it:

Count György Thurzó of Bethlenfalva, Palatine of the Kingdom of Hungary, Judge of Kumans and Arva, and perpetual governor of the same county (Arva), and councilor of the current Prince and Lord, Lord Mátyás, by the grace of God King of Hungary, Dalmatia, Croatia, Slovakia, etc., appointed King of Bohemia, Archduke of Austria, Duke of Burgundy, etc., and governor of Hungary.

To the honorable Master, Mózes Cziráky, our Deputy Notary, with gracious greetings. You know how, both in the past and the present time, several serious complaints have come to us regarding the noble and glorious Lady Erzsébet Báthory, the widow of the late, noble and glorious Lord Ferenc Nádasdy, etc.; namely, that this same Lady Erzsébet Báthory, through some sort of evil spirit, has set aside her reverence for God and man, and has killed in cruel and various ways many girls and virgins and other women who lived in her *Gynaecaeum*; also that we, both by the will of said Royal Majesty and by virtue of the laws and regulations of the Kingdom of Hungary, said Palatine of the same Kingdom of Hungary shall be responsible in fulfilling our duties and we are entitled under Palatinal authority, in accordance with the customs of the Kingdom, to punish said unbearable and serious crimes which have been committed. Thus, we can legitimately and duly proceed in the aforementioned matter; and, thus, regarding said Lady Erzsébet Báthory, once a proper verdict - if it should be necessary – is spoken and can be achieved, we begin by ordering you in this matter to collect and make inquiries of witnesses, as the law of the Kingdom requires. Therefore, we exhort you earnestly and instruct and authorize you, by virtue of our Palatinal authority that, as soon as you receive this letter, to question every member of both the ecclesiastical state as well as the nobility and other honorable people of all classes and of both sexes in the counties of Györ, Sopron, Vas, Zala and Veszprém, concerning the above-mentioned killings of girls and women by the said Lady Erzsébet

Báthory; by members of the spiritual state, may they answer in the purity of their conscience; by the upper and lower nobility, and those of other classes of both sexes, out of respectable secular ethos in their God, and with due reverence and loyalty to the said Royal Majesty and the sacred Crown; the whole, pure truth is to be fully explored, and you should bring your experience to the inquiry (we add our Palatinal authority by virtue of the seriousness of the matter and strictly impose a penalty of 16 marks - - such as this is available in a general decree – a heavy weight imposed immediately thereafter upon those whom it affects, as we are adamant that only the pure truth be given on the issue points without having the slightest sacrifice of the oath). After implementation of these interviews and witness interrogations, you are obliged to faithfully report and to make announcements to us. This matter calls for justice. Anything else shall not proceed. Given at Bratislava, on the 5th day of the month of March, the year of the Lord 1610.

APPENDIX

LAST WILL AND TESTAMENT OF ERZSÉBET BÁTHORY
SEPTEMBER 3, 1610

I, noble and gracious Erzsébet Báthory, the widow of the former noble and gracious Ferenc Nádasdy, covered by God's grace, now in old age and without strength, in an ailing state, am obliged to tend to matters that cause me excruciating suffering due to the passing of my blessed and beloved husband, weakening me from day to day. Many restless concerns came over me as to my three beloved children, when my two unmarried daughters and my un-tutored son came into the care and custody of my widowed hands. Until now, I have supplied them, with God's gracious help, by assiduous care and motherly love, despite my widowed standing, not only for their good and their physical nourishment relating to their benefit; especially also, as the almighty God in His gracious goodness with my two daughters Anna and Kata Nádasdy therein showed luck, praised and blessed be His holy name, for all the orphans and widows to whom He graciously provides. I have provided decently for them at appropriate times, through their father's house, and their parents bore the appropriate costs of marriage—my older daughter Anna to the highly well-born and gracious Miklós Zrínyi, Kata to the most high-born and gracious György Homonnay, where I paid the expenses and took care of the major concerns. I cared, thanks to the gracious help of God, praised and blessed be His holy name, also for the education of my son Pál Nádasdy, such that he, as the almighty God declared the time to have come, at twelve years of age took the oath of office of County Chief at the county of Vas in a proper manner and with corresponding costs paid. And because for all these things I zealously bore these concerns, my awareness now dwindling, thanks to the strength and holy grace of God, from day to day without ceasing I am still able to think about the end of my earthly life with all my heart, and have decided that to the end of my life, I shall think only of the holy, gracious God, the Savior and Creator, and prove to Him my gratitude. For this reason, I renounce earthly concerns and clarify hereby by this Testament that I have renounced the care and possession of the father's portion for my children, including all of his movable and immovable goods, and, as of this day, wish to be carefee of worries about such desires, save for all the managers, assistants, and other faithful servants of my beloved husband's blessed memory who have been entrusted to me for their care and custody.

Since the father's portion has not yet been divided amongst my children, and while also my two daughters currently live distantly away with their husbands, since Pál Nádasdy my son lives with me, I have left him in possession of the goods, and he shall let it remain so until God allows my three children to come together and divide the goods with the help of their pious, God-fearing relatives and friends of the most important neighboring men with whom in loving kinship this agreement has been made.

Hereby, I have asked both my daughters and sons-in-law to wait for their brother to come of age before distributing the goods acquired from Sárvár, Kapuvár, and Leka and not to cause any harm to come to them. May they among one another find an equitable manner in which to share, such that the rights of a child living after the death of another child be not diminished. The remaining goods, both the father's portion as well as the mother's portion, that have come to be located everywhere in this country, no matter which county they are located, are to be divided in three portions. As for my bridal gown, which I shall wear until my death, what a reward it would be for me to allow my three children, from their share of goods, both to me, not as their mother, as well as other relatives to pay nothing; because I have them and because I have them naturally and also frequently equally permit, that they in the future never need to pay for the goods coming into their hands.

APPENDIX

As far as inherited property and legacies that came to me by my father and my mother are concerned, everything I've previously owned, and everything in the future that would go to me after my due share of inheritance and, whether by virtue of blood, whether by virtue of a Testament, blessed by my parents or brethren, as I could or would have had a claim—I have transferred all of this with full inheritance rights to my three children, Anna Nádasdy, Kata Nádasdy and Pál Nádasdy, and I also pass into their hands all my castles, together with their revenues. I also have included all of my property owned since childhood into their respective shares of ownership; I have also put into their hands all of the deeds, titles, and letters, as the decree so provides, and for which the law provides. The gold works, I have bequeathed to Pál Nádasdy because my two daughters have already received their shares; i.e., rings, hangers, etc. I have also bequeathed all my moveable goods, silver works, gems and however they may be called, to my three children in equal shares, except for the horse harness and weapons, since I had already bequeathed that to my son, Pál Nádasdy.

These are my orders and my Last Testament, shown by their own free will that I did call as witnesses certain important nobles, so that they could witness my orders and my Last Testament, from my mouth were words that were put in writing here, present together with me with their original seals and reaffirming their names as thus follows:

first: Bálint Récsey from Gátosháza
second: Kristóf Cicheo from Gulács
third: Márton Szopory from Fölsö-Szopor
fourth: István Döry from Jobaháza
fifth: István Tompa from Bódogfalva
sixth: János Bácsmegyei from Simaháza
seventh: Gergely Piterius, a preacher from Keresztúr
eighth: Benedek Deseö from Haraszt
ninth: Gergely Pásztori from Bozd

tenth: Vid Andy de And
eleventh: Miklós Madarász.

This testament is given at Keresztúr, 3 Sept. 1610.

Erzsébet Báthory

REPORT OF ANDRÁS OF KERESZTÚR
(34 WITNESS STATEMENTS/DEPOSITIONS)
SEPTEMBER 19, 1610

After he received and faithfully and dutifully handed over this
letter, the notary of record handled such in the following manner. According to the demands and orders of the said royal
Palatine, he summoned on the below-listed days the following
witnesses in accordance with the foregoing provisions of said
Palatine, under heavy penalty of 16 marks (given under general
decree) for those who refused to respond to the questions from
the notary of record, according to the content of the decree to be
summoned and assembled, monitored and interrogated sepa-
rately, so that each would speak the pure truth of what he knew,
experienced, and was interrogated upon, including the clergy in
the purity of their conscience, and the people in their faith in
God and their loyalty towards our royal Majesty and our holy
Hungarian royal crown.

The first was the noble Mátyás Muraközy, 46 years old, residing
on his property in Apaj and Alsócheppen who personally appeared, was sworn and interrogated; he said that he heard from
the nobles Melchior and Pál Nagyvathy that their own sister had
been entrusted to and passed on to the *Gynaecaeum* of said Mrs.
Erzsébet Báthory, and that their sister was killed there at the
court in this *Gynaecaeum* of Mrs. Erzsébet Báthory. Melchior

and Pál Nagyvathy further reported that they had undertaken extensive and thorough inquiries regarding said sister, but could not find out anything about her whereabouts or what came of her; they were certain, however, that she had been killed by Mrs. Erzsébet Báthory.

Eventually, on the 30th day of the month of March, in the market town of Újhely, the venerable István Raczyczenus, provost of the Church of the aforementioned Újhely, 55 years old, as second witness, was interrogated under the purity of his conscience and testified in a similar way to the next. He said that he had heard much about the cruelty of the aforementioned Ms. Erzsébet Báthory from all sides and that many said that this Lady Widow Nádasdy had killed or allowed to be killed approximately 200 virgins and women at her Court or *Gynaecaeum*.

The third witness was the honorable György Predmerczky, 45 years old, subject of Lord Dániel Pongrácz, a resident of the market town of Újhely, sworn and interrogated; he said he knew nothing more, except that this year after the wedding ceremony of the daughter of said Mrs. Erzsébet Báthory and her son-in-law György Homonnay, the judges and jurors of the market towns of Csejthe and Újhely and the Russo property met in order to hold Judgment Day. From Csejthe, three jurors took part, one of whom called was Mattheus Foglar. These three jurors reported to the court that during the wedding celebration of Lady Widow Nádasdy, two virgins were so severely tormented and tortured that they died. Then Lady Widow Nádasdy caused the dead to be brought to the market town of Kostolány, as the same witness had heard before, to be buried among other virgins, also killed by this same woman, the Widow Nádasdy.

The fourth witness was the honorable Georgius Casparowych, subject of the illustrious Franciscus Magochy, residing in the borough of Újhely, about 70 years old, sworn and interrogated;

he said that the cruelties of which the Lady Widow Nádasdy was accused had been rumors that were in general circulation for a long time; however, whether these were true, he does not know; however, regarding the two girls who died during the said wedding ceremony and were buried in Kosztolány, he said the same as the previous witness, Gocrgius Predmerczky.

The fifth witness was the honorable Mátyás Chad, about 45 years old, subject of the illustrious Peter Rattkay, residing in Újhely, sworn and interrogated; he said that recently, during the wedding ceremony of the daughter of the said Mrs. Nádasdy, he was at the court in Csejthe and heard from local officials and servants that two virgins had died due to excessive beatings and cruel tortures from said Mrs. Nádasdy, and that after they died, they were taken in the night to Kosztolány to be buried there. The same witness also said that the pastor of Csejthe named Janós had told him that he had heard from the preacher of Sárvár that said Widow Nádasdy had killed over 100 virgins and women by her outrageous and cruel torturing.

The sixth witness was the honorable Nicolaus Kokhanowsky, about 30 years old, subject of the aforementioned Dániel Pongrácz, residing in the said Újhely, sworn and interrogated; he testified in all ways like György Predmerczky, the third witness.

The seventh witness was the honorable Georgius Blavar (also Blanar), about 50 years old, subject to the aforementioned Dániel Pongrácz, sworn and interrogated; he testified in all ways like the previous witness, Nicolaus Kokhanowsky.

The eighth witness was the honorable Jacobus Hromady, about 40 years old, subject to the aforementioned Franciscus Magochy, sworn and interrogated; he testified in all ways like the previous witness.

APPENDIX

The ninth witness was the honorable Nicolaus Kuzkleba, about 50 years old, subject to the aforementioned Dániel Pongrácz, sworn and interrogated; he said that he had heard for the first time from a certain Potoczky, a former servant of István Illésházy, that the Lady Widow Nádasdy took into her *Gynaecaeum* two noble virgins from Liptov (county), upon whom this Lady Widow inflicted various tortures and outrageous beatings. He also said that his son György Pellio had told him that he had seen how, shortly after the end of winter, when the Lady Widow Nádasdy came to the city of Trencsén, a girl was bound and was very violently beaten and lashed, and then submerged into ice cold water in her clothes, and then not permitted to remove the wet clothes.

The tenth witness, the honorable Petrus Hamerda, clerk in the said market town of Újhely, about 40 years old, subject to the aforementioned Dániel Pongrácz, was sworn and interrogated; he said that he himself was once in Kosztolány and heard from the inhabitants of this same market town of Kosztolány that Lady Widow Nádasdy, who no longer stayed over in Kosztolány, inflicted cruel and terrible blows upon a girl, whipping her with nettles, until she finally died after suffering various other tortures.

The eleventh witness was the noble Nicolaus Mezarych, Tricesimator (a type of tax collector), about 40 years old, sworn and interrogated; he said that when at the house of the nobleman János Zluha, residing in the city of Verbo, it was recounted in Prandio that he had once received letters from the administrator of Csejthe, by which he was charged to go to the pharmacy in Tirnau to pick up a particular drug; this drug was denied to him, however, when the doctor, Martinus, was told which drug it was. Eventually, after János Zluha showed the doctor the letter from the administrator, the pharmacist handed him the medicine; however, Doctor Martinus told him that he should tell his mistress that one in possession of such a drug could kill a hundred people if he wanted to.

The twelfth witness was the noble András Somogy, counterclerk (controller) of the Tricesima (tax office) in Újhely, about 35 years old, sworn and interrogated; he testified in all ways like the previous witness Nicolaus Mezarych and added that, after the death of Count István Báthory, the Widow Nádasdy traveled herself to the property of the former Count and, on the trip, while traveling through the town of Trencsén, this witness had seen two girls, both of whose hands were burned so badly that they could not touch anything with the hands; while climbing into the carriage they could not use their hands, but rather someone had to help them into the carriage, and definitely not the carriage in which the Lady Widow was riding. On the question to the witness of what had been done to the hands of the girls, he said that the Lady Widow Nádasdy had burned their hands.

The thirteenth witness was the nobleman Peter Daynter, about 40 years old, residing in said Újhely, sworn and interrogated; he said that he knew nothing except what he had heard from rumors; for example, that after the wedding celebration of Lord György Homonnay some girls had been buried in Kosztolány without ceremony and funeral bells.

The fourteenth witness was the noble Ladislaus Saary, residing here in Újhely, about 50 years old, sworn and interrogated; he said that once, Stephanus Pesti, servant of the Lord István Dóczy, told him he had heard the mistress, Lady Widow Nádasdy, once gave such a strong beating to a girl that it caused very heavy bleeding. After that, she rubbed the girl with nettles, then tied the outstretched hands of the nude girl to a pole and let cold water pour over her. She was made to stand there until the water froze. Furthermore, the same witness heard from people living in Kosztolány that in winter, around the time of the Sunday Invocation, she left Csejthe and traveled out to the other side of the Danube river where her property was located, staying over here in Kosztolány; a girl had angered her was taken and forced to completely disrobe and was submerged into the frozen stream that flows through the city, after a hole had been hewn into the ice.

The fifteenth witness was the honorable Janós Morawczyk, subject of the above Rattkay, 35 years old, sworn and interrogated; he said, he heard from a certain Mazalak, servant of said Lady Widow Nádasdy, who told him, and then recounted the same again under oath, that Lady Widow Nádasdy had killed a girl and that the witness himself was compelled, at the command of the Lady Widow, in winter, to bring naked girls in the cold, and pour cold water over them; the same witness added that when he went to Liptov to buy salt, he heard from the salt merchants that Lady Widow Nádasdy, during her trip to the property of the late Count István Báthory, had buried two girls here in Lipov.

The sixteenth witness, the honorable Janós Mezar, about 50 years old, subject of the above Rattkay, resident of the said Újhely, was sworn and interrogated; he said he knew nothing about the cruelty of the Lady Nádasdy, except for that which is known by hearsay; she has abused living girls in her *Gynaecaeum* with blows, and that these naked girls were made to roll on the floor scattered with nettles; and he had also heard that after the wedding ceremony of her daughter, two girls died and were buried in Csejthe.

The seventeenth witness, the noble Janós Pesty, about 35 years old, resident of the said market town of Újhely, was sworn and interrogated; he said that he knew nothing.

The eighteenth witness was the honorable Nicolaus Csíszár, about 30 years old, residing in the market town of Újhely, sworn and interrogated; he said he knew nothing but that he had heard rumors that Mrs. Nádasdy is very cruel and that she had some girls killed.

The nineteenth witness was the honorable Janós Benkó, about 50 years old, subject of the aforementioned Peter Rattkay, residing in the market town of Újhely, sworn and interrogated; he said he knew nothing, except from the stories told by many, that each crime, as is generally claimed, really was committed by the Lady Widow Nádasdy.

The twentieth witness was the honorable Janós Kraychowych, about 33 years old, subject of the aforementioned Dániel Pongrácz, residing in Újhely, sworn and interrogated; he said a certain carpenter named Nicolaus Krestyan, who is now established in the market town of Galgocz, had told him that he once worked at the court in the city of Csejthe, owned by the Lady Widow Nádasdy, and there he heard from the staff of the Lady Widow Nádasdy that this Lady Widow had so cruelly whipped and tortured two girls that they were dying; the same witness had also heard that Lady Widow Nádasdy had killed two girls in the market town of Beckov on her way to the more northerly parts of the Kingdom and buried them somewhere along the way without funeral ceremony.

The twenty-first witness was the honorable György Maidanek, about 40 years old, subject of the above Rattkay, residing in Újhely, sworn and interrogated; he said that he knew nothing more except that which he heard: Lady Widow Nádasdy had killed some girls in a cruel way.

The twenty-second witness was the honorable Janós Hlavach, about 30 years old, subject of the above Rattkay, residing in Újhely, sworn and interrogated; he said that he had heard from different people what Lady Widow Nádasdy did to the girls under her care in her *Gynaecaeum*; namely, that she stuck needles under their nails and submerged some naked girls in ice-cold water. He had also heard that she killed some girls.

The twenty-third witness was the honorable Nicolaus Kleko, about 30 years old, subject of Franciscus Magochy, residing in Újhely, sworn and interrogated; he said he knew nothing except what he heard from others; namely, that Lady Widow Nádasdy, on her way into the more northerly parts of the country last year, killed a girl who had fled, and buried her in Kosice; regarding her atrocities, he replied as the previous witnesses.

The twenty-fourth witness was the honorable Pál Kwachkowy, about 28 years old, subject of the aforementioned Dániel Pongrácz, residing in Újhely, sworn and interrogated; he said the same as the third witness, György Predmerczky.

The twenty-fifth witness, the honorable György Hladny, about 40 years old, subject of the above Franciscus Magochy, residing in Újhely, was sworn and interrogated; he said that he knew nothing except that he heard that, at the time of the wedding celebration of Lord György Homonnay, Lady Widow Nádasdy had whipped and tortured two girls so much that they died and that they were finally buried in Kosztolány; by whom he had heard this, his recollection is no longer accurate, because this rumor was generally in circulation.

The twenty-sixth witness was the honorable Stephanus Mokor, about 60 years old, subject of the aforementioned Dániel Pongrácz, residing in Újhely, sworn and interrogated; he said that he heard both in Csejthe as well as in Verbo, and also in Kosztolány from various and numerous people that Lady Widow Nádasdy was very cruel, as is generally said, that she methodically processed living maidens in her *Gynaecaeum*; he had also heard that at the time of the wedding of Mr. György Homonnay, two girls were killed by whippings and torture and were buried without funeral ceremony.

The twenty-seventh witness was the honorable Nicolaus Drebnyczky, about 50 years old, subject of the aforementioned Dániel Pongrácz, residing in Újhely, sworn and interrogated; he said he knew nothing and saw nothing, but he had heard many of the Lady Widow Nádasdy's atrocities perpetrated on the living maidens and girls in her *Gynaecaeum*.

The twenty-eighth witness was the honorable Martinus Komarek, about 30 years old, subject of the aforementioned Dániel Pongrácz, residing in Újhely, sworn and interrogated; he said he knew nothing and heard nothing of which was brought into circulation about the Lady Widow Nádasdy.

The twenty-ninth witness was the honorable György Chaba, about 20 years old, subject of the aforementioned Dániel Pongrácz, residing in Újhely, sworn and interrogated; he said he knew nothing except what he heard about her.

The thirtieth witness was the honorable Georgius Zlaty, about 40 years old, subject of Dániel Pongrácz, residing in Újhely, sworn and interrogated; he said he definitely knew nothing except that he heard from many regarding the atrocities of the Lady Widow Nádasdy which she perpetrated on living virgins and girls in her *Gynaecaeum* virgins.

The thirty-first witness was the honorable György Zamochnyk, about 40 years old, subject of Dániel Pongrácz, residing in Újhely, sworn and interrogated; he said he heard about the cruelty of the Lady Widow Nádasdy, but does not know whether all of this was true. The same witness also said that at the time of the wedding ceremony an official said Lady Widow Nádasdy brought him a boot to be fitted with an iron. As the witness was asked whether it was true if Lady Widow Nádasdy murdered girls, he, the witness, replied that this was perfectly true, and now two were dead. The same official also recounted that, prior to the wedding, when she went from Sárvár to Csejthe, two had been killed and buried along the way. Furthermore, this witness had heard from Adam Pollio, residing in the city of Verbo, that, once when he was working as a craftsman for the Lady Widow, he saw a naked girl with her feet shackled to a table, and that this girl was then never seen again.

The thirty-second witness was the honorable Ladislas Holechny, about 55 years old, subordinate to the aforementioned Franciscus Magochy, sworn and interrogated; he said that he knew nothing except that he had heard from many, that this Lady Widow Nádasdy would perpetrate cruel deeds.

The thirty-third witness was the honorable Michael Haleman, about 40 years old, subject of the aforementioned Peter Rattkay, sworn and interrogated; he recounted the same as György Zamochnyk, the thirtieth witness.

The thirty-fourth witness was the venerable Michael Fabri, pastor in the city of Kosztolány and who, in the purity of his conscience, testified that it was well known that after the wedding ceremony in Csejthe, two girls died; afterwards they were brought to Kosztonány and were buried without funeral ceremonies, and were laid into the grave wearing only the clothes in which they supposedly died. He also heard from others in earlier years that, when coming from Csejthe to Kosztolány, a girl was undressed in winter and submerged naked in a frozen brook after the ice was removed, and that after her death, she was buried here in the cemetery. He had also heard that many were killed by her; recently, an injured girl, bound and with a knife in her foot, had escaped and told many in Kosztolány that she would have died if she didn't flee, and she reported unprecedented butchery.

About which we are faithfully informed, the above notary of record gives these, our letters of testimony of our investigation, under our judicial seal on the general judicial interrogatory.

Given at Bratislava, on the 5th Weekday after the Feast of the Raising of the Cross (Sept. 19) in the year of the Lord 1610.

REPORT OF MÓZES CZIRÁKY
(18 WITNESS STATEMENTS)
OCTOBER 27, 1610

After he had received this assignment, the master, our notary public, reported to us, faithfully fulfilling his duty in the following manner, as set forth over the following days in accordance with the contents of our letter and issued orders for the below-mentioned witnesses under acceptance of the usual fixed oath, thus carrying out the subsequent witness interviews and interrogations.

And as the first, the notable Benedictus Bicsérdy, Castellan (warden) of Castle Sárvár, said under oath: since he had been Castellan of Sárvár, 175 dead girls and women were taken out from the house of the Lady in Sárvár; as to how they died, he could not know because, unless she called for him, he was not permitted to go into the house of the Lady; in such a case, however, where it might be possible to see something that had happened previously, it remained hidden from his eyes and everything had been re-adjusted. Once he saw that the wall was bloody, and he could think of nothing other than that this was the blood of some people who had been tortured. He knows that the girls were so cruelly beaten that if he were walking around the castle, he could hear the slapping noises of a lashing coming from inside the castle through the walls, and, previously, such a beating could continue sometimes for up to six hours. He also said that the mistress kept a kind of "secret house" in the interior

APPENDIX

of the house itself where the tortured people were kept hidden, but he had no access to that because the doors were guarded, and he definitely had no desire to go in there.

Gregor Paisjártó, Vice Castellan of the same Sárvár Castle, said under oath that he is not permitted in the house of the mistress, and cannot testify to anything wrong about the conditions and practices inside there. He knows, however, that one girl was taken out in a coffin in order to bury her, but could not say anything on whether it was an illness or the cause of her death, because he was not allowed to enter the mistress' house without being called, and had also not seen anything.

Benedict Zalay, Paymaster at the same castle, said that his function and his ofice is to be concerned with ensuring supplies, which he performs, that he does not pay attention to such incidents and regarding it cannot say anything.

Gergely Balás said under oath that he had seen girls taken out on the cart, accompanied by the scholars singing, but he does not know how they died.

Ambrus Barbély said under oath that he entered the mistress' house when she called for him but would not be there otherwise, and when he gave a sick girl medicine, he only saw the face and mouth but not the rest of the body, and he does not know whether the girls were beaten or tortured or not, because he has not seen such, and did not notice any signs of it on them.

Michael Zvonaric, preacher at the same castle, said that if he or someone else went into the house of the Lady, everything was cleaned and there was nothing to see, and that she demanded great care to be taken by her people; the outer door was guarded by Drabont, and no one could enter without his knowledge. Inside again, there was a separate "secret house" in which she, as the witness has heard from others, had the girls tortured; he could not see anything; just once, the news went around that three girls had been nailed together in a coffin and that they were thus transported to the Sárvár church for the funeral. When he heard this, accordingly under his office as preacher, he could not remain silent, but had gone into the castle to complain to the mistress; and when he had asked her what was the reason why she buried the three girls in a single coffin -- because before the whole world, she already had a bad reputation because of such deeds, and even those who belonged to the servant status would therefore suffer ignominy, and he also sought the will of God to ask the reason behind such statements and shame by seeking out a better explanation – the Lady replied that it was not the truth because she had not nailed three but only two girls in a coffin, and this had been done so because they saw that a girl was already dead and the other would die not much later, and so they waited to take two out in the same coffin rather than two coffins in quick succession such that even more gossip would arise.

On April 3rd, Adam Zelesthey from the area of Dienesfalva was sworn and interrogated and said that he heard that the daughter of Mrs. István Szoltay and the two daughters of Gábor Sittkey were put to death under cruel torture. He had also heard from one of her coachmen named Peter, when he returned from Ecsed, that she tortured a child there, the daughter of a noble, for so long that she died. She was then buried midway on the same trip. He also knows that when she went to the last coronation (i.e., in Bratislava) came, she so victimized a girl with a knife and burned her with the fire iron, that she was brought back from Bratislavas in a very miserable condition. She could hardly stand on her feet and had to remain at home for days because of the great pain; nonetheless, she was moved to Keresztúr. He also knows that not long ago, a respectable German woman was with her who, from the very beginning, stood well in her favor. Once, however, when he was entering the foyer of the mistress' house, she had fainted from being seriously ill. When he asked who she was, she answered by giving him her name; this was the German

APPENDIX

woman, but she did not have it easy. Also, he had heard from others that she was one of those who had been burned on the abdomen with a hot burning iron, so that she would suffer a terrible death.

Ferenc Török was sworn and interrogated and said that the Lady would not have been so open in front of him as with the others in this matter that he saw and heard. He knows, however, that the first time she traveled to Ecsed after István Báthory's death, two girls had died because of the cruelty of Her Grace; they carried the corpses for three days in the freight car, and finally buried them somewhere between Branyicska and Sirok. And evenso, the daughter of a nobleman was obliged to her court; when she came back home, she killed the girl at Keresztúr through much torment. When they traveled the second time to Füzér, the Lady made them stay over in Sirok, and the relatives of the girl went to her and asked where their relative was, whereupon the Lady said she could not deny that she died of typhoid. On the first trip, when she was staying over at Veranno, she also tortured a girl severely; as the witness had gone hare hunting, upon his return, the officials told him: Mr. Ferenc, the girl that you saw tortured yesterday may not otherwise have died, were she not (killed) in the Turkish manner. A young woman from Bratislava who was no longer a servant at her court, whom she had taken to Varanno, was forced to dress in the manner of a girl. The young woman apologized, "But certainly, my dear high and gracious lady, I cannot be a girl, since I already have a little son, my little Ferenc." In her anger she went and brought her a piece of wood and commanded her to suckle it, even put the stick in diapers and made her carry it around the castle, saying, "Suckle your child, you whore. Don't let it cry." She woke her up in the night, violently forcing the piece of wood to her breast as though it were a child. Later, as he heard from others, she departed the world after much suffering. And not long ago, before the wedding of Homonnay, she hid two dead girls in the inner chamber at Csejthe and then buried them at night. The witness has often

215

seen wounds on the girls from torture and burnings, and he has also heard that they were burned on the abdomen with a fire iron. Moreover, he heard from the servants of the inner house, that she has already killed two hundred. From Sittkey's wife and many others he knows with certainty that they have not died from disease, but that they were taken from this world by torture. Regarding the manner and type of torture, he had seen some of them with their arms tied up such that their hands were blue and blood came from the fingers. Only the Lord God can count up all of her atrocities.

The notable Balthasar Poky (Poby), the other warden of Castle Sárvár, was sworn and interrogated, and said that the number of those from the Lady's court that have been buried are now much more than two hundred, if not already amounting to nearly three hundred. And he had also heard from others that they had died because of many tortures.

István Waghy (Vagy) was sworn in and said that he knew by hearsay that she had killed many with her torturing. In addition, she possessed a cake of gray color, like a pretzel, which she was obsessed with, which contained a wafer (host) in the middle; then she put it before her and looked into it, whereupon she prayed both against the Palatine, as well as against our King, and also against the judge of the county. The words of the prayer in turn went in this manner: "Herein show me (whereupon at this point she said the name against whom she prayed), so that I cannot be seen by you, so that you cannot cause any harm against me." And she muttered more such prayers, sometimes continuing for up to an hour.

Another citizen of the market town of Sárvár, István Chiszar, Deputy Mayor, says that he has not seen anything but has heard from others that she tortured and martyred the girls, and that they themselves had suffered death, but he only heard from others and never saw anything.

APPENDIX

Emericus Zabó, Judge, says the same as the previous witness.

The noble Michael Zabo confessed under oath that he had heard from a German woman that she had forced her to dress up and act like a girl; thereupon she apologized that she was not a girl, because she already had a child; but when she came back from Upper Hungary, (the woman) died from the many tortures.

Georgius Csizmadia *auditu audivit eadem, quam praecedens testis.* (Georgius Csizmadia has heard the same as the previous witness.)

Lucas Vargha (Varga) *nihil scit, neque audivit.* (Lucas Vargha knows nothing and has heard nothing.

Peter Kowach was sworn and said that he had heard that girls from the court had been buried, but he does not know for certain, nor has he heard with certainty, how and if this happened.

Janós Szücs knows nothing and has heard nothing.

Andreas Lakatjáró, teacher, was sworn in and said that he had heard that the girls were tortured through a woman named Anna, who was also called Darvolia, and also the younger sister of Máté Fekete was killed through her and several others.

The noble Ferenc Bornemissze was sworn and interrogated, and said that one day, at the end of his sermon to the congregation, the preacher, István Magyari, asked her to wait a moment because he had something else to say: "It is said about us as preacher that we know other people complain, but that Your Grace is not reproached. Therefore, I cannot conceal it, it must be even moreseo announced that, regarding the girl, Your Grace should not have so acted, because it offends the Lord, and we will be punished if we do not complain to and criticize Your

Grace. And in order to confirm that my speech is true, we need only exhume the body, and you will find that the marks identify the way in which death occurred." Says the mistress: "You will soon see, Preacher István, that I will make you pay for this; my husband and I have relatives who will not tolerate it, that you bring such shame on me and denounce me so; and I will also write to my husband." The Preacher replied: "If Your Grace has relatives, then I also have a relative: the Lord God. But for better proof of what I say, let us dig up the bodies, and then we will see what you have done." And after she got back to the castle, the Lady wrote her husband, because the Lord was in Vienna at the time. He did not see anything further, since he was frequently employed by the Lord, except that once, as he arrived into the house of the Lady, he witnessed the girls with their hands bound, wrapped with rein straps and hanging from the iron lattice at the window by their hair. From a scholar named János, his clerk, he probably had their names and numbers (i.e., how many victims there were) but, since then, he has forgotten them. And this servant is still with him.

The highly literate Paul Beöd, Vice Warden of said Sárvár Castle, was sworn in, interrogated, and said that he had often seen how the scholars carried the girls from the Lady's house with singing and procession to the funeral. But as to how they died, of course he cannot know from his own knowledge, because he did not enter into the inner chambers of the mistress. Also, he had heard from others that it was said the deaths happened due to the cruelty of the mistress, but he himself has never seen anything like this. At another time, the blessed János Mogyoróssy and Gergely Jánossy who, at the time, were senior professors at Sárvár and had criticized the mistress quite heavily, were also with the preacher, István Magyary, and they were talking amongst themselves: "It is feared that the Lord God will punish us, along with you; let us rather go away from here, or you, good Mr. István, since you are a man of the church, and would be guilty, you must warn her, and if she does not stop, then you must announce her deeds down from the pulpit, because it offends the Lord God, and he will not tolerate it." And so he then talked to her after the sermon; the preacher laid the burden upon the poor Lord Count, who was then still alive and had returned very quickly from Vienna, but it was not very long before the preacher and the Lord reconciled.

Super qua quidem attestatione, Pressburg in profesto Beatorum Simonis et Judae apostolorum anno Domini millesimo sexcentesimo decimo (October 27, 1610).

ZRÍNYI'S LETTER TO THURZÓ
DECEMBER 12, 1610

The gracious God should abundantly bless Your Grace's desires. At your command, I sent my main men and servants to Csejthe so that Mrs. Nádasdy can remain there in peace, as we have agreed with you. Also so that no harm will come to the property and that the Royal Treasury cannot assess anything against it, and above all, so that no further injustice will be added to the family. For all this time off, we feel as you do, Your Grace, regarding your advice on Csejthe, in this sense, the problem should resolve. However, I would like to remind you that we have not yet agreed concerning the allocation of property – indeed, it may not even happen quickly, and I would object to that. I do not know in which way Your Grace will decide; in any case, I am convinced that I am to receive an equal share along with the other relatives, and I also want the same part of the property on this side as well as the other side of the Danube. I am aware of Your Grace's benevolence certainly, and in my heart, I hope that you   are   pleased   with   my   advantage. God grant that I can serve Your Grace my entire life; this is also my desire. God should let you live long with all of your property. Monyoròkerék, 12 December anno 1610

Count Nicolaus de Zrínyi (manu propria/written by his own hand)

APPENDIX

PONIKENUSZ'S LETTER TO ÉLIAS LANYÍ
JANUARY 1, 1611

(Lanyí is a famous theologian at Bitca, also the religious super-intendent of the counties of Trencén, Arva and Liptov)

To us is born and sent Emmanuel (Jesus Christ), the Redeemer, favorable to our salvation and my office. I greet your venerable and worthy glory with all my soul.

Long live, long live the radiant Lord, the Lord Viceroy, our protector, to God the best and most desirable. From him, namely, the Palatine, there is truth, and justice shines from the sky, peace and mercy kiss; all this should not only be present in Hungary at this time, but forever! Let us pray. God's will be done. Amen.

The devil has exercised in the sons and daughters his mighty works of unbelief, but he is overcome by one more powerful, our Savior. But what am I talking about, noble man? The pious are never lacking in war and fighting.

And when man struggles, you always sense his devotion. On the first Sunday of Advent, as I read the Scripture in the Vesper, Andreas Priderovith revealed to me - me? No, by the Holy Ghost! - a tool of Satan; during which he declared with a clear voice: "Is this pastor preaching the truth? I do not understand it!" I showed him the New Testament and said: 'See, here is the text'; but when I wanted to say something about the text, A.P. says: "It only annoys me!" and leaves the church amidst numerous insults. On the next day, a nobleman greets me at a wedding without reason: "You whore's son of a pastor, I will see you out of this parish, grabbed by the hair and dragged out like a dog." (May chaste ears be spared), whereupon I left. I referred the matter to the domestic magistrate at the Synod of Tolna, who promised me full assistance.

But, good God, what a change beyond expectation! Signs and miracles have happened: Our Jezebel (I mean, Erzsébet Báthory) receives the punishment according to her crimes. She will be led into the keep (tower) and into eternal prison, walled in, locked up. What more? After I had considered my occupation, I called on one of the brothers so that we could comfort her with prayers and support so that she does not fall into temptation. No sooner are we in the Godless one's presence, she welcomes us and says that her situation is our fault; specifically: "You two priests are the cause of my captivity." The venerable Mr. Zacharias, pastor of Leszetice, apologized in Hungarian. His apology calmed her down, and she says: "If you're not (at fault), then the pastor of Csejthe." And she was excited by her words about me. Mr. Zacharias replied: "Your Grace should not believe this." She said: "I can prove with witnesses that it is so." I reply, "I have preached God's word, and if it caused Your Grace to examine your conscience once, I have nothing to do with it, because I never named you." The prisoner replied:" You, you will die first, then Mr. Megyeri. You two have brought all this trouble upon me and are the cause of my arrest. What," she said," don't you believe me that because of this situation a revolt will soon take place? The Hajduk (Transylvanian farmer soldiers), who have already gathered beyond the Theiss, have written to me yesterday that even the Prince of Transylvania will avenge my wrong." I remained silent as this was spoken; my interpreter did not tell me everything that she spoke in Hungarian. However, when she wished to send off letters and called for a knight, she said nothing, and she was also not questioned about it. I think it was someone from her entourage, whom she called. After she was imprisoned, however, much more came to light. First, however, the following should not be missed: On the 29th of December, 1610, before she was taken, she was given a magic spell, issued by the Mistress from Miava. While this happened, a scribe was summoned so that he could immediately take down the words heard from her mouth. Both women, engaged in the magic arts, would not immediately speak, but as expected, after the last half

APPENDIX

of the night had passed, they considered the stars and watched the clouds, then took the floor and called the writer to write:

Help, oh help, you clouds! Help, clouds, give health, give Erzsébet Báthory health! Send, oh, send forth, you clouds, 90 cats! I command you, Leader of the Cats, that you hear my command and assemble them together, from wherever they may be, whether they are on the other side of the mountain, beyond the water, beyond the sea—that these 90 cats come to you and, from you, should go straight into the heart of King Mátyás and also the heart of the Palatine! In the same way should they chew to pieces the heart of the Red Megyeri and the heart of Mózes Cziráky, so that Erzsébet Báthory shall not suffer any grief. Holy Trinity, so it is done!

Similarly, I have also heard from the report that our Provisional Master has more in written form. You see, Your Grace, how the devil hides his presence, and how and what he seduces. Before the same scribe came and reported the magic words (and he was ordered under penalty of death to faithfully write out everything that was said), she had already been caught and brought into the keep. Another wicked woman named Torkoss, who resides miles beyond Sárvár, gave the following advice: "Find a black cat, kill it with a white stick, keep the blood, and smear it on your enemies. And if not their body, then at least the clothes - and not so stained with blood that your enemy can hurt you more."

You see, Noble Sir, that this wicked heroine is accused of many crimes. Nevertheless, she is still confident in her case and named the priests as the cause of her imprisonment, even as the heathens accused the messengers of faith to be the reason for severe weather and unrest. Yesterday, we spoke of many things with her in the dungeon. Among other things, said the venerable Mr. Zacharias: "Do you believe that Christ was born for you, died and rose for the forgiveness of sins?" She replied: "I also know Peter Faber (Catholic priest, co-found of the Jesuit order, who worked to bring Protestants back to the Church)." Immediately Mr. Zacharias gave her the Holy Bible and asked her to read it in prison, but she answered: "I need it not." Then I said: "I want to know who has caused Your Grace to have so much contempt for me, by claiming that I am the cause of your detention." She replied: "I will not tell you. Now you have angered me and soon both of you will have angered me." I said that I did not wish to anger her, but rather, to clear myself of the accusation of having been the reason for her detention. She replied: "I have been a mistress and mother to all my staff. I have never been treated right, neither in the small nor the large. By either of you." I insist that she think well of me, because I prayed to God for forgiveness of her sins. She replied: "To ask God for the salvation of someone else – especially in a special case—is a good work." So many words were exchanged. But it would be better to speak rather than write them.

But coming to the end, I write that only those three old women as well as the young Ficzkó were taken away and thoroughly interrogated: they confessed that this despicable woman felt delight in such killings, and that they had nurtured a monster. Specifically, we have heard from the virgins who were still alive by then, that they were forced to eat their own flesh, roasted in the fire. Other girls had virgin flesh placed before them, served with mushrooms, chopped into pieces and boiled. Without knowing this, they ate it. O what a Thyestian banquet! (From Thyestes of Greek mythology) What outrageous cruelty! No butcher under heaven was, in my opinion, more cruel. Here I could go on, except for the pain it causes my senses. Soon I will have many enemies, so I commend your venerable jurisdiction immediately and ask that His Highness deign to support me, unworthy as I am, including the Lord Homonnay as well as the mighty son or daughters, and not to refuse the protection of his power. Preferably, the truth is, that for the past ten years or longer now, Erzsébet Báthory has been a witch, or better, that she acted as a murderess. Even my predecessor in Christ, Andreas Barosius, who was 90 years of age, was in the church at night secretly burying virgins, as our fellow citizens probably know. Also, the venerable Mr. István Magyari, a priest in Christ some eight years after the death of Lord Ferenc Nádasdy, frequently accused Erzsébet Báthory publicly (in the church) of sins and murder, witnessed by the existing domestic servants.

The situation will take its course. But I commend my God, because the good always wins. I eagerly greet Mr. Samuel Hammelius and Mr. Balthasar Grelnercius and the servant of your Gracious Highness. Live well and happy in the Lord. Csejthe, 1 January, 1611.

Always willing to serve your venerable Highness. Janós Ponikenusz, priest of the church at Csejthe and citizen.

P.S. Paper cannot capture what I wish to communicate verbally with your Venerable Grace. Whether it is honor or burden, I add this confidential note: After I came from the dungeon on the last day of December and the two brothers, the pastors of Leszetice and Verbo, were sent home, I formed my opinion: Soon I will be feasting in another fire; that when the family had prepared to pray, from there I returned from my study to hot prayers to God to judge. Soon, my wife was following me and telling me about the signs and wonders which happened in this situation. Still, I do not know if signs from the highest vault will guide me. Perhaps I can express myself better by being simple: I know that the voice of malice is not natural. From everything I have experienced, nothing is invented: I say what I, along with my family, have heard, and write:

"This was no ordinary cat voice." I go look, but find nothing. I call my servant, whom I had taken with me, and tell him: "Jano, if you see cats running in the yard, beat them dead! Fear nothing!" But we have found nothing. My servant says: "My Lord, in this chamber, many mice are whistling." I run out, but find noth-

ing there. I cry: "There is nothing in here either!" And as I went down the staircase from the house, just two steps from me, suddenly six cats - on my honor – started biting my right foot, and I cried then: "Go to hell, you devil!" And I beat them with a wooden stick next to my foot. As they all pushed from the lowest level in the crowded courtyard, my servant, who came up from behind, was unable to see or find anything.

You see, Your Highness, Satan's works. But they will be undone.

On Christmas Eve, the House Mistress of Miawa had the Countess bathe in various herbs, and then she desired, as I have heard, to bake bread with this bathwater so that her opponents and enemies should eat it, but in this endeavor, she was betrayed. So Satan fell into his own trap.

Above all else may Your Grace, along with God and myself, expect that they are going to want to harm us; or, should they want to convert, that they are converted, let us pray. The Lord be with us, Amen.

Meanwhile, the aforementioned House Mistress, as I have heard, is already completely shriveled up.

APPENDIX

TRANSCRIPT OF THE WITNESS INTERROGATIONS REGARDING THE CRUEL DEEDS WITH ERZSÉBET BÁTHORY, WIFE OF COUNT FERENC NÁDASDY, IS ACCUSED. 1611.

(Published in 1817; originally written in Hungarian and Latin. In some places, natural context and logical order are missing, and written in the curial (abbreviated) style of the time.)

Confessions given below in order by specific persons against Erzsébet Báthory, married name of Nádasdy.

In the year 1611 on January 2nd in the market town of Bitcá, an assembly was held.

First. Janós Ujváry, otherwise called Ficzkó, was interviewed on the following points by his own admission:

First. How long has he been in the service of that Lady, and how did he come to her court?

Answer: Sixteen years, if not longer, he lived with the Lady, having been brought there to Csejthe by the wife of the teacher, Martin Deak, taken there by force.

Second: Since that time, how many girls and women has she killed?

Answer: He does not know of women, but girls, he knows 37, while he was with her. In addition, when the Lord Palatine traveled to Bratislava, they buried five in a pit and two in the small garden under the eaves. A girl who they found there and she placed before them, and two others were taken to Leszetice in the church, where they buried the same; they brought down the

227

same from the castle, because Mrs. Dorkó (Dorottya Szentes) killed them.

Third: Who were those which they killed, and where?

Answer: He does not know to whom the girls belonged.

Fourth: How were those, the same women and girls, enticed and brought to the court?

Answer: Six times, the declarant went looking for girls with Mrs. Dorkó; they attracted them with the promise that they would either marry a merchant or that they would be brought somewhere as a chambermaid. The now-deceased girl was brought from a Croatian village beyond Rednek; the girl worked for (the Lady) for a month, and then they killed her. Others who looked for girls, along with Mrs. Dorkó were: The (wife of) János Barsony, residing in Taplanfalva next to the Gyöngyös, except for once at Sárvár, they found a Croatian woman living with Mátyás Otvos, across from János Szalay. Also, (the wife of) János Szabo brought girls, even her own, who was also killed, and though she certainly knew it, she still gave more and brought them. The wife of György Szabo gave (the Lady) her own daughter at Csejthe, who also was murdered, but she did not bring anymore. The (wife of) István Szabo, however, brought many there. Mrs. Ilona brought enough. Ms. Katalin never brought any, but only buried those murdered by Dorkó.

Fifth: By what torture and what manner did they kill these poor (unfortunates)?

Answer: The same were tortured as follows: the arms were bound were Viennese cord (woven cotton?); when she lived at Sárvár, Anna Darvolia tied their hands backwards, they were deathly pale, they were beaten until their bodies burst. On the soles of the feet and the flat of the hands, these imprisoned women were given 500 strikes in a row; they learned this torturing first from Darvolia, and beat the same so long, until they died. Dorko cut with the hands of the girls with sheers, which at Csejthe is no different.

Sixth: Who were the instruments of this torture and murder?

Answer: In addition to these three women, is one from Csejthe, Mrs. Ilona, (wife of the one) called the Bald Coachman, who also martyred girls. The woman herself pricked them with needles when they were not finished with their stichery. If they didn't take off their hair covering, if they did not start the fire, if they did not lay the apron straight: they were immediately taken to the torture-chamber by the old women, and tortured to death. The old women burned them with the curling iron and she herself the mouth, the nose, the chin of the girls. She stuck her fingers in the mouth and tore it apart. If they were not finished with their needlework by 10:00 p.m., so were they also brought into the torture chamber. They were taken to be tortured even ten times in a day, like sheep. Sometimes there were four to five girls standing naked there, and in this way they had to sew or knit. The Sittkey girl was killed, because she had stolen a pear; in the same way, she was tortured and murdered in Piastány with an emaciated old woman, and Ilona. The milliner Modli from Vienna was killed at Keresztúr.

Seventh: Where were the dead bodies buried or where were they were taken? Who hid the same corpses and where were they buried?

Answer: These old women hid and buried the girls. He, Confessor, had himself helped bury four here and in Csejthe, in Leszetice two, one in Keresztúr, and also one in Sárvár; the others were buried with singing at the three last-named places. When the old women murdered a girl, they were given gifts by the Lady. She herself even tore the girl's face and scratched it all over. Then, the tortured girl was made to stand in the frost and splashed with water by the old women; also, the Lady herself poured water on her until she froze and died. When she was here at Bitcá, she was ready to depart when one of her girls escaped to Ilava, but was brought back, put up to her neck in water, and doused; she died afterward at Csejthe.

Eighth: The Lady herself also tortured and murdered? And how did she torture the poor (ones) and kill them?

Answer: When she herself did not torture them, she transferred them to the old women who tortured the girls, whom they put in the coal storage for a week without food, and whoever gave them something to eat in secret was immediately punished.

Ninth: In what sort of places at Csejthe, Sárvár, Keresztúr, Beckov and elsewhere, were the poor (ones), tortured and killed?

Answer: At Beckov, the same were tortured in the chamber next to the (wash)-kitchen; at Sárvár, this happened in the interior of the palace, where not everyone had access; at Keresztúr, in the toilet area; at Csejthe, in the kitchen. Even while we were traveling, she tortured the girls in the carriage, and beat them and stuck them in the mouth with needles.

Tenth: Who, of important people, knew or saw the same deeds of the Lady?

Answer: The Courtmaster Benedikt Deseö knew best over the others; however, no one ever heard him say anything about the Lady. Also, the other servants knew about it in general, even the riff-raff. A certain "Obstinate István," now beyond the Danube, who recently left the Lady's service, knows everything better than even the witness; he also talked freely with the Lady, and carried several dead bodies away but, where? The witness does not know.

APPENDIX

Eleventh: For how long have they known or learned of, that the Lady began committing these cruel deeds?

Answer: She had tortured the girls even during the lifetime of the late Lord, but not so often murdered them, as now. The poor Lord had spoken to her about it, but did not forbid it. But when the woman, Anna Darvolia, came to her, she (Anna) killed the girls, and also the Lady became more cruel. Something like a pretzel was kept in a box, with a mirror in the middle, before which she prayed for two hours. - Item: The Mistress of Miava made some sort of water in the morning, and at approximately four clock the lady bathed in a baking trough, then she poured the water in the creek. She wanted to bake two cakes in the trough, of which she wanted to poison both the King, the Lord Palatine and Imre Megyeri. But these gentlemen became aware of it and bested the Lady with the physical; because once they had eaten the first baked item, they all got stomach aches, and so she dared not permit the second backed item to be prepared.

Second: Ilona Jó, widow of István Nagy, testified on the above points in order, as follows:

Regarding No. 1: She lived ten years with the Lady and was the nursemaid for the three girls and also Pál Nádasdy.

2: She does not know the number of victims, but she has killed enough.

3. She does not know of which families they were; but she knows two Sittkey women; then a sister of Gregor Jánosi; also, two noble girls were brought to her from Vécsei, also two from Cheglét: the one she killed, the other is still alive. Also, the Lady Szell had brought a girl, and one was also brought from Poland. The (wife of) Janós Bársony also brought a large, tall girl, the

daughter of a nobleman, from where Janós Poliani lived; she was also killed. In sum she knows fifty or more who were murdered.

4. The (wife of) Janós Szalay, then (brought) a Jewish and a Slovak woman to live at Sárvár. The (wife of) Janós Szalay also brought two or three girls, although she knew that the same would be killed, but the one named Chiglei is still alive. She went away with Janós Bársony and remained there, but the (wife of) Janós Barsony herself brought a noble girl from south of Poland. Stablemaster Dániel Vas brought many around; the Lady Homonnay looked for girls but found none, except for a little one from Vécsey.

5. Also she herself brought girls when the Lady ordered it, but Darvolia in particular murdered the same; she put them in cold water all night, bathed and beat them. The Lady herself heated a key, and then burned the hand of a girl. She also did the same with coins when the same were found with them and did not give them to the Lady. In addition, she herself murdered the Lady Zichi, along with an old woman, at Ecséd. At Sárvár, she killed the Lord's sister (translation mistake: it was a sister of Ilona Jó) - which he saw with his own eyes - in the summer stripped naked, covered with honey, and made to stand the whole day and night in great pain until she fell sick and dropped to the ground. The Lord punished her, lighting oiled papers between the toes, which would make her stand up even if she was half dead. István Szabó brought enough girls from the Verpén area, for gifts, the rest for payment. One (girl) was given a petticoat, the other a little winter skirt. Also, the (wife of) Balthasar Horváth, who lives in a village near the monastery, has brought many girls. Szilvásy, as well as the Court Master, have seen that the Lady herself tortured the girls, stripped naked, and made to stand before them. Dorkó cut the swollen bodies of the girls with a pair of scissors, and once, when the Lady allowed it, the servants here gave the girls mouthclamps. She threw the girls to the ground naked and beat them so violently that one could scoop

handfuls of blood from her bed, and ashes had to be strewn. In a village near Varannó she also killed one of them, and left the Declarant behind in order to bury her. She herself stuck a knife into the girls, and beat them and tortured them in many ways.

6. After Darvolia went blind, the women Dorkó and Kata beat the girls, as well as the Declarant, so long as she was healthy.

7. She does not know where the corpses are now buried, but they were first carried to a wheat shaft. The women Dorkó and Kata took five corpses to Sárvár during the day with singing and also buried them at Keresztúr accompanied by (ministry) students.

8. She herself, the Lady, beat and tortured the girls so much so that she was covered in blood, even having to change her shirt, and the bloody wall had to be washed. When Dorkó beat the girls, the Lady herself stood nearby.

9. Overall, anywhere she went, she looked immediately for a place where they could torture the girls. In Vienna, the monks even threw pots at the window when they heard the frightened cries. Also at Bratislava, Mrs. Dorkó beat the girls.

10. Namely, Balthasar Poki (Poby), IstvánS Vaghi, the Court Master, and all officials and servants knew of the atrocities; also Kozma knew about it.

11. She does not know when they Lady began committing these cruelties, because by the time the Declarant had come to her, she had already begun the same: but Darvolia had instructed her in cruelty and was her confidante. The Declarant knew and saw that she burned the genitals of the naked girls with a burning candle.

The third, Dorottya Széntes, the widow of Benedikt Szócs, confessed on the following, above-asked questions in order:

Regarding No. 1. It has been five years since she has been with the Lady. Mrs. Ilona lured her to the castle with beautiful words that she would be taken on by Lady Homonnay.

2. She knew of approximately 36 young women and sewing girls killed by the Lady.

3. From which families they came and to whom they belonged, she does not know but, rather, said the same as the above, that they came from many places.

4. The (wife of) Janós Szalay, the (wife of) Janós Bársony, and the Widow Keöcsé living in Dömölk. The (wife of) Janós Liptay brought some to Csejthe. She confessed the same way in all matters as the previous two Declarants.

5. Consistently she admits what the two previous Declarants had confessed, with the addition that the Lady also tortured the girls at Chian, and that if the Declarant would not beat the same, then (the Lady) would do it herself with a club, like a chair leg. She stuck the lips of the girls together with needles and also tortured them in this way. When the Lady was sick and could not beat anyone, she ordered the Confessant over to her (the Confessant had dragged the victim onto the bed) and bit a piece out of the face and the shoulder. She pricked the girls through their fingers with pins, and said: "If it hurts the whore, then she can pull it out"; if she did so, the Lady would beat her again and cut off the finger.

6. Soon, they were all helping the Lady with torturing, first one and then the other, along with the Declarant herself, because she forced them to do it.

APPENDIX

7. Within a week and a half, five girls died at Csejthe, which they stacked one on top of the other in the storage room. She then went to Sárvár, and Kata dragged the same, right past the house staff, into the wheat pit. Confessant was with the Lady at Sárvár at the time. The remaining corpses, which they could not hide, were often publicly buried through the Preacher. The servants, along with Kata, carried one to Leszetice and buried it there.

8. The Lady herself beat the girls -- in general, the Confessant testified the same as the previous two.

9. In regard to the places of torture, she said that the Lady tortured wherever she was.

10. She said the same as the others.

11. She does not know when the Lady began her cruelties, because she was only with her for five years.

The fourth: Katalin Beneczky, the widow of Janós Boda, confessed on the previously-asked questions as follows:

1. It has been ten years since she has been with the Lady; the (wife of) Valentin Varga, mother of the current pastor at Sárvár, had appointed her to be a washerwoman at the palace.

2. Since she was a washerwoman, she doesn't know how many were murdered; she believes, however, that during her time with the Lady, it could be fifty that the Lady killed.

3. She does not know from which families or from where they came, because she did not bring any; she knew only the Sittkey women.

4. In all matters, she said the same as the others. The (wife of) Janós Liptay brought a girl, and she adds: that (the wife) of Miklós Kardos also brought two, such that she dared not even go into the village; however, the woman, Dorkó, brought in the most, and she brought in all of the ones that are now dead.

5. Continues identically with the foregoing, with the addition: that after Darvolia became blind and the two previous female Confessants had fully learned how to torture, the same forced this Declarant to perform beatings; indeed, the woman, Ilona, had them carry on with beatings until they were tired. Also, the women forced her into the beatings, constantly yelling at her and screaming: "Hit her! Hit her! Harder!" The girl who has now been found dead was so terribly beaten that, when she was already half-dead, Lady Nádasdy went inside and also started beating her, so that by 11:00 p.m., she had given up the ghost.

6. Mrs. Ilona was the most wicked in her bragging; even though she could do nothing by her own hand, she received permission from the Lady to control Sárvár. The Lady Nádasdy even married two daughters of the same and gave them 14 beautiful gowns. She was above all others an advisor (to the Lady). Mrs. Dorkó beat the girls and also the Declarant when she was forced to do so; she herself was beaten when she refused to do it and once spent the entire month in bed because of the beating suffered. Once, when the Lady Zrínyi came to Csejthe, she sent her entire staff of housegirls, along with Dorkó, up into the castle, where Dorkó kept the girls in strict captivity like criminals, washing and making them bathe in cold water and then forcing them to stay outside, naked, for entire nights. "May the thunder," she said, "slay anyone who gives them something to eat!" She guarded the same so strictly that neither the castle steward nor anyone else could feed them. But when the Lady wanted to travel to Piastány with Mrs. Zrínyi, she sent the Declarant up to see if one of them could go with her; she found all of them having fainted from lack of food, and said to the Lady, when she

returned: "Not a single one is in a position to travel with Your Grace. " The Lady clapped her hands together; she was very angry with Dorkó and said that this should not have happened. The girls were brought out and died in a room of the castle. Because both the Lady and Dorkó beat them, and now that they had gone without food, they had to give up the spirit. A young lady from Dömölk, who was with the Declarant in a coach, died on the journey from Piastány to Csejthe. This girl had already collapsed at Piastány, but was propped up again and beaten by the Lady.

7. Two of the dead girls were buried in Leszetice. The rest was as the previous. Regarding five girls, of whom Dorkó knows are dead because she was with them, she stacked them one on top of the other under the bed and threw oakum (a kind of tar) on them. Nevertheless, they brought food every day as if they were still alive, no matter how long things were different. Then the Lady went to Sárvár and ordered that the Declarant break up the floor and bury them there; she did not do it, however, because she was too weak. The poor corpses remained in this way such that a foulness was given off, and it caused such a stench in the manor that one also felt the same. Now the Declarant did not know what she should do, so she buried all of the bodies, by God's will, in a wheat pit with the aid of Bulia, (and) the servant-women Barbara and Käte, who were together with Dorkó daily and when they died. At night they buried the same. Dorkó herself even had a corpse buried under the eaves, which the dogs dug up, and which was seen by the servant of Lord Zrinyi. This one was then buried in the wheat pit, which was now filled with these five bodies. At Csejthe, where she had been only a short time, eight were killed.

8. Same as the previous.

9. The same, with the addition, the she had tortured her girl, Ilona Harczi, in Vienna.

10. The same as the others.

11. She learned torturing and the other forms of cruelty from Darvolia.

These voluntary confessions were given before us on the day and year above.

Magister Daniel Eördeögh, m.p., Caparus Echy, Castellan at Bicsa, m.p., Kaspar Kardos, Elias Vaniay, sworn Kanzellist, m.p.

The contents of the second writing is as follows:

We, Theodosius Szirmay of Szulio, Royal Presider; Kaspar Ordody of Trencsén, and Janós David of St. Peter; Georgius Lehotzky, Janós Záturetzky, Nikolaus Hrábovszky, Janós Borsitzky, judicial chair; Gábor St. Mariai, also known as Hlinitzky, Trencsén court presider; Michael Prusinszky, Raphael Kvasovszky, Benedikt Kozár, István Mársovszky, Georgius Záluszky, Janós and Michael Hlinitzky, Apollo Milicius, Janós Draskovszky, Nikolaus Mársovszky, István Akay and Janós Medveczky, decree through all here present: that we, on the 7th day of this month in the Year of the Lord 1611, at the request of His Grace, the Lord György Thurzó of Bethlenfalva, Palatine of the Kingdom of Hungary, Judge of Kumans, Count of Árva and everlasting presider of the legal committee, senior confidential advisor to His Royal Majesty and governor of the Kingdom of Hungary, in the distinguished market town referred to as Bitcá, for the investigation and trial of certain subjects who were assembled, there in the name and under the authority of his Lordship, the beneficent Georgius Závodszky, against Janós Ficzkó and against Ilona, Dorottya, and Katalin, women from Sárvár, do hereby issue the following order:

APPENDIX

It is evident that the supreme God, through His Royal Majesty, with the determined wishes and elections of the national occupants and estates of our homeland Hungary, His Grace, through the honor and dignity of the palatinal office, called this summit, so that in the furtherance of the requirements of His office, without regard for the person, to protect the good and innocent, should punish the guilty: so we, the above, who desire to sufficiently accomplish His order have made, among other things, so far a salutary undertaking and fortunately finished this public matter, having heard about and questioned regarding the one who, unheard of from the beginning of the world by the female sex, committed outrageous, inhuman rage and satanic cruelty against Christian blood, the high noble, Lady Erzsébet Báthory, widow of the high-born and high noble, Lord Ferenc Nádasdy who, to this kingdom and fatherland, was otherwise a much-deserved man, which she perpetrated, for many years now in a nefarious, inhuman way against her female servants, other women, and other innocent young souls, wretchedly killing an unbelievable number of many of the same. Given such a huge, unspeakable atrocity, this committee in no way wanted to (as one may care to say) see through the finger (i.e., make a rash decision). They set up a much more rigorous investigation, from which evidence could be shown that the Lady Widow Nádasdy had really committed the crimes of which she was accused, according to the confessions of her own servants. After His Grace heard of it, the committee applied His directive from Bratislava to the legal proceedings, and the designated high nobles and gentlemen, Count Nicholas Zrínyi and György Drugeth of Homonnay, relative of the above Lady Widow and Mr. Imre Magyeri, guardian of the orphaned Pál Nádasdy, and also a not insignificant number of troops, accompanied him to overtake the castle at Csejthe. Right at the entrance to the manor was the truth of what the witnesses had offered. There, a young lady was found, maiden name of Doricza, miserably killed from beatings and torture, and two others, also tortured to death in different ways in the said manor at Csejthe, by the aforementioned Lady Widow Nádasdy. This inhuman, more than tiger-like ferocity and anger moved His Grace, with the well-mannered advice of the above-mentioned, to hand over the blood-thirsty, highly nefarious Widow Nádasdy, caught in fresh atrocity (i.e., red handed) and to condemn this woman to eternal imprisonment in Castle Csejthe. János Ficzkó, however, as well as Ilona, Dorottya, and Katalin, as assistants and murderers of innocent people, knowledgable and participatants in such Godless deeds, henchmen in this terrible execution and butcher shop, are set against their Lord Judge and in need of fair punishment for their horrible and nefarious crimes. Specifically, we the Committee, both because it is the sacred course of justice and fairness, as such entails, as well as to send a warning and example to those who have acted, or plan to act, in a similar way; for these, however, who have perpetrated such monstrous deeds, they shall receive the sharpest punishment and eternal shame, based on the document submitted by us, including the legal writings and copies, both of which have been brought against the Widow Nádasdy, as well as the voluntary confessions given by the defendants. After such was publicly read, the defendants individually interviewed on all points of the confessions and, in turn, heard, all being in agreement and nothing from the same confession omitted or modified, but set down just as they had been taken, regarding all that they had commited, in everything they violently perpetrated and forced by threats by their mistress; has the Committee finally determined from the aforementioned testimonies and confessions and also established from witnesses who appeared before us in the following order.

History.
Transcript of the Witness Interrogatories regarding the cruel deeds which Erzsébet Báthory, wife of Count Ferenc Nádasdy, is accused. 1611. (Decision No. 31)

APPENDIX

The first witness, the honorable György Kubanovich, resident of Csejthe has acknowledged under oath: he was in attendance at Csejthe Castle when he saw the corpse of the last murdered girl, full of blue welts and burn marks and strangled execution-style, carried out in a trough, while the Lady Nádasdy was being taken into custody.

The second witness, Janós Valkó; the third, Martin Jankovich; the fourth, Martin Krsskó; the fifth, Andreas Ukrovich; all residents of Csejthe, have been sworn and testified the same as the first witness.

The sixth, Ladislas Centalovich, residing also in Csejthe, was also been sworn and testified like the others, with the addition: he had seen the girls when they were still alive, and had also seen the welts and burn marks on the shoulders of the same.

The seventh, Tamás Zima of Csejthe testified as the others, and also stated that two female servants of the Lady were buried in the cemetery at Csejthe, while the third was buried at Leszetice, specifically because the preacher at Csejthe challenged the murder.

The eighth, Johann Krappmann, church servant at Csejthe, testified as the previous sworn witnesses, and added that, regarding the girl martyred execution-style, he had spoken with one of the assistants while still alive and received this answer: the Lady herself had perpetrated such, with the aid of a certain woman in a green dress which, however, she did not identify.

The ninth, Andreas Butora of Csejthe, in general testified in all things the same as the rest.

The tenth, Susanna, a young girl, was sworn and testified that the executions, which the Widow Nádasdy perpetrated against her handmaidens, was horrifying, and that her execution henchmen were: Ilona, Dorottya, Anna with the surname Darvolya, and János Ficzkó, who was also sent out to steal girls and bring them back. Kata was milder and gentler, but while alive had thrashed the girls enough, but was so merciful that she brought food in secret to the martyred dead. She remembered also that she had heard that Jacob Szilvásy had found a list of the dead girls in a box of the imprisoned Lady, numbered at six hundred and fifty, which number the Widow Lady Nádasdy signed with her own hand.

The eleventh witness, Sara Baranyai, widow of Peter Mártiny, testified the same as the previous girl, Susanna, with the addition: she knew for certain that in the previous four years (namely, during her entire time of service), while she was with Lady Nádasdy, over eighty girls in the women's quarters were killed, which is confirmed by the testimony of a certain Bichierdi, Warden of Sárvár, which agrees with the number, and that this is completely true, with her claiming conscientiously to repeat several times. Finally, it also strengthens the admissions of the defendants.

Twelfth, Ilona, Widow Kotsis, said under oath: she could comment on so many things over the past three years, namely during her time of service; over 30 girls were killed from multiple torture-executions by Lady Nádasdy and her assistants. The Lady Nádasdy was very knowledgeable in magic and the art of poisoning, of which there are many examples but, in particular that, through magic and poisoning, she wanted to take the lives of His Royal Majesty, and the Lord Palatine, and also Imre Megyeri and others, too, against whom she prayed a certain wishing formula/spell. In all ways, she confirmed the confessions of the defendants.

The last witness, Anna, widow of István Geonczy, recounted generally as the previous witnesses, regarding the butchery perpetrated by the Lady Nádasdy and her female helpers, and also

APPENDIX

confesses: among the number of slain victims, was also her ten-year-old daughter, cruelly tortured to death, whom she wanted to visit but, to her greatest pain, was not permitted in. The rest was the same as the previous.

After all that we have heard and considered, we have set forth the following recommendation.

As apparent from the defendants, and also the strong evidence before the present Tribunal, as well as repeated testimonies, but especially the confession of Dorottya, as the one guiltiest of so many cruelties against the innocent blood of the female sex, through her Lady and mistress clearly perpetrating crimes in which she and Ilona, as well as Janós Ficzkó, the secret helper, were not only knowledgable, but also participating in and hushing up such cruel deeds; because of such an obvious suspect and from the defendants themselves who made clear and apparent declarations on suspiscious matters, including the overall secret and cruel deeds shown, first and before all others this Dorottya, then Ilona, and finally Janós Ficzkó were taken in for interrogation. The interrogations here are unlike anything contained in the indictment, and the interrogated ones themselves previously acknowledged, including said witnesses who also claimed and strengthened, abbreviated and withdrawn, even more so in view of the ways of the often-named Widow Nádasdy through which was perpetrated terrible slaughter and maltreatment; thus, the following judgment is passed upon the defendants, through us, and publicly pronounced:

After the confessions of the defendants, which were given either voluntarily or after torture, as well as the revelations from the witness interrogations regarding the defendants' crimes and, indeed, crimes which exceed all notions of inhumanity and cruelty consisting of multiple murders, butchery, and sophisticated execution-style torture — such atrocities require horrible penalties: thus, first, Ilona and Dorottya, as primary participants in so many misdeeds and as tools of such serious, ongoing atrocities perpetrated against Christian blood, shall have the fingers of both hands torn out by the executioner, and shall then be executed and burned.

Regarding Janós Ficzkó, his age and fewer crimes somewhat lessen his punishment: he shall be beheaded, the corpse placed on the pyre, and burned together with the other two criminals. Regarding the last, Katalin, the statements of both of these two defendants, as well as some witnesses will be excused, and the statement of Janós Ficzkó alone cannot convict her: it seems to us that she should be returned to the dungeon and remain there for some time until perhaps other more clear evidence is given against her. - This is our verdict on the accused, publicly pronounced and soon thereafter to be duly completed.

Given in the aforementioned market town of Bitcá on the 7th of January in the year of the Lord 1611. Theodosius Szirmay, Georgius Lehotzky, Kaspar Ordody, Janós Záturetzky, Nikolaus Hrábovszky, Janós Borsitzky, judicial chair; Gábor Hlinitzky, Assessor; Michael Prusinszky, István Mársovszky, Benedikt Kozár, Nikolaus Mársovszky, István Akay and Janós Medveczky, Janós St. Mariay, István Akay, Janós Draskovszky, Georgius Záluszky, and Michael St. Mariay, also known as Hlinitzky.

APPENDIX

MÁTYÁS' LETTER TO THURZÓ
JANUARY 14, 1611

Mátyás II, by the grace of God King of Hungary, Dalmatia, Croatia, Slavonia, etc., designated King of Bohemia, Archduke of Austria, Duke of Burgundy, Marquis of Moravia, Count of Tyrol.

Venerable and distinguished one, loyal subject sincerely devoted to us. What you tell us about the lofty and well-known Widow Nádasdy in writing, we have not heard without serious displeasure, paralyzing fear and internal shuddering; namely, that she has put behind any reverence for God and man, driven by animal crudity and diabolical influence, killing more than 300 innocent virgins and women, of both noble and lower levels, who served her as maids, and of whom no such action was deserved, without any involvement of the judiciary, in a most monstrous and cruel manner, their bodies mutilated, burned with hot irons, their flesh ripped out, roasted on the fire and this roasted flesh then allowed to be served. We would have certainly preferred that mortals never heard of such an atrocity of so many miserable virgins who perished, whose innocent blood and misery could not be held by the vastness of the heavens; but after this became so widely known and, as a result, the fear that if we do not render punishment the avenging wrath of God will come upon us, we are determined to bring justice and, by this example to cut off other such outrageous acts of sacrilege, that the woman known as Lady Erzsébet Báthory (after the others had already been caught in the act, convicted and arrested by you), 15 days from when this copy was created or the date on which your decision to the court against the notable Peter Zokoli falls, under the law and in accordance with the custom of the Kingdom and, finally, on the basis of the matter there being no grounds in which to delay a verdict for her outrageous sacrilege and deeds, and through our faithful one, the excellent Magister Joannes Kythonich of Kostanicza, the President of the Court Chamber (*director causa-*

rum nostrarum regalium) of the Crown of the Holy Kingdom of Hungary, to our knowledge will do as follows: we instruct you earnestly and we give you the emergency order as soon as you receive this letter, that you immediately summon this woman Erzsébet Báthory on the said date or through dates of letters to your bondsmen and by warrant of the honorable Chapter of the Metropolitan Church of Esztergom to appear at Castle Csejteh with leave to discover and discuss her aforementioned immense and outrageous deeds and that the judgment proceed and be carried out in fulfillment of the law, whether she appears personally or sends someone or not, and warn at the front where you set the date and place that she personally or by legal representation appear before you. Your handling of the matter, however, given the insistence of the parties involved, has to be done in accordance with the law. Anything else shall not proceed. Given in our City of Vienna on the 14th day of the month of January in the year of the Lord, 1611.

Mátyás

P.S. We also wish to inform you, that we benevolently instructed the well-known notaries of record, Mózes Cziráky and András Keresztúr, to stay on – to collect testimonies from all of the Nádasdy places of residence on both sides of the Danube as soon as possible, so that at the time your court date is set our Court Legal President has all of the necessary and sufficient information at its disposal. We also benevolently urge you if you know something suitable regarding what the witnesses were asked and their answers, to share this with the notaries as soon as possible in writing. And the earlier testimony either already designated by the notaries or gathered by the torture of the old women should not be neglected, with a sufficient designation of the names and circumstances of the death of virgins, in which these crimes are involved, and to send authenticated information to the said Legal President.

APPENDIX

ZRÍNYI'S LETTER TO THURZÓ
FEBRUARY 12, 1611

God bless you and all your family along with all your property! I have received and understood your sincere letter along with the copy of the letter from His Royal Majesty to you and the copy of your answer to it. And although with sad heart and suffering I heard the news of the shameful and miserable situation of my wife's mother, Mrs. Nádasdy - in view of her immense, shameful deeds, I must confess that, regarding a penalty, you have chosen the lesser of two evils. The judgment of Your Grace served us for the better, because it has preserved our honor and shielded us from too great a shame. When, in your letters, you made known to us the will of His Royal Majesty, including punishment by horrible, judicial torture, we, her relatives, felt that we must all die of shame and disgrace. But Your Grace, as our benign, truly beloved cousin and Lord, has prevented our shame, having imposed the best kind of punishment in *perpetuo carceri inclusa delineatur* and not public punishment, which would shame all of us, including her children and the memory of her pious, blessed and good, knightly husband. We want to thank Your Grace for the rest of our lives and repay you with all our available strength; we wish to offer you a humble token of our mortal existence. We ask that you, therefore, implore His Majesty to reconsider his decision so that it is in accord with your previous verdict and to be content with your judgment and not to litigate against her in public. This would, as you can imagine, cause much shame and harm to us. By God have we placed our hope in you that you and His Majesty will decide this case in our favor, as we trust you will govern. For a more detailed discussion of this matter, I send my devout servant, Mr. András Milley, to you. I ask you as my benevolent, beloved Lord and brother, to believe his words and allow him to return to me with the desired answer. Lifelong will I repay you. May God grant Your Grace long life.

Csákvár, February 12, 1611

Illustrissimae Dominationis vestrae servitor addictissimus

Nicolaus de Zrínyi (m.p.)

NÁDASDY'S LETTER TO THURZÓ
FEBRUARY 23, 1611

I wish Your Grace and my Lady, as well as your beloved children, all the best from God, as you yourself desire. I took from your letter what His Majesty has ordered you to do to my miserable mother. I have your response to His Majesty, and realize how often you are well disposed toward me and my sisters. God grant that we, I and my sisters and brothers-in-law, can reward your kindness by obedience from a pure heart throughout our entire lives. It is true, as you wrote to His Majesty, that the *Citatio* (court summons) should have been issued sooner and that it is now inappropriate, because Your Grace, as the country's Chief Justice, has already done enough *extentio*. It is no longer necessary to continue, since the present punishment of my poor mother is worse than death, and not necessary to proceed according to the command of His Majesty since a judgment on her life has already been made. Turning now to her property, there is no need to fear, because before her arrest, she turned it all over to the three of us. Nevertheless, we, the relatives and humble subjects of His Majesty, wish to ask that your use of legal force against my mother not impose eternal shame on our family. However, we do not want to act without the knowledge and advice of Your Grace; it is not fitting. I therefore implore you, please, write us your opinion on how my sisters and I should proceed with our intercession to His Majesty so as not to cause Your Grace any grief; indeed, as we learned from your letter, which we have kept secret. I await a favorable response from you, as my beloved father and Lord. God grant you many years in good health. Castle Keresztúr, February 23, 1611.

Count Paulus de Nádasd manu propria.

MÁTYÁS' LETTER TO THURZÓ
FEBRUARY 26, 1611

Venerable and distinguished one, our sincerely devoted, loyal subject. What you shared with us in writing regarding Mrs. Nádasdy's case, namely, those urgent reasons and considerations for which you are not accountable and that which can be brought before the court, we have heard favorably. However, we do not want you to conceal your loyalty—that it has become known to us that nothing precludes nor should prevent said woman from appearing in court, so that we can be assured she receives her sentence. Indeed, clarification on the matter, including the gathering of testimony to show evidence of what happened, makes it possible to show the soundness of judging her before a court known to be competent, which would then enable a proper punishment to be imposed in light of her crimes. We ask firmly, that you handle this Nádasdy complaint no differently and that you proceed according to the way of the law, despite any above-mentioned concerns or other important reasons. What is uppermost in mind and consideration is that, hereafter, we expect your loyal and immediate response. We do not doubt your assurance that the appropriate time and due effort will not be neglected and, in particular, that you will act in the pursuit of the conventions and expectations of the law. We remain under leave of our royal grace and benevolent affection. Given in our City of Vienna, on the 26th Day of February, the year of the Lord 1611.

Mátyás

MÁTYÁS' LETTER TO THURZÓ
MARCH 18, 1611

Respected and magnanimous one, our faithful, sincere and valuable subject. Regarding the necessary and obvious common sense reasons why it is necessary to re-open the case of the noble and dignified Lady Nádasdy, and why we desire to and must bring this case to court, we provided such details in our previous letter dated the 26th of February. In addition, the observance of divine law and its compliance now require us to proceed according to the laws and customs of the Father, to carefully weigh, and to investigate and conclude the matter by judicial review. In order for the meeting of judges to take place with you in Bratislava on the agreed date and time, we have instructed our Hungarian Court Chamber with seriousness and vigor, under application of the royal legal authority, to proceed immediately in this case with the proposed process and, to ensure compliance, in accordance with the laws of the Father. We also do not doubt your devotion, to which we seriously and zealously urge all of this, and to which you are called to do in the interest of the laws and statutes of the Kingdom, such being necessary to fulfill your duty and responsibility to us. We will continue to weigh all other respects in your favor, with our affections sympathetic toward you. Given in our City of Jihlava (Iglau), the 18th Day of March, the year of the Lord 1611.

Mátyás
Valentinus Leepes, Bishop of Nitra
Laurentinus Ferencz

APPENDIX

THURZÓ'S LETTER TO MÁTYÁS MARCH 30, 1611

Many factors in the case of the well-known and noble Lady Nádasdy were reviewed in a rather narrow time period and were neither settled nor brought about for all the various reasons in the world, because neither could the witness statements be gathered in due time, nor were they made available during the prisoners' stay in the dungeon when they were sentenced to death. Moreover, I received Your Majesty's order only yesterday evening after the court had already resumed from the holiday due to the failure of the sitting judge of the kingdom. But that Your Majesty can be satisfied, based on known considerations, with the perpetual prison sentence, may Your Majesty graciously receive the unanimous ruling by the Council of Lords and sitting judge from my letter dated the 23rd of the current month. There is also no risk that complaints about her innocence should reach the ears of Your Benevolent Majesty, since when, in this matter, the judicial investigation of the Council of Lords and sitting judge prompted by Your Majesty became necessary as a result of the horror of the atrocities perpetrated which demanded divine punishment, I, as chief judge next to Your Majesty, arranged her imprisonment after careful deliberation with the common consent of her relatives and her sons-in-law. The same Council of Lords and sitting judge confirmed for me today that I have taken the correct approach. The difficulty in this case, when weighing justice, is that it very rarely happens that highly regarded women of our time, as a result of their way of life, find themselves in such a highly alarming situation that the death penalty should be imposed on them, as well as to ask, what benefit would the government (treasury) receive in this case. Your Majesty will receive a full report on everything contained in this message upon the return of the sublime and dignified (*Magnificus ac generosus*) noble directors and their associated Council of Lords of the Court Chamber of Pressburg (Bratislava). Nevertheless, I leave everything to the gracious decision of Your Majesty; to decide what is incumbent on the Treasury of your Majesty and the *director causarum regalium* (royal administrator of the goods); in accordance with the law in this matter, I will act as judge and justiciary and not deviate from my duty.

Bratislava, 30 March 1611

Count György Thurzó

HUNGARIAN COURT CHAMBER'S LETTER TO MÁTYÁS MARCH 31, 1611

Sacred Royal Majesty, our gracious Lord!

As loyal servants who humbly receive the grace of Your Holy Royal Majesty, we subjects take note of the benevolent command of our Sacred Royal Majesty issued on the 19th of this month, regarding the accused Lady Nádasdy. As to which causes and by which means this matter can and must proceed and be encouraged through the royal officials of your Majesty, the both of us diligently, faithfully and sensibly discussed and considered the matter in careful negotiations with the Assembly of the Chamber of Your Royal Majesty and, as before, simultaneously with the designated Council of Lords of your Majesty, and also with the master notaries. But because of the occurrence of very many difficulties involving the jurisdiction and legal traditions of the Kingdom, we note that this process has not been treated with appropriate or sufficient care by said officials of Your Majesty for a number of reasons, but most especially because of the following: Because when the original, commissioned master notaries of record began taking witness testimonies, public knowledge regarding the case became known; however, they had not yet concluded the matter, thus rendering the state action ineffective. In the situation in which one has committed murder, such as in the case of persons of low birth accusing the noble of commiting a crime, which ordinarily would result in the death penalty at the court of your Majesty, it is a matter for the parties to settle amongst themselves and not for the State to decide, since it is feared that the relatives of the deceased would not feel as though they were bound to the judicial decision; thus, it is easier for them to agree with one another than would be possible with the State. And, although in this case, the state would be allowed to impose the death penalty against her, nevertheless, no major advantage can be hoped for as only the third portion of the property, according to the usual estimate, of the one condemned to death, goes to the Kingdom, which, strictly speaking, is only after deducting the respective portions of the remaining sons and daughters, under the laws of the Kingdom, Part 2, Title 60, of which those two parts of this estimate will be discussed by the illustrious Lord Palatine, as judge of this case in accordance with the ancient customs of the Kingdom and in accordance with Part 2, Title 57. Indeed, it seems that the Treasury of Your Majesty will not even receive this benefit because, a few years ago, the above-mentioned Mrs. Nádasdy transferred all her possessions over to her sons, including her total and complete rights to it, so that the now-incarcerated prisoner has nothing to be found in the way of property. From there it follows that, even if convicted, nothing could be confiscated by the Treasury, nor could the Treasury take possession of anything. Thus, any trouble and expense which would arise would be entirely in vain. Nevertheless, however, as to the remaining matter, it would be what Your Majesty graciously determines as to how to proceed against her; if we may suggest, she is already a prisoner of those in power over her after previous approval, but not confirmation, of the first general council of the Parliament of the Kingdom and publicly presented as, so to speak, caught red-handed, and so the favor of a guilty sentence will be deemed worthy, with the con-

sent of the Parliament, whether it be a mild sentence or the death penalty, in accordance with the aforementioned laws of the Kingdom, Part 2 Title 75. Ultimately, however, we have no suggestion regarding a method by which to bring her to justice, both because of time constraints, and also because the witness interviews against her have not yet been reported or even completed by the master notaries of record. However, since nearly all of the judges of the Kingdom and Assessor of the Royal Court are so inclined and, thus, since we hardly have to do anything to secure a ruling, I recommend a mild verdict on the part of Your Majesty in consideration of the gracious, faithful and useful services of the deceased husband of this woman and her minor sons and daughter, one of whom is married to the illustrious and glorious Lord Count Nicolaus de Zrínyi, the other to Lord György Homonnay, both important nobles and Your Holy Majesty's faithful servants and useful and good citizens of your country, who are against the extreme punishment of putting this woman to death, but rather beseech you to decide her punishment so as to effectively remain at life-long imprisonment, respectively. We ask for the royal instruction of your gracious Majesty in the near future; which in the grace of God always be in full glow and receive a happy reign.
Pressburg, March 31, 1611.

Your Royal Majesty's faithful and devoted servants, directors and associates of the Council of the Hungarian Chamber,
Tomás Vizkelety
Franciscus Leranth

APPENDIX

ANDRÁS OF KERESZTÚR'S REPORT TO MÁTYÁS II (224 WITNESS STAEMENTS) JULY 28, 1611

After this message was issued and delivered to him, said notary of record proceeded to faithfully fulfill his duty on behalf of our Royal Majesty, and in furtherance of this faithful endeavor, on the third day of the week after the Sunday Sexagesima (February 9, 1611) and the days following, initially in the city of Kosztolány, and thereafter in the cities of Csejthe and Beckov, the testimony below was taken under the heavily-weighted penalty of 16 marks, as stated under general decree, only after the following were called and gathered in his presence, in order to discover, from the clergy in the purity of their conscience, while the people in their faith in God and conscious of their loyalty to our Holy Majesty and the Crown of our said Kingdom of Hungary, whether the magnanimous and noble Lady Erzsébet Báthory, widow of the illustrious and famous, late Ferenc Nádasdy, Stable Master, who with disregard of her reverence for God and man, as with animal savagery directed and driven by devilish sense, cruelly killed numerous innocent virgins, nobles as well as lower-class maids alike without the slightest blame upon them, their bodies mutilated and burned with hot iron, pieces of flesh torn from them, roasted in the fire and given to them to eat, in order to discover the truth, to inquire, to learn and to know.

And the first was the venerable Michael Fabri, pastor in the city of Kosztolány, who was questioned in the purity of his conscience; he said that he heard freely and, in general, far and wide of the alleged cruelty of said Mrs. Erzsébet Báthory; but whether all that is said regarding Lady Erzsébet Báthory is true is certainly not known to him. But he does know well that after the wedding celebration of the illustrious György Homonnay, two dead girls were brought from Csejthe to Kosztolány and were buried there without funeral ceremonies; he had also heard from others that, in previous years, while this woman Erzsébet Báthory was on a trip from Csejthe to Kosztolány, a virgin was undressed in winter here in the city of Kosztolány, submerged in the frozen stream that flows through the city after the ice was removed, and finally killed; they had also buried her here in Kosztolány.

The 2nd witness was the honorable Tamás Jaworka, Judge of the City of Kosztolány, about 40 years old, sworn and interrogated; he spoke of the cruelty of the woman Erzsébet Báthory in the same way as the previous witness, the Pastor of Kosztolány; regarding the virgins, however, at the time of György Homonnay's wedding celebration in winter in the stream where they were submerged and died, he added to the pastor's report that after the death of these two girls, the two women were released after the arrest of this woman and handed over to the illustrious Palatine. The judge of Kosztolány said, in addition, that he had heard from some young servants of the said Mrs. Erzsébet Báthory how extremely cruel this woman was with her maids; namely, that she burned some of them on the abdomen with a red-hot iron; others she seated in a large, earthen tank and poured boiling water over them and scalded the skin, in this way causing them to suffer; the same witness had also frequently seen the appearances of the virgins in her retinue disfigured and covered with blue spots from numerous blows.

The 3rd witness was the honorable Michael Kwryo, about 30 years old, sworn and interrogated; he said, regarding the two maidens, that they had died at the time of György Homonnay's wedding celebration, the same as the previous witness, the judge of the city of Kosztolány; he knew nothing of burns but only what is generally recounted on the matter.

The 4th witness was the honorable Michael Palenyk, 45 years old, sworn and interrogated; he said, he knew nothing more re-

APPENDIX

garding the questions, except that, 13 years ago when said Mrs. Erzsébet Báthory stayed in the city of Kosztolány, a girl from amongst her maids died and was buried here, and that the witness himself saw that the body of the dead girl was covered with bruises and black and blue marks.

The 5th witness was the honorable Stephenus Kressko, about 43 years old, sworn and interrogated; he said—-as the 3rd Witness--he had heard very much regarding the cutting out, frying, and eating of human flesh.

The 6th witness was the honorable János Mraz, about 50 years old, sworn and interrogated; he spoke on all things the same as the judge of Kosztolány.

The 7th witness was the honorable Georgius Markowych, about 50 years old, sworn and interrogated; he spoke of the cruelty of the Lady Widow the same as the judge from Kosztolány; he had heard the least regarding the virgins who died at the time of the wedding celebration of György Homonnay; however, he had seen the girl that was forced to bathe in winter in a frozen river, then carried away bound; the next day she was dead.

The 8th witness was the honorable Paulus Jeczko, 33 years old, sworn and interrogated; he said the same as the first witness regarding the two maidens who were buried in Kosztolány.

The 9th witness was the honorable János Palenyk, 30 years old, sworn and interrogated; he said the same as the 1st witness and added that he himself saw that the bodies of girls who died at the time of the wedding celebration of György Homonnay were covered with horrible wounds, their faces crushed, burned and full of blue spots; and he had also heard from many that the Lady Widow inflicted various sufferings upon her maids and tore off their body parts with forceps.

The 10th witness was the honorable Georgius Mladých, about 45 years old, sworn and interrogated; he said the same as the previous witness regarding the cruelty, and also in all things like the first witness; at the time, however, when the two aforementioned virgins had died during the wedding of György Homonnay, the witness was the sexton in Kosztolány, and he himself had dug graves for them in the middle of the night in Kosztolány; they had been buried in the early dawn at Kosztolány, without any funeral ceremony. The witness had himself seen their disfigured appearances, shattered and covered with stains.

The eleventh witness was the honorable Martinus Vurzko, about 40 years old, sworn and interrogated; he said that he knew nothing, that he had not lived long in Kosztolány.

The 12th witness was the noble Michael Horwath, *Officialis* (official) in Kosztolány, 40 years old, sworn and interrogated; he said the same as the judge of the city of Kosztolány and added that he himself heard from the same young servants, mentioned by the judge of the city of Kosztolány, that the Lady Widow sometimes tore off the girls' limbs with glowing tongs; he also added that last year at the same time as the illustrious Palatine came in for the eight days of court, two girls were buried in Leszetice.

The 13th, 14th, 15th, 16th, and 17th witnesses were the honorable Nicolaus Syny, 35 years old, Stephanus Belwczky, 30 years old, Johannes Hronyak, 30 years old, Michael Dubrawczky, 30 years old, Nicolaus Kwochka, 40 years old, Janós Mychalowech, 20 years old, all residents of the said city of Kosztolány, sworn and interrogated; they unanimously said the same as the first witness regarding the cruelty of Lady Erzsébet Báthory.

The 18th Witness was the noble Michael Horwoytth (also Herwoyth), Provisor (administrator) of Castle Csejthe, 38 years old, sworn and interrogated; he said that the rumors of the cruelty of

the Lady Widow Nádasdy were already in circulation far and
wide for several years; the same witness also knew that whenever the Lady Widow stayed in Csejthe, one could hear everyday
the sounds of beatings being heard from her *Gynaecaeum*, including the crying and lamenting of the beaten girls; the fact that
they were beaten more and more often and that they could be
heard crying changed nothing; the same witness had also seen
that almost every day the Lady Widow was briefly bound together with switches, which the girls got to feel; he had also
heard from the noble, Michael Horvath, who lived in the castle
of the city of Csejthe, that last year when the Lady Wife of the
illustrious and famous Count Zrínyi stayed with the Lady
Widow in Csejthe, five virgins were killed and buried here in
Csejthe in a grain cellar; also in this year, two more virgins were
cruelly killed and buried in a similar way in Leszetice; this witness also added that he had heard from the same noble that a
dead girl had been buried in the small garden behind the castle
courtyard; however, as it had not been buried deeply enough, the
dogs dug it up again; this witness also reported that the Lady
Widow Nádasdy went into the dungeon, where a coat was placed
over a dead girl and, before the eyes of even this Lady Widow,
the body was placed into a carriage and, thereafter, the Lady
Widow departed; however, after the Lady Widow's departure,
the witness and many others were able to see these dead bodies
down there more closely, that on their cheeks, between the
shoulder blades and other parts of the body cruel injuries caused
by torture were visible; he had also seen another girl that had
been cruelly tortured, with two rather large wounds between the
shoulder blades and also burned hands, which, when asked how
these wounds and this injury had come about, he answered, by
cruel blows; and then had the Lady Widow, through her old
women, torn the flesh from the body with pliers, the body already swollen and reddened from beatings.

The 19th witness was the honorable Emeritus (retired from service) Ocskay of Ochko, encountered in the city of Kosztolány,

about 32 years old, sworn and interrogated; he said, regarding the items included for questioning, he had seen none of it with his own eyes; he had only heard about everything from others.

The 20th, 21st, 2nd, 23rd, 24th, 25th, 26th, 27th, 28th, 29th, and 30th witnesses were the honorable Paulus Horvath, about 50 years old, Mattheus Morawczik, about 40 years old, Martinus Blanar, about 60 years old, Michael Janychowyk, about 50 years old, János Janychowyk, 33 years old, Gasparus Lyptaak, 36 years old, Martinus Sebanowyk, 40 years old, Mátyás Swecz, 30 years old, Adamus Kowach, about 80 years old, György Lehoczky, 33 years old, Martinus Koryttko, 30 years old, all residing in the city of Kosztolány, sworn and interrogated; the first, Paulus Horwath, said that to his knowledge he could not confirm, but that he had heard from others, two dead girls have been buried in the city of Kosztolány; but at least he knew that in the last year, a girl from Schar who was a maid of the Lady Widow was buried in Leszetice, whose coffin the witness himself had prepared; he knew also that the boy named Ficzkó came into Leszetice with the dead girl; Mattheus Morawczik said the same as the 9th witness, János Palenyk; Martinus Blanar said the same as Paulus Horwath, the 20th witness, regarding the two virgins buried in Kosztolány, and nothing more; Michael Janychowyck said the same as the previous witness; Gasparus Lyptaak said the same as the previous witness; János Janychowyk said the same as the previous witness; Mattheur Sebanowyk said the same as the previous witness; Matthias Swecz spoke of the two virgins who were buried in Kosztolány at the time of the wedding celebration of György Homonnay, like Paulus Horvath, the 20th Witness; Adamus Kowach said the same as the previous witness; Georgius Lehoczky said the same as the previous witness, adding that he heard from the wife of Stephenus Literatus, Mrs. Barbara, a relative, that she herself had seen, in the city of Trencsén, two virgin maids of the Lady Widow Nádasdy with pierced hands; Martinus Koryttko said that he knew nothing other than the fact that whenever one heard of the arrival of the Lady Widow in this

APPENDIX

area, some of the female servants fled the property in fear of her arrival.

The 31st, 32nd, 33rd, 34th, 35th, 36th, 37th, 38th, 39th, und 40th witnesses were Petrus Hrenkaar, about 70 years old, Nicolaus Podhoczky, 40 years old, Stephanus Gasparowych, 65 years old, Janós Seban, 30 years old, Georgius Peczyk, 80 years old, Georgius Porwbzky, 50 years old, Nicolaus Blaho, 28 years old, Martinus Knyebko, 40 years old, Petrus Lybay, 30 years old, Mattheus Janowych, 50 years old, all residents of the city of Kosztolány, sworn and interrogated; the first, Petrus Hrenkaar, said that he knew nothing regarding the questions, except what he had heard from others; regarding the content of the questions, Nicolaus Podhoczky and Stephanus Gasparowych said the same as previous witness; Janós Seban said he knew that at the time of the wedding celebration, two girls were buried in Kosztolány; he also heard from others that Lady Widow Nádasdy tore apart the body of her maid with pliers; Georgius Peczyk, Georgius Porwbzky, Nicolaus Blaho, Martinus Knyebko, Petrus Lybay, Mattheus Janowych said the same as Petrus Hrenkaar, the 40th witness; Nicolaus Blaho said, in addition, that he had heard 300 maidens had been put to death by the Lady Widow Nádasdy.

The 41st, 42nd, 43rd, 44th, 45th, 46th, 47th, 48th, 49th, and 50th witnesses were the honorable Georgius Pepliczky, 40 years old, Adamus Panychowek, 45 years old, Stephanus Dyenak, 40 years old, Janós Urbanowych, 28 years old, Janós Janychowek, 40 years old, Michael Pepliczky, 28 years old, Adamus Janychowych, 32 years old, Janós Potoczky, 25 years old, Janós Rekra, 30 years old, Martinus Zaryeczky, 20 years old, all residents of the city of Kosztolány, sworn and interrogated; they spoke unanimously that they could not confirm the questions from their own knowledge but that they had heard much about the Lady Widow's cruelty; Michael Pepliczky also said that this autumn, after the Lady Widow had come to Csejthe, he saw two ladies from her entourage with bruises and black and blue marks, and their faces scratched as if by nails.

The 51st, 52nd, 53rd, 54th, 55th, 56th, 57th, 58th, 59th, 60th, 61st, 62nd, 63rd, 64th, 65th, and 66th witnesses were the honorable Janós Kadlwecz, 40 years old, Martinus Gonda, 50 years old, Janós Petryk, 50 years old, Janós Gazda, 50 years old, Nicolaus Zmatana, 30 years old, Mattheus Stephanozowych, 30 years old, Martinus Polyak, about 40 years old, Janós Hawran, 40 years old, Janós Kubychokowych, 30 years old, Janós Morawchyk, 25 years old, Martinus Hornyak, 55 years old, Jonas Zlatynsky, 28 years old, Felix Kowach, 55 years old, Janós Sebanowych, 30 years old, Georgius Horenyczky, 60 years old, Georgius Habdak, 33 years old, all residents of the city of Kosztolány, sworn and interrogated; The first, Janós Kadlwecz, said that recently and not so long ago that he was in the city of Bitcá, having come from the city of Zolna; there in Bitca, he had heard that the boy Ficzko, servant of the aforementioned Lady Widow Nádasdy, had been interrogated and had confessed to killing 130 virgins in this Lady Widow's *Gynaecaeum*; however, the old women of this Lady Widow, who were burned in Bicsa, admitted to having killed 50 and 70, respectively; he had also heard that the Mistress of Miava, after they interrogated her under torture, had confessed that she sent many girls with cheese and cheese products from the estate to Csejthe, all of whom came to the court of the Lady Widow and were killed there. Martinus Gonda said that, after the Lady Widow came to Kosztolány, he himself often saw virgins with swollen faces and hands covered with blue patches; regarding the girl who had been plunged into the stream in the winter, he said the same as the judge of Kosztonány; the second witness from this group, Janós Petryk, said that he knew nothing more except what he had heard about her, that two dead virgins had been buried during the wedding celebrations of György Homonnay in Koszolány; Janós Gazda said the same as the previous witness; Nicolaus Zmatana said, overall, he knew nothing; Mattheus Stephanozowych said the same as Janós Pettryk; Martinus Hornyak said he knew by hearsay the same as Martinus Gonda, the 52nd witness; Jonas Zlatynsky said the same as Janós Pettryk, the 53rd witness; Felix Kowach said he knew nothing; Janós Seban said the same as Janós Pettryk; Georgius Horenyczky said the same as the previous witness; Georgius Habdak said the same as Georgius Markowych, the 7th witness, regarding the girl who was forced to swim in the creek in the winter, and added that he had seen girls who were cruelly shattered and covered in bleeding wounds; this same witness had also personally seen girls who had been kept shackled by the creek and asked why this was happening, and was told, their mistress could neither eat nor drink if she had not previously seen one of the virgins from amongst her maids killed in a bloody way.

The 67th, 68th, 69th, 70th, 71st, and 72nd witnesses were the honorable Adamus Mojzes, 50 years old, Kosztolány property owner, Janós Werwrowech, 52 years old, Janós Steffanczowech, 30 years old, Janós Stywgel, 40 years old, Martinus Kyswkha, 40 years old, Janós Nedoraz, 36 years old, all residents of the city of Kosztolány, sworn and interrogated; the first, Adamus Mojzes, said the same as Michael Horwath, *Officialis*, the 12th witness, regarding the maidens buried here in Kosztolány; regarding the rest, he said the same as Michael Herwoyth, Provisor, the 18th witness; Janós Werwrowech (also Wendrowych) said the same as Janós Pettryk, the 53rd witness, regarding the two dead maidens buried in Kosztolány; Janós Steffanczowech (also Stephanowych) said the same as the previous witness; Janós Stywgel said that he knew that two dead maidens were buried in Kosztolány at the time of György Homonnay's wedding celebration because he himself was one of the gravediggers; Martinus Kyswkha said that he knew nothing; Janós Nedoraz said that he heard that the boy Ficzkó confessed under torture that he sealed the lips of girls together with large-headed nails so that they could not scream; eventually, their flesh was cut out, whereupon the Lady Widow Naáasdy ground it up and gave it to the servants to eat.

The 73rd witness was the noble Balthasar Zelessy, living in the city of Verbo, about 50 years old, sworn and interrogated; he said, regarding the questions he was asked, that he had seen nothing with his own eyes, rather had only heard from others.

The 74th witness was the noble Chrisophorus Zelessy, 20 years old, sworn and interrogated; he said the same as the previous witness.

The 75th witness was the noble Georgius Rathkay, living here in the city of Verbo, 43 years old, sworn and interrogated; he said, regarding the girls who were forced to bath in the brook in winter, the same as the pastor and the judge of the city of Kosztolány.

The 76th witness was the noble Daniel Rathkay, living here in Verbo, 28 years old, sworn and interrogated; he said that he knew nothing.

The 77th witness was the noblewoman Anna Welykey, former wife of Nicolaus Kardos, and now the wife of Georgius Hodossy, about 45 years old, sworn and interrogated; she said, regarding the questions asked, that she had seen nothing with her own eyes, but, regarding the Lady Widow Nádasdy she knew the following: When she asked this Lady Widow if she would bring her girls and let them be introduced, (the Lady) said: "Ah, how could I trust or introduce you girls, after so many bad and terrible things are told far and wide about you"; then (the Lady) said to this witness: "These whores lie"; this witness added that she herself had often seen tortured virgins with swollen and bluish colored faces; nothing further.

APPENDIX

The 78th witness was the noble Mátyás Sakathyartho, Verbo city official, 28 years old, sworn and interrogated; he said he knew nothing regarding the questions posed, other than, while for the past 7 years he served as cellar master at the court in Csejthe, a maiden named Lady Sittkey died and was brought to the town of Csejthe and buried there.

The 79th witness was the honorable Stephanus Puskas, residing in the town of Verbo, about 45 years old, sworn and interrogated; he said he knew nothing at all regarding the questions posed.

The 80th witness was the honorable Mátyás Gabansky, residing in the same Verbo, about 45 years old, sworn and interrogated; he indicated that he knew nothing.

The 81st witness was the venerable Nicolaus Barosius, pastor in the town of Verbo, sworn in by the purity of his conscience; he said he had heard much regarding the tremendous cruelty of said Lady Widow Nádasdy; regarding the questions posed, he cannot state anything further except, he himself came to the Lady Widow at her court at Csejthe, six days before she was put in prison, together with other pastors because of her terrible deeds, which, as we know, have been committed by her, and to exhort her to pray for her salvation, and later, there he himself saw a virgin at the time of her incarceration, found as if dead, but still alive yet very weak and frail; he also saw other virgins in similar condition; he, in turn, after this Lady Widow had been brought to the prison (dungeon), they urged her to consider how much suffering she accomplished and what terrible deeds she had committed, and counted all of them that are included in the points in question and what they heard from the witnesses. Next, she retorted to the witness and the other pastors with him: "You," she said, "you nefarious and wicked priests are the cause of my captivity, but have you not yet heard of the Hajdukes at the Theiss? I gave my brother Gabor Báthory a message, and you'll soon have realized that you and your children will regret my fate." A little later, however, as the witness and the others present with him called this Lady Widow not to despair, but rather to repentance and to partake of Holy Communion, she said: "How could I do this when all of you are my enemies." As the witness then recounted to her what outrages were already discovered and those of which she had already been convicted and how much and what terribleness were confessed under torture by her old women and the servant Ficzkó, she replied that she would not admit to anything, whether she was tortured by fire or otherwise; and the witness asked her whether she had also considered and still stood by her statement; she replied that she stood firmly by it and nothing else; the witness also said, he asked her why she allowed her old women to do such things; whereupon she replied that she let them do it because even she herself was also afraid of them.

The 82nd witness was the noble Janós Zluha, residing in the town of Verbo, 29 years old, sworn and interrogated; he said the same as the previous witness and added that he would be sent from Csejthe, and from the Official of the town of Verbo, letters would be sent; upon a response, he would be instructed to travel to Tirnau to the local pharmacy to obtain antimony which would be sealed for the return trip; letter in hand, the witness went to Doctor Martinus and showed him the letter with the instructions to obtain this drug; after he had read this, Doctor Martinus asked for what purpose he wished to have this drug, which the witness answered, he knew not how it was to be used; thereupon Doctor Martinus told the witness, because many people can be killed with this drug, it would be delivered once by the pharmacy and then issued to the administrator of Csejthe.

The 83rd witness was the noble Janós Felon, 52 years old, encountered in the town of Csejthe, sworn and interrogated; he said he saw a maiden whose hands were maimed, wounded, and dismembered through excessive beatings and torment, and as if by cutting, and had been rendered useless; he had seen three dead girls who were brought to Leszetice to be buried there; also, he knew and had seen the two virgins who had died at the time of the wedding celebration of György Homonnay, and afterwards had been brought to Leszetice to be buried there; the witness added that a few years ago, he took a virgin from Tirnau with him, who remained with him for a few years and was regarded as a talented embroiderer; as this girl was twelve years old, the Lady Judith Pogan, wife of John Lyptay, tempted this girl to come to her with flatteries and then handed her over to the said Lady Widow Nádasdy; she was then killed, to the knowledge of the witness, in her court or *Gynaecaeum*; he knew also, and has also seen that the Lady Judith Pogan brought over a bourgeois girl from the upper parts of the country who, afterwards, was introduced to the Lady Widow Nádasdy by those old whores who were burned in Bicsa; and the witness had heard that this girl had been killed after about a week in Varanno; this witness also reports that, at the time when he was in the service of the former Ferenc Nádasdy, the son of the former János Trombitás, named Vitus, was also employed by the former Ferenc Nádasdy, and that he had heard, Lady Widow Nádasdy had an adulterous relationship with this Vitus Trombitás, who was later killed while serving as a soldier of the said Ferenc Nádasdy.

The 84th witness was the noble Valentinus Jelon, encountered here in Csejthe, about 90 years old, sworn and interrogated; he said, with my own eyes I have seen nothing and, regarding the specific questions, he also knew nothing except what he had heard from many others.

The 85th witness was the noble Johannes Bula, encountered here in Csejthe, 35 years old, sworn and interrogated; he said that same as the previous witness, Valentinus Jelon.

The 86th witness was the noble Nicolaus Bula, 28 years old, encountered here in Csejthe, sworn and interrogated; he said he knew nothing else regarding the specific questions, except that he had seen a maiden at the doctor in the town of Újhely, who said that the Lady Widow Nádasdy had inflicted cruel torture and torment on her.

The 87th witness was the noble Martinus Waychko (Vychko), residing in Zolnafalva, about 50 years old, sworn and interrogated; he said that, when the Lady Widow Nádasdy was taken to the dungeon, he himself was present at the court in Csejthe and saw how before the eyes of the Lady Widow, a dead girl lying in a box, who had been killed by cruel blows, was put into a cart; he had also seen another girl who had been tormented by similar cruel torture; the witness had himself seen wounds between the shoulders where the flesh had been cut out, and also that the hands were torn apart, especially the right, and that the flesh between the fingers and the muscles on the upper arm and forearm, along with the tendons, were cut such that no hope seemed to exist that the healing and renewal of the former power of this hand could ever be restored. He asked this girl who had cut her flesh; she responded, the woman named Katarina had cut her with pliers, ripping out the black and blue marks and festering flesh; however, the Lady Widow Nádasdy hit and beat me with her hand.

The 88th witness was the noble Gasparus Ztubyczay, 20 years old, sworn and interrogated in the town of Csejthe; regarding the questions posed, he knew only from hearsay; he knew only that one of his sisters named Anna was killed at the court or *Gynaecaeum* of said Lady Widow Nádasdy.

The 89th witness was the noble Martinus Lofaak, 30 years old, sworn and interrogated; he said the same as Valentinus Jelon, the 84th witness.

APPENDIX

The 90th witness was the noble András Pryderowyth, about 30 years old, sworn and interrogated in the town of Csejthe; he said that he himself was in attendance at the court at Csejthe when the Lady Widow Nádasdy was led into the dungeon, and he had seen a dead girl lying in a box who, before the eyes of the Widow Lady Nádasdy, was placed on a cart; he had also heard from those who were standing closer that her body had been cut over and over and that injuries such as traces of shackles could be found around the neck, as confirmed by the doctor regarding the other surviving girls, as well as Martinus Vychko, the 87th Witnesses; he had also seen a woman who, after she was freed from having her feet bound together, recounted that she had been so tied because she had refused to hand over her daughter to the Lady Widow Nádasdy; he had also seen another virgin upon whose body he discovered, after looking closer, wounds so deep from the flesh being cut out that one could easily stick a fist through them.

The 91st witness was the noble Stephanus Pryderowyth, about 28 years old, sworn and interrogated; he said that he knew nothing more except that he had seen a girl being treated by a doctor in Újhely, and said the same as Martinus Vychko, adding that he saw that her right hand was scarred over.

The 92nd witness was the noble Gasparus Arokhathy, 32 years old, sworn and interrogated in the town of Csejthe; he said that he knew nothing more, except that he had seen a girl at the doctor's in Újhely who could not move her right hand.

The 93rd witness was the noble Janós Andachy, Castellan of Castle Csejthe, about 50 years old, sworn and interrogated; he said that he knew two girls died at the time of the wedding celebration of György Homonnay and that they were brought to Újhely and buried there, but he did not know how they died; he also saw a girl, treated by the doctor in Újhely, and he recounted the same as Martinus Vychko, the 87th witness, regarding the mutilation of her hand.

The 94th witness was the noble Michael Horwath, Castellan at the court of Csejthe, about 45 years old, sworn and interrogated; he said that he knew seven girls died at the *Gynaecaeum* of the Lady Widow, and that they were not buried deep enough in the little garden behind the courtyard at Csejthe such that the dogs dug up the bodies. He had also seen the girl taken out at the same time when the Lady Widow was brought to the dungeon, whose face was overall destroyed, appearing blue in color; regarding the girl who was treated in Ujhely, he said the same as Andreas Pryderowyth, the 90th witness, adding that her right hand was severely injured and rendered unusable.

The 95th witness was the noble Stephanus Bobochay, about 40 years old, living in the town of Zolnafalva, sworn and interrogated; he said that he had been present at the court in Csejthe when the Lady Widow Nádasdy was led into the prison, and he had seen a dead girl laid in a box that, before the eyes of the Widow Lady, was taken out on a wagon; after the Lady Widow had been taken away, the witness himself and others there present undertook a detailed examination, and they saw wounds and injuries from blows to the face, thighs, the buttocks and other body parts; the hands were also broken, blue colored and swollen; regarding the other girl treated in Újhely, the witness said the same as Martinus Vychko and added that her hand had been destroyed and rendered completely useless.

The 96th witness was the noble Janós Mlynar, residing in the town of Csejthe, about 30 years old, sworn and interrogated; he said the same as the previous witness, except that, regarding the girl treated in Újhely, he had not seen her.

The 97th witness was the venerable Janós Abrahamides Ponikenos (Ponikenusz), Pastor in Csejthe, about 38 years old, sworn in by the purity of his conscience. He said that he had been in Csejthe for eight years and had heard about the many vices and terrible deeds of the Lady Widow Nádasdy. His predecessor had told him about this woman, that the Lady Widow buried dead girls in her *Gynaecaeum* and, in secret, even several times in the church cemetery in Csejthe; after the witness had assumed the pastorship here in Csejthe, he had forbidden the Lady Widow these clandestine burials, both in Csejthe as well as for the other areas of his parish diocese; but then he had heard that she had buried someone in Leszetice, and he, therefore, scolded the parish priest of Leszetice, who then sent him this reply, that he informed the old women of the Widow Lady that the funeral in Leszetice could not take place since there is a burial place in Csejthe; to which they responded, you must permit the burial, both in Csejthe and in Leszetice alike, because both places are in our possession. Regarding the virgins, particularly the ones found in her Gynaecaeum at the time when the Lady Widow was taken to the dungeon, the witness said the same as Martinus Vychko; regarding the threat of the Hajdukes, the reminder to exercise restraint, remorse, and to take Holy Communion, he said the same as the pastor from Verbo; he had also heard from Martinus Gablyowych, once the servant of the Lady Widow, who told him how once in one of the buildings of Castle Csejthe, the old women undressed some girls and put burning candles around them and since one could observe through the cracks of the door - because the blades/blinds were closed - he saw that the burning candles were placed on the girls' abdomen and that something happened, but what they did, he could not exactly make out.

The 98th witness was the noble Martinus Chanady, living in the town of Beckov, 48 years old, sworn and interrogated; he said that he, along with Janós Belanczky, had visited the aforementioned Lady Widow Nádasdy there in the city of Beckov so that Janós Belanczky could get his sister back, but that this Lady Widow had refused to return her; then Janós Belanczky de-

manded that the Lady Widow at least show him his sister, something also nearly impossible to achieve; after they waited nearly
an hour, they finally got to see her; she was very severely weakened because of the great pain from torture and torment, so
much that she could hardly hold out her hands, bitterly whining
and crying; and soon thereafter she was so terribly tortured that
she died and was buried in Beckov; the same witness also knew
that a daughter of the noble Georgius Tukynzky was killed by
the cruelty of this Lady Widow Nádasdy; he knew also that this
Lady Widow had also killed the daughter of Benedictus Barbel,
the brother of Janós Chapordi, once the castellan at Castle
Verbo, torturing her through a red-hot iron to the abdomen; the
same witness had also heard that this Lady Widow Nádasdy had
torn the flesh from the bodies of the virgins, ground it into
minced meat and allowed it to be set before her servants.

The 99th witness was the noble Nicolaus Mednyansky, notary of
Trencsén county, sworn and interrogated; he had no knowledge
of and could say nothing regarding the questions posed, but he
had heard from everyone what this Lady Widow had done.

The 100th witness was the noble Janós Kenesey, about 42 years
old, sworn and interrogated; regarding the sister of Janós Belanczky, he said the same as Martinus Chadanay; regarding the
other questions posed, he knew of it only through hearsay.

The 101st witness was the honorable Georgius Keery, living in
the town of Beckov, about 63 years old, sworn and interrogated;
he said that he had not seen anything posed in the questions but
that he had heard that the Lady Widow Nádasdy had allowed the
murder of Georgius Tukynzky's daughter and Janós Belanczky's
sister in an unspeakably cruel manner; he had heard that their
parents and relatives frequently tried to investigate their death;
but to the best of witness' knowledge, the Lady Anna Welykey,
former wife of Nicolaus Kardos, had entrusted both of these

girls, as well as the daughter of Benedictus Barbel, to the *Gynacaeum* of the Lady Widow Nádasdy were they were killed.

The 102nd witness was the noble Georgius Zombach, official of the honorable Dániel Pongrácz, about 35 years old, sworn and interrogated in the city of Beckov; he said that he knew nothing except that which he had heard from noble Georgius Tukynzky, that the said Lady Widow Nádasdy had killed his daughter through various tortures and cruel torments and buried her in Beckó; regarding the rest of the questions posed, he knew about them in general from hearsay.

The 103rd witness was the noble Franciscus Symanoffy, Castellan at Castle Beckó, about 35 years old, sworn and interrogated; he said the same as Nicolaus Mednyansky, the 99th witness.

The 104th witness was the noblewoman Soffia Chehy, former wife of the noble Franciscus Kardos, about 50 years old, sworn and interrogated in the city of Beckov; she said the same as the previous witness.

The 105th witness was the noblewoman Anna, wife of the noble Stephanus Hydweghy, living in the city of Beckov, 33 years old, sworn and interrogated; she said the same as the previous witness, and added that she knew of many virgins who had been taken to the Lady Widow Nádasdy but none, however, had returned from there.

The 106th witness was the respectable Lady Dorottya, wife of Georgius Ztankowsky, residing in the city of BeckOV, 18 years old, sworn and interrogated; she said that she knew that Lady Anna Welykey brought the daughter of Benedictus Barbel and sister of Janós Zabo or Chapordy to the *Gynaecaeum* of Lady Widow Nádasdy and that they were killed there but in which way, however, she does not know.

The 107th witness was the respectable Lady Dorottya, wife of György Phylippowych, residing in the market town of Beckov, 19 years old, sworn and interrogated; she said the same as Nicolaus Mednyansky, the 99th witness.

The 108th witness was the respectable Lady Chrystina, widow of Georgius Polyak, 28 years old, residing in the city of Beckov, sworn and interrogated; she said the same as the previous witness.

The 109th witness was the respectable Lady Katalin, wife of Blasius Kochys, about 42 years old, sworn and interrogated; she said the same as the previous witness.

The 110th witness was the venerable Georgius Kromholcius, Pastor in the town of Beckov, 53 years old, sworn by the purity of his conscience; he said the same as Nicolaus Mednyansky, the 99th witness.

The 111th witness was the prudent Tamás Nycrcghjárto, 35 years old, sworn and interrogated in the town of Beckov; he said that he heard from many in general about the Lady Widow Nádasdy; he had nothing else to report from his own knowledge except that the girl he saw was treated in Újhely because the flesh on her right hand between the fingers and arm was torn out and the tendon had been destroyed.

The 112th witness was the honorable Janós Zabo, citizen of the town of Beckov, sworn and interrogated; he said the same as Nicolaus Mednyansky.

The 113th witness was the honorable Georgius Tarnoczky, first judge in the town of Beckov, 66 years old, sworn and interrogated; he said that he had previously worked as a judge for the Lady Widow Nádasdy and had frequently stopped at the court of this woman; when he was in Csejthe or Beckó, he frequently

APPENDIX

heard that the Lady Widow Nádasdy tortured and tormented the virgins amongst her maids in various and horrific ways, such as binding them naked to a ladder and burning them them with a red-hot iron, the kind used to press women's collars, burning them on the abdomen and torturing them thus; regarding the daughter of Benedictus Barbel named Anna, he said the same as Dorottya, wife of Georgius Ztankowzky, the 106th witness.

The 114th witness was the honorable Petrus Zabo, Senator (Council Member) of the town of Beckov, about 55 years old, sworn and interrogated; he said the same as Nicolaus Mednyansky, the 99th witness, and added that when the Lady Widow Nádasdy spent some time in Beckov, he saw a number of virgins with smashed and blue-flecked faces; he had also heard that the wife of Nicolaus Kardos had sent the Lady Widow Nádasdy two girls from the other side of the mountains located in another part of the country, who died at the court or *Gynaecaeum* of this Lady Widow.

The 115th witness was the noble Valentinus Newedy, 55 years old, sworn and interrogated; he said the same as Nicolaus Mednyansky.

The 116th witness was the noble Janós Kun, Provisor of the glorious Franciscus Magochy in Beckov, 50 years old, sworn and interrogated; he said the same as the previous witness; regarding the girl who was treated in Újhely, he said the same as Tamás Nyeregjartho, the 111th witness; also, he had heard from the noble, the former Alexander Kun, Court Master of the said Lady Widow Nádasdy, that this Lady Widow Nádasdy put some virgins from amongst her maids into containers carved from rough stone, which were filled with water, and made them sit there, while others were made to lie naked on burning coals which were brought into the house, so that she could pull out the flesh of the upper- and underarms and between the shoulders of some of them, allowing them to be so cruelly tortured and tormented.

The 117th witness was the noblewoman Katalin, wife of said Janós Kun, about 36 years old, sworn and interrogated; she said the same as her husband, Janós Kun; however, regarding the girl who was treated in Újhely, she said that she had seen the hand of this girl and that the flesh between the fingers as well as the upper- and underarms together with the tendons and also between the shoulders was cut out, and that the right hand of this girl was completely destroyed.

The 118th witness was the noblewoman Anna, wife of Georgius Posgy, about 40 years old, sworn and interrogated; she said the same as Nicolaus Mednyansky.

The 119th witness was the noblewoman Dorottya, widow of the noble Ladislaus Zemenyei, about 56 years old, living in the town of Beckov, sworn and interrogated; she said the same as the 117th witness and added that the girl who was treated in Újhely told her that she was cruelly tortured not only with a red-hot iron but also with burning candles.

The 120th witness was the noblewoman Katalin, wife of the noble Valentinus Newedy, sworn and interrogated; she said the same as Nicolaus Mednyansky.

The 121st witness was the noblewoman Erzsébet, wife of the noble Nicolaus Vachay, 35 years old, sworn and interrogated; she said the same as the previous witness.

The 122nd witness was the noblewoman Soffia, wife of the noble Georgius Kopach, 24 years old, sworn and interrogated; regarding the questions posed, she said the same as Nicolaus Mednyansky and added that she knew that the noble girl, Susanna, daughter of Georgius Tukynzky, was killed in the *Gynaecaeum* of Lady Widow Nádasdy.

APPENDIX

The 123rd witness was the noblewoman Soffia Rakolubzky, wife of the noble Franciscus Symonffy, 26 years old, sworn and interrogated; she said she knew that the daughter of Benedictus Barbel was killed in the *Gynaecaeum* of Lady Widow Nádasdy; regarding the other questions, she knew only from hearsay.

The 124th witness was the noblewoman Anna, wife of the noble Martinus Köszeghy, 32 years old, sworn and interrogated; regarding the girl treated by the doctor in Újhely, she said the same as Lady Katalin, wife of János Kun, the 117th witness; she added that she herself often stopped at the court and *Gynaecaeum* of Lady Widow Nádasdy and saw that the girls had been cruelly tortured and tormented, that all of their hands and broken fingers had been burned such that the fingers could no longer be used, and that they had told her that Lady Widow Nádasdy had allowed them to be burned with a red-hot iron.

The 125th witness was the noblewoman Dorottya Jezernyczky, wife of the noble Franciscus Bardy, 45 years old, sworn and interrogated; she said that she had given up her own daughter named Erzsébet to the *Gynaecaeum* of this Lady Widow Nádasdy in the year 1590 (1610?), where she was killed; in which way she died, she does not know; regarding the remaining questions posed, she knows only from hearsay.

The 126th witness was the noblewoman Eufrosine Lattkoczy, wife of the noble Georgius Bereczk, 45 years old, sworn and interrogated; she said that she often stopped at the *Gynaecaeum* of Lady Widow Nádasdy and had always seen that the young girls living there had bruised and blue-marked faces; she also knew that the sister of János Belanzky and the daughter of Georgius Tukynzky were killed here in the *Gynaecaeum* of the Lady Widow Nádasdy.

The 127th witness was the respectable Georgius Zayecz, about 40 years old, sworn and interrogated; he said the same as Nicolaus Mednyansky.

The 128th witness was the honorable Adamus Zoblahowzky, 50 years old, sworn and interrogated; he said the same as the previous witness and added that three years ago, Lady Widow Nádasdy had resided here in Beckó upon returning from the upper parts of the country; after her departure, he had seen a girl who had been left behind, in the house of Nicolaus Chaktornyory, whose entire body was blue from beatings.

The 129th witness was the honorable Paulus Lyzkowzky, 60 years old, sworn and interrogated; regarding the girl who was treated in Újhely, he said the same as Lady Katalin, wife of János Kun; regarding the other questions posed, he reported from hearsay.

The 130th witness was the honorable János Ztolar, 40 years old, sworn and interrogated; he said the same as the previous witness.

The 131st witness was the honorable Martinus Zamechnyk, 50 years old, sworn and interrogated; he said that he himself had seen the girl treated in Újhely and knew that her right hand was completely mangled; when the witness asked, who did that to her hand, the girl answered that the Lady Widow Nádasdy had done it.

The 132nd witness was the honorable Georgius Gero, 40 years old, residing in the town of Beckov, sworn and interrogated; he said the same as Nicolaus Mednyansky.

The 133nd witness was the honorable Osvaldus Matthwsowych, residing in the town of Beckov, 60 years old, sworn and interrogated; he said the same as the previous witness.

APPENDIX

The 134th witness was the honorable András Golyas, residing here in the town of Beckov, 32 years old, sworn and interrogated; he said the same as the previous witness.

The 135th witness was the honorable Georgius Chada, residing here in the town of Beckov, 40 years old, sworn and interrogated; he said the same as the previous witness.

The 136th witness was the honorable Janós Plank, residing in the town of Beckov, 40 years old, sworn and interrogated; regarding the girl treated in Újhely, he said the same as Janós Kun, the 117th witness; regarding the other questions posed, he reported from hearsay.

The 137th witness was the honorable Michael Galyk, residing in the town of Beckov, 32 years old, sworn and interrogated; he said the same as Nicolaus Mednyansky.

The 138th witness was the honorable Blasius Chyzmazia, Captain in the town of Beckov, 33 years old, sworn and interrogated; he said the same as Nicolaus Mednyansky.

The 139th witness was the noble Janós Baranyai, 40 years old, sworn and interrogated; regarding the daughters of Benedictus Barbel and Georgius Tukynzky, as well as the sister of Janós Belanzky, he said the same as Martinus Chanady; regarding the questions posed, he only knew a little from hearsay.

The 140th witness was the noble Franciscus Bardy, residing in the town of Beckov, 34 years old, sworn and interrogated; he said the same as his wife, Lady Dorottya Jezernyczky.

The 141st witness was the noble Georgius Kopaach, residing in the town of Beckov, 29 years old, sworn and interrogated; he said the same as his Janós Baranyai.

The 142nd witness was the noble Georgius Bereczk, residing in the town of Beckov, 30 years old, sworn and interrogated; he said the same as his Nicolaus Mednyansky.

The 143rd witness was the noble Michael Horwath, residing in the town of Beckov, 50 years old, sworn and interrogated; he said the same as the previous witness.

The 144th, 145th, 146th, 147th, 148th, 149th, 150th, 151st, 152nd, and 153rd witnesses were the honorable Blasius Kochys, 45 years old, Nicolaus Zamochnyk, 40 years old, Janós Sargawych, about 90 years old, Martinus Tekol, 40 years old, Jacobus Buol, 40 years old, Janós Sysska, 40 years old, Martinus Walach, 23 years old, Janós Andrassowych, 23 years old, Adamus Vadomzky, 40 years old, all residing in the town of Beckov, sworn and interrogated; they said the same as Nicolaus Mednyansky.

The 154th, 155th, 156th, 157th, 158th, 159th, 160th, 161st, 162nd, and 163rd witnesses were the honorable Zacharias Halgaff, 50 years old, Martinus Zwolyenzky, 30 years old, Andreas Hojan, 24 years old, Martinus Pusztaczky, 20 years old, Felix Sedyk, 50 years old, Michael Sodykowych, 35 years old, Martinus Walagowych, 65 years old, Nicolaus Buyak, 34 years old, Martinus Megarowych, 24 years old, Michael Warga, 34 years old, all residing in the town of Beckov, sworn and interrogated; they said the same as the previous witnesses and, in particular, like Nicolaus Mednyansky.

The 164th, 165th, 166th, 167th, 168th, 169th, 170th, 171st, 172nd, and 173rd witnesses were the honorable Nicolaus Motychka, 24 years old, Andreas Sedykowych, 23 years old, Andreas Hlawathy, 26 years old, Daniel Jakwbykh, 40 years old, Janós Zamechnyk, 28 years old, Janós Blawar, 20 years old, Nicolaus Petruskowych, 26 years old, Martinus Sedykowych, 26 years old, Janós Ztankowych, 35 years old, Janós Ztankowych, 23 years old,

APPENDIX

sworn and interrogated; they said the same as the previous witness and, in particular, like Nicolaus Mednyansky.

The 174th, 175th, 176th, 177th, 178th, 179th, 180th, 181st, 182nd, and 183rd witnesses were the notable Jacobus Voyko, 35 years old, Adamus Boffaczky, 20 years old, Martinus Kral, 26 years old, Ladislaus Morawchyk, 30 years old, Stephanus Kehalyowych, 28 years old, Paulus Kukharowych, 35 years old, Nicolaus Hlawathy, 65 years old, Mattheus Haycheck, 30 years old, Georgius Kawalecz, 32 years old, Jacobus Golyas, 40 years old, all residing in the town of Beckov; they said the same as the previous witnesses and, in particular, like Nicolaus Mednyansky.

The 184th, 185th, 186th, 187th, 188th, 189th, 190th, 191st, 192nd, and 193rd witnesses were the noteable Martinus Vesowych, 30 years old, János Ptaczek, 25 years old, Nicolaus Troyan, 60 years old, Adamus Malyk, 50 years old, Michael Malyk, 28 years old, Nicolaus Thykhy, 28 years old, János Balasykowych, 35 years old, Georgius Sedyk, 35 years old, János Frastaczky, 23 years old, János Hrodko, 35 years old, all living in the town of Beckov, sworn and interrogated; they said they knew about the content of the questions posed only through hearsay.

The 194th, 195th, 196th, 197th, 198th, 199th, 200th, 201st, 202nd, and 203rd witnesses the noteable Martinus Mlynar, 28 years old, Nicolaus Sedyk, 40 years old, Tamás Györkeos, 31 years old, Michael Twrkowych, 23 years old, János Wawrowych, 25 years old, János Hornyachek, 40 years old, János Myhalyowych, 32 years old, Martinus Swanczar, 35 years old, Vosommanus Mayer, 40 years old, Martinus Gonyo, 35 years old, all residing in the town of Beckov, sworn and interrogated; they all said the same as the immediately-preceding witness.

The 204th, 205th, 206th, 207th, 208th, 209th, 210th, 211th, 212th, and 213th witnesses were the honest women Dorottya Hornyakowych, wife of Nicolaus Vybarowych, 30 years old, Katalin

Hornyakowych, widow of Janós Horniak, 60 years old, Katalin, widow of Janós Zechaar, 33 years old, Katalin, wife of Martinus Cherny, 20 years old, Anna, wife of Janós Frastaczky, 62 years old, Dorottya Semkowa, wife of Martinus Sanko, 70 years old, Susanna, wife of Martinus Zwolyenzky, 32 years old, Katalin Korchochka, widow of Georgius Korchok, 40 years old, Orsolya, wife of Adam Nowottnyk, 44 years old, Susanna Krannarowych, wife of Janós Sankowych, 40 years old, all residing in the town of Beckov, sworn and interrogated; they all said the same as Katalin Hornyakowych as well as the immediately-preceding witness; Katalin Hornyakowych, however, said the same as Lady Katalin, wife of Janós Kun, the 117th witness, regarding the girl who was treated in Újhely.

The 214th, 215th, 216th, 217th, 218th, 219th, 220th, 221st, 222nd, and 223rd witnesses were the honest women Soffia Hlawatha, wife of Nicolaus Hlawatha, 42 years old, Anna Klwkowa, widow of Janós Klwka, 45 years old, Margareta, wife of Martinus Barbel, 40 years old, Margareta Gonyowych, wife of Martinus Gonyowych, about 50 years old, Marta, wife of Felix Sedyk, 38 years old, Katalin, wife of Janós Wokhath, 40 years old, Dorottya, wife of Adamus Voykowych, 50 years old, Anna Hlawatha, wife of Andreas Hlawatha, 40 years old, Katalin, wife of Georgius Horywasakowych, 28 years old, Anna, wife of Adamus Korbel, 40 years old, all living in the town of Beckov, sworn and interrogated; regarding the content of the questions posed, they all said that they knew of it only from hearsay.

The 224th witness was the honorable Paulus Sankowych, living in the town of Beckov, sworn and interrogated; he said that he knew well that the daughter of Benedictus Barbel was killed by the Lady Widow Nádasdy in her *Gynaecaeum*; regarding the other questions posed, he knew only from hearsay.

These witness interrogations and demonstrations testify to the truth, and we declare that we have faithfully undertaken our duty

APPENDIX

as the Notary of Record with these, our letters, under our judicial seal in the service of general justice.

Given in Bratislava on the 3rd weekday after the Feast of the Holy Apostle Jacobus, in the year 1611 (28 July 1611).
Reviewed and completely corrected by me,
Master András of Keresztúr
Royal Notary of Record
By My Own Hand

REPORT OF MÓZES CZIRÁKY
(12 WITNESSES)
DECEMBER 14, 1611

After he was in receipt of this order, the master notary of record reported in faithful and appropriate fulfillment of his obligation in this way, as it appears from the testimony below, in compliance with the Royal Majesty and the Holy Kingdom, having dutifully been made to ensure that in this case those above-mentioned witnesses speak to our Majesty of what they have experienced, heard, and may possibly know regarding the guilty so that all may recognize how everything has been taken down and, thus, the truth and certainty in all ways be fully satisfied.

The first witness, the honorable Mrs. Erzsébet Reta, widow of Janós Siido, residing in Sárvár outside the castle, some 36 years old, was sworn and interrogated, and said that she knew nothing, except that Mrs. Erzsébet Báthory herself personally beat the girl named Kata Berényi, the girl called Szabattkay and the daughter of Mrs. Draskóczy, of which she (the witness) knows with certainty that their noses, lips and fingers were pierced with needles, and she (the Lady) beat and whipped them for so long that they departed from this world. She heated the pliers and likewise the fire iron glowing hot, and burned them on the stomach. As for what the others saw, she (the witness) knows nothing about it, except that from the Lady's court came plenty of very bad news of her many atrocities.

The second witness, the honorable Mrs. Susanne, wife of Janós Eötvös of Csejthe, residing in the above-mentioned city of Sárvár, some 25 years old, was sworn and interrogated. She said: She knows well that the younger daughter of Gábor Sittkey died from the many beatings of Lady Erzsébet Báthory, but she does not remember the first name of the girl because at court she was always called Lady Sittkey.

The third witness, the noblewoman Helena, married first to Janós Zalay, and then to the noble Paul Gerczej, residing in the said town of Sárvár, about 45 years old, was sworn and interrogated, and said: She knows that Kata Fekete died in chains at Keresztúr; she has also seen Erzsébet Báthory torture and beat the girls, and that she scorched their hands with a burning iron when the frills were not done well. She has seen her (the Lady) wash the girls with nettles, and she also saw how she stuck pins into their shoulders and flogged the girls on their breasts; regarding the young girl from Bratislava named Modl, she knows that Mrs. Báthory flogged and held her in chains.

The fourth witness, Ambrosius Borbély, residing in the aforementioned city of Sárvár, about 35 years old, was sworn and interrogated and said: E. Báthory frequently called him to court with paving/plastering requests, but he does not know what for. About the rest, he does not know anything exactly, because he never entered her house.

APPENDIX

The fifth witness, the magnanimous Lady Anna Zelesthey, widow of the honorable Janós Zelesthey from Mihalifalva, residing in the area of the above-named market town, about 54 years old, was sworn and interrogated, and said that her own daughter, Zsuzska, was given at the court of Mrs. E. Báthory, from which she can say with certainty and also what she was told by certain people that, namely, E. Báthory beat, tortured, and tormented Zsuzska with blows for so long that her flesh fell from the bones, which is why she had to suffer death. She has also heard from many that, from the beginning, E. Báthory killed several hundred girls with the same kind of cruelty; she, however, did not see it, because she never went to the court, but has only heard from others.

The sixth witness, the honorable Benedikt Deseö, residing outside of Castle Keresztúr, 50 years old, was interrogated under oath and said: Even though he had worked as E. Bathory's Court Master in the past, when he entered her house he indeed saw some monstrous deeds with his own eyes; some he had only heard about from others, and it would be an impossible thing to count every single evil deed on the Mistress' shameful list, because there was enough to fill an ocean. Among other things, the following shameful deeds were clearly seen by him with his own eyes: that the mistress took a shoemaker's daughter named Ilonka, stripped her naked and, in this way, cruelly tormented her by taking a knife and, beginning with the fingers, shoving the knife into both arms; thereafter, she flogged the girl, and then held a burning candle to her hands until they were burned and singed, torturing her until she put an end to her life. He has also seen with his own eyes that a girl, her name no longer known to him, had her lips pierced on two sides with needles, thus fastening her mouth shut; when she moved her tongue between her lips to let it extend out, the tongue was also perforated with a needle. So the poor girl had to suffer. The witness has seen countless cases in which girls were made to stand naked before Lady Báthory as she beat them, many times beating them on the hands and nails so long that they became swollen and infected, and then she forced them to sew, commanding them, "Sew, you whore!" And if the poor girl with her broken hand could not sew because she was in such a pitiful condition, it led Lady E. Bathory to complain in front of her attendants: "What a useless, spoiled whore she is. She can't even sew!" And then she began to stick the girl with the needle from her arm up to her shoulder, thereafter whipping, flogging and tormenting her. She withheld water from many of them until they became very thirsty. When she eventually and finally (on my honor!) brought them water, each one standing naked before her, even better it was that the hand was held underneath and then used to drink from it. The witness also heard from others that the wide fire iron was heated and the girls' two arms burned to smoke and ash. Yes, we are also told that the smaller, round fire iron was also heated until very hot and (on my honor!), shoved into their vaginas. As to the following, he also knows this with certainty that the noble lady brought in two girls from Regede. Once, on one occasion, while traveling in the direction of Bratislava, Ferenc Zemptey gave Lady E. Báthory two potato *pogácsa* (*Pogatsche* in German; a type of sweet appetizer) to take along. The mistress gave these to the German girl to hold. The girl ate one and could therefore no longer present it. As a result, the mistress heated the other until it was very hot, and then shoved it, nearly flaming, into the girl's mouth. She subjected these two girls to all sorts of different torments until they finally breathed their last. Regarding one young lady named Modl, the lady herself used a knife to cut into the raw hindquarters of a giant piece of meat and gave it to the poor woman to eat. After much suffering, she finally died at Sárvár. When the parliament meeting was held in Bratislava, she tormented a girl so long that she finally died in Cseplez. Last year, on St. Luke's Day in Csejthe, a laundry woman named Ilona buried the corpse of a girl next to the latrine; later, the dogs dug it up, as many saw with their own eyes, dragging around parts of it. Those women knew of her many heinous misdeeds, such as the laundry woman and the others that she knew, and could probably be very accurate if they wanted to tell the truth. Also, particularly those who were tortured and executed at Bitcá; they were able to report many atrocities. Jakob Zylvasy, Mátyás Nagy and Gergely Páztory also know something about it. The Lord God could enumerate as to how many innocent people's death she was to blame. We, the staff, said this witness, warned and asked her, by God's will, not to commit such huge atrocities and to stop, because she certainly would be arrested. She replied that she was not afraid because she had two good advisors in Transdanubia ae well as on this side of the Danube. And also, so she said, a noble could not be arrested without a judicial sub-poena. Finally, we wanted to leave her service, but the Lord Megyeri asked us not to leave until the mistress went to Csejthe. As soon as we went to Csejthe, she would then be arrested.

The seventh witness, the honorable Gergely Páztory, residing in Bathyfalva, 40 years old, was sworn and interrogated, and said: At the time he was the court judge at Sárvár for E. Báthory, be-cause he had to take care of external affairs, he only very rarely entered the mistress' house, and when he went in, he never saw cruelty exercised before him; the girls were only slapped by the mistress when something was not done according to her mood. He heard from others, however, that the girls were terribly beaten, and he also heard that a whole row of them had been buried. But later, when he was no longer the court judge, when the mistress visited Füzér, she also took him with her, and while she waited for Mr. Homonnay in Füzér, a young woman from Bratislava named Modl, a shapely (full-figured) housekeeper, remained with her. The Lady Báthory had forced her to act like a girl and to dress up like a young girl. Modl said, pleading for forgiveness, that she could no longer pretend to be a girl, that she already had a husband and also a child. In her anger, the Lady scolded her very much and even called her a whore, and when she then returned to Csejthe, she tied a pot around her neck and stuck a piece of wood against her womb; she let her carry the wood to Csejthe and hold it like it was a child, and there, where they remained over night, she let the woman expose her breast and lay it on the piece of wood as if it were a child suckling. Finally, he heard from others that this young woman named Modl had her breast cut off by her, but he himself had not seen this. Once, at the time of the last parliament meeting, as they traveled Csejthe, so the witness knows, a girl died on the journey, but he had not seen this death. While they were on the same trip, a servant of the mistress named János Ficzkó beat a servant of the witness in Csejthe, after he made Ficzkó very angry. And as he (the witness) became angered in return and wanted to beat him for it, Ficzkó ran to the lady inside to complain, and the mistress called to him (the witness) and said, "Why have you upset Ficzkó?" and thereupon he answered, "Because he is a bad person who hit my servant; if my servant does something wrong, I can punish him for it. I am rather surprised that Your Grace keeps such a bad man in your court. You should have a chat with him about the things he sees and hears around here. Just now he spoke of things, which, if Your Grace knew, would certainly not be good to publicize." (He had told us that five dead girls would be hidden under the hemp.) The lady said, "Tomorrow I will ask him what he said." The day after the mistress summoned him, but said not a single word and asked him nothing, but rather talked about other things. Likewise during the war, when we had fled to Sárvár, I saw in the Lady's house an unsealed crate, and it was said that was where the dead girls would be shut in. And once Mrs. Ilona, who had been burned, was actually taking the box from the castle, when a nobleman from Zopor named Sebestyén Orbán said to her: "What is really in the box, Ms. Ilona?" Whereupon she said: "Ask not, on my soul, your Honor!" The witness heard that even then just such a dead girl was being taken out in the box. When they were traveling and took overnight accommodations, once he saw that a bag was packed with small chains and locks, and when the loaded bag was taken from the carriage and brought into the house, all was silent, and he asked Mrs. Ilona, "For what do we need these chains and locks?" She said that at night, all the girls were put in chains. The witness does not know any more.

The eighth witness, the honorable Jakob Zylvasy, administrator of the castles Léka and Keresztúr, 37 years old, was sworn and interrogated, and said that regarding the atrocities which he saw or heard about from others, he cannnt remember them all, and that he might need a long time to think about and recall all of Erzsébet Báthory's outrageous deeds, because there were so many of them, like sand on the sea. Nevertheless, he would speak of what came to mind and he certainly knows the following: in 1606, when he was with Erzsébet Báthory in Ecséd, there was an old soldier, accompanied by an innocent girl of thirteen years. He knows neither the name of the old soldier, nor the girl. The girl was in the custody of the old soldier, because he himself was also a relative of the girl. This girl was being brought to be given over to the mistress who, the next thing we saw, was being very loving and very friendly with her, and said even among us, that certainly this little girl might very well win the mistress' favor and work out quite nicely with her. After a few days, however, we saw that the girl was always weak and run down. The old soldier and his relatives pleaded by the will of God to let the girl be dismissed from the court because she was very weak, and even though Her Grace knew about their request and pleasure to serve, she still refused to release the girl. Thus, the old soldier said he would like to see her and asked at what gate she would be brought out. When they then departed from Ecséd, she brought the girl to the witness' carriage, and she sat at his feet. The witness saw the burns and the brand marks on the girl and asked her why she was so despondent and what were those marks on her hands? The girl said that papers had been set between all of her fingers, and they had been burned as such. As they began to travel along the street, said the girl: "My dear sir, by God's will, stop the carriage and give me something to drink, because it is already the fifth day that no one has given me anything to drink." Meanwhile, cherries were picked, and he said to the girl: "I'll fetch cherries, if you eat them." And the girl said: "I'll eat them, dear sir." During the trip he came with the girl so far but then, before Eperjes, in a village in Szerderke, she died. Also had the witness heard from others, but not seen himself, that in the hour of her death when the poor girl died, Erzsébet Báthory had stood on her throat, killing her, and that she was then buried. During the same trip, on the way there, two other girls died, whose bodies were taken on board a long way, past Branyica, and finally buried in Sirok. He has also seen how she (the Lady), when she traveled in great cold, had the girls wipe her running nose with their bare hands, tormenting them with the cold. One of these girls who was tormented thus, was found dead in Csejthe when she was arrested. He saw traces of beatings criss-crossed over the girls, but since he did not serve inside the house, and no servant was allowed entry into the inner chambers, he had never been in there: only when he was called. The daughter of the bootmaker died on Füzér the last time they were there. He heard from others that this girl, during his own lifetime, said right to the face of the mistress, "You beast, you notorious whore, Erzsébet Báthory, you'll go to hell, but I know where I'll be going because I will enter into the kingdom of heaven." The mistress said:"Why do you call me a whore?" "That," said the girl, "is because when you were mistreating and torturing me, you made me come." Regarding the young woman called Modl, says the witness: because she did not want to be like a girl, she made her carry a stick around like a little kid, all the way from Füzér to Csejthe, and then breastfeed it; from another, he has also heard that she had cut out her flesh with a knife and roasted it. He heard that there are two Germans girls he can no longer identify from Regede who died by her, but where and how they died, he knows not. In Csicsva, her body was smashed with a large needle. The other thing seen by the witness, at Keresztúr, was a dead body in the doorway that was secretly wrapped in a rush mat in the early morning dawn. From his housemates he has heard that in the past year the bodies of five dead girls were thrown in a grain pit at Csejthe; indeed, even a derelict recounted how the corpses had been kept for two weeks and were already so rotten that, as the bodies were thrown into the pit, they were falling apart. He has also heard, but did not personally see, that while he was with the Lady at the spa to Pöstyén (Piastány), meanwhile back at Csejthe, the corpse of a dead girl was secretly buried in the flower garden, but because it was not quite buried deeply enough, the dogs came and dug up the head and hands before the eyes of many, and carried them around. He has also seen, when he sometimes entered the Mistress' house, that all the girls stood naked in front of her and were covered with wounds. Regarding the two German girls, he knows that they died at Csejthe; and they already lay dead, as the Lady Homonnay married, at the time of the wedding. They celebrated the wedding and also held the feast, and then the girls were buried in Kosztolány. When she traveled up to Csejthe for the Homonnay wedding, he had seen with his own eyes that the mistress, staying over at Bratislava, stuck a knife into the body of one of the German girls, who were still alive at the time. All her deeds and misdemeanors were told as soon as they happened, that they were burned at Bitcá because they were around in the house day and night.

The ninth witness, the honorable Stephanus Martonfalvy, Warden (castellan) of Castle Leka, 35 years old, was sworn and interrogated, and said: He had not seen anything further, except that she slapped the girls left and right; after that, he is aware of the many atrocities recounted about her, and that she caused the suffering of many girls who died, such that he no longer wished to serve here and thus left her.

The tenth witness, the noble Janós Deseö, Warden (castellan) of Castle Keresztúr, 47 years old, was sworn and interrogated, and said: that he had a niece named Kata Berényi, the daughter of Mihály Berényi, at the court of Erzsébet Báthory. I learned, he said, that the mistress beat my poor niece severely and went to the old woman to ask that they allow me to see my niece, be-

cause I had heard that my Lady was going to travel up to Csejthe; so possibly they would let me speak with her and let me
give her a little money. The old woman said, if I valued my
head, I should not dare to try this without the knowledge of Her
Grace, my mistress. After the mistress had arrived back in Keresztúr, I begged Her Grace that she might allow me to meet with
my niece, because Her Grace was going to take her along to Csejthe and no one knew when I would be able to see her again.
Also I wanted to give her a certain sum of money." The Lady
said: "You definitely cannot speak with her now, but if you want
to see her, you can see her when she climbs into the carriage."
Meanwhile, she went down, as if she wanted to burst. There
were only two horses fixed, and the mistress ascended the carriage because she believed the horses were already fixed, while
there stood my poor niece, dejected, freezing and in tears, and I
also could not bear it without crying, so I said: Merciful Lady,
please do not take my niece with you! I implore you in the Name
of God--not by me alone but on behalf of all my relatives. We
indeed see that she does not know how to serve the will of Your
Grace. She said: "I certainly will not give her back, because she
has already escaped from me three times; all the more will I kill
her." And she cried to the coachman that they should hurry on,
while I implored her, weeping and begging. She indeed took her
away and never brought her back, beating and thrashing her so
much that she died. He has also heard that she tormented the one
with and pushed the knife into the other, and they were severely
tormented, but he himself did not see it because he was the servant of the Lord and did not enter the Lady's house.

The eleventh witness, the nobleman János Zamabory, residing in
said Castle Keresztúr, 40 years old, was sworn and interrogated,
and said that at Keresztúr, he worked part-time as paymaster and
part-time as provost. He knows that they had to bury two girls
and also that sometimes they were wrapped in mats and secretly
taken out in the night. He only heard from the mistress, Erzsébet
Báthory, that he was to make a coffin and bury them. And as far

APPENDIX

as his memory goes, he buried at least twelve of them, if not more, but as to how they died, he does not know, because at the time when she tormented them, he was not permitted to enter the Lady's house.

The twelfth witness the honorable Lady Barbara, wife of the upstanding H. Bixi, residing at Castle Keresztúr, 25 years old, was sworn and interrogated, and said that she was the the attendant of the mistress and had been traveling with her the last four months. She had seen those poor girls who had been banished to Bitcá and, at the behest of Mrs. Erzsébet Báthory, were beaten and thrashed, that she cut their bodies, stabbed the unfortunates with needles, put stinging nettles into the girls' wounds or covered them with nettles, so as to torment them. She did not know their names because, in general, the girls were grabbed from anywhere and brought there. She had also heard that she burned them with a hot fire iron and she also saw the burn wounds on them. János Ficzkó has said that typically the girls were grabbed from everywhere and brought there, and they do not even know where they came from, because they had dedicated girl catchers. The girl, who was found at Csejthe during the arrest of the Lady, was also a girl from Zala, but whereshe originated from and what she witnessed, she does not know. She has heard that of the dead girls, five were thrown in a grain pit.

Regarding these confessions and statements of the aforementioned witnesses made faithfully and in accordance with the truth, we certify the report of our Notary of Record, Magister Mózes Cziráky, to our Royal Majesty and that our confirmation is given and completed.

Given under the Jurisdiction of Pinnie (Hungary), on the Saturday after the Feast of the Blessed Maiden and Martyr Lucia (14 December) in the year of our Lord 1611.

Executed by me, Master Mózes Cziráky, Notary of the Excellent Lord Palatine of the Kingdom of Hungary.

Manu propria (with his own hand).

REPORT OF THE COURT OF ÚJHELY
(1 TESTIMONY)
JANUARY 9, 1612

We, Judge and Jury of the City of Újhely on the Riverway, send our greetings, hereby making known what presently occurred at the meeting of our full Advisory Board. Regarding the questions asked by the honorable Mr. Nicolaus Bornemissza, Tricesimator, and András Somogyi, scribe, to our barber (surgeon) Thomas, who answered our call, and said in our presence and under oath regarding the injured girl under the Widow Nádasdy, we herewith submit this honestly as well as reliably and not unwillingly, what was recorded in our presence, under the lesser seal of our city.

Our aforementioned surgeon Thomas said the following: regarding the individual points raised in the letters which were sent to us, which he, in turn, was asked: who this girl was, he answered: from the village of Dubmicza, which is in the vicinity of Trencsén. Whose daughter was she; to which he said that she was the daughter of a certain Barbara, Widow of Dubmicza; what her name was; to which he said that she had the name Anna. About her social standing and her origin, he said she was not noble, rather of the lower class, namely, a peasant girl. When asked about her age, he replied that she had reached 18 years. However, as to whether she was healed yet, he replied, one of her hands appeared to be cut into pieces, which was also confirmed by the girl herself. On her back, pieces had been cut out on both sides of her shoulders. On her buttocks, it seemed as well that flesh had been cut out on both sides, such that for the past two months, she was very badly ill at home, so ill that she could not even get out of bed once. Because of this treatment, she received 56 guilders and 15 pounds of wheat, guaranteed by the Újhely measure, from the Administrator of Csejthe by command of the illustrious Lord Palatine. After her recovery she was given, along with her mother, a small farm in Csejthe as free property.

Nothing further. Given at Újhely on the Riverway on the 9th day of January in 1612.

THURZÓ'S CERTIFICATION OF COURT DOCUMENTS: BÁTHORY CASE FEBRUARY 5, 1613

Under the intent of the gracious order and will of the said sacred, imperial and royal Majesty, our noble Lord, having performed sufficiently and submissively, provide all the above interviews, witness interrogations, and confessions of the above-mentioned persons, after they were first sworn to us faithfully, and to report it, recorded and collected in the form of a little book and written authentically, under our Palatinal seal and handwritten signature, to protect all those involved. Given at our Castle Bitcá, the 5th day of the month of February, the year of the Lord 1613, Count György Thurzó.

APPENDIX

ADDENDUM TO BÁTHORY WILL
JULY 31, 1614

We, the Cathedral Capital of Eszertgom, commemorate the following: that we, on the amiable request of the noble lady, Countess Erzsébet Báthory, the widow of the former illustrious and noble gentleman, Count Nádasdy, who, because of her captivity is not personally able to come to us, sent two of our Venerables, namely Messrs. Andreas Kerpelich and Emericus Agiens, our brothers and fellow clerics, who took the following confession that the lady gave to us; this, in turn, made it appropriate for them to serve witness to what this finally reported, after they were returned to us, under oath, as set forth in a general decree:

That in the current year of the Lord, 1614, on the 31st day of July in the castle called Csejthe, having been built in County Nitra, where the aforementioned Lady Countess Erzsébet Báthory, in the personal presence of our brothers voluntarily and on her own initiative stated the following and in this way expressed: that she bequeathed the City of Keresztúr in the County of Abauj to her daughter Katalin Nádasdy, the wife of the illustrious and venerable György Drugeth of Homonnay; and that this bequest had already been transferred and assigned during her captivity but in such a way that, up to this point, merely released it and that they were not yet in their full and permanent possession. Also, she bequeathed nothing more to Lord György Homonnay; rather, after they put her in prison, she made her assignments only to her heirs and passed along nothing further.

Therefore, if she desired, and even if she still wanted to exclude someone from her property, nor could she have so wished in the least; her intention therefore continues to be that the entire property will be divided among them (her heirs). Finally, had she established in documents of the aforementioned Lord György

Homonnay, in the journal of 1610, what property she had assigned, which is why we have kept for ourselves these writings on these dispositions aforementioned by Lady Erzsébet Báthory to the knowledge of our trusted brothers, in writing referred to under the seal of our chapter and entrusted to them. Given on Sunday after the Feast of St. Peter in Chains (*in vinculi*), in 1614.

STANISLAS THURZÓ'S LETTER TO GYÖRGY THURZÓ
AUGUST 25, 1614

Servitiorum meorum paratissimam commendationem. God give Your Grace, your wife, and your beloved children good health and a happy, long life. I received melons from my garden in Sempte and, with this coach, I send you some. I beg you, take it with my great pleasure. With God's blessing should you, your wife and your children eat in good health. If Your Grace knows of any news, I request, as my Lord and benevolent patron, that you please share it with me, as well. With us, there is no news of which I should notify you. The death of Mrs. Nádasdy may already be known to you and how she unexpectedly resigned from this life. In the evening, said she to her bodyguard: "Look, how cold my hands are!" The bodyguard told her: "It's nothing, Mistress. Just go and lie down." She then went to sleep. She took the pillow that was under her head and put it under her feet. As such, she lied down and, in the same night, she died. In the morning, she was found dead. They say, however, she prayed imploringly and praised God with beautiful singing. Regarding her funeral, we still have no information.

APPENDIX

I commend myself and my services, along with my wife, to Your Grace, your wife, and your beloved children. God grant Your Grace a long and healthy life. Pöstyén (Piastány), 25 August, Anno Domini 1615.

Illustrissime Domi(natio)nis vestre servitor et Frater addictis-simus
Count Stanislas Thurzó
By his own hand (manu propria)

Some memorable events, which in this (17th) century have taken place in the dominion of Csejthe (*Chronicle of Castle Csejthe*)

April 25, 1603: Ferenc Nádasdy I assumes possession of Csejthe and died in January 1604.
April 17, 1608: The Hungarians went to Prague to get to the crown.
June 27: The emperor gave Hungary the crown.
July 10: The Hungarians have returned from Prague.
July 29, 1606: The flooding of the brook in Csejthe tore bridge, houses and scarecrows in the field.
January 6, 1610: Mr. George Homonnay has married: he took Kata Nádasdy as his wife.
December 29: Mrs. Erzsébet Báthory was captured during dinner and next day brought into the castle.
January 7, 1611: There were two women and Ficzkó, and then also on 24 January, Mistress of Miava, burned because they were accomplices of Mrs. Báthory, in the torturing of girls.

Oct. 8: The Dominium of Csejthe was divided in half between Pál Nádasdy and Mr. Zrínyi. Mátyás Töttösi was steward/manager of Mr. Zrínyi's estate.

October 18, 1613: Gábor Báthory, Prince of Transylvania, was murdered.

August 18, 1614: Mr. Nádasdy gives Mr. Homonnay one third of the dominion of Csejthe and Beckov.

August 21: Erzsébet Báthory died at Csejthe Castle at two after midnight.

November 25: She was buried in the church of Csejthe.

January 29, 1615: Pál Nádasdy releases Brezova to Mihaly Nagy.

August 13: Mrs. Zrínyi died.

In December, Palatine Thurzó died. On February 19, he was buried.

March 9, 1616: The goods of Csejthe and Beckov were divided between Homonnay and Pál Nádasdy.

August 3, 1620: His Grace Pál Nádasdy was betrothed to his wife, Judith Revay.

December 15, 1621: My mistress, Mrs. Pál Nádasdy, bore a son, György Nádasdy.

January 14, 1623: She has a second son, Ferenc.

APPENDIX

A BRIEF HISTORY OF LITERARY WORKS ON THE COUNTESS

1729: Lászlo Turoczi writes *Ungaria suis cum regibus com pendia data*.

1744: Lászlo Turoczi writes *Báthory Erzsébet*.

1796: Michael Wegener writes *Beiträge zur Philosophischen Anthropologie*.

1839: John Paget publishes an account of his European travels, devoting a chapter to the history of Countess Báthory.

1894: Ferdinand von Strobl Ravelsberg, under the pseudonym of R.A. von Elsberg, writes the essay, *Die Blütgrafin (Erzsébet Báthory): Ein Sitten und Charakterbild*.

1932: Slovak writer Jožo Nižňanský publishes *Cachtická Pani* (Lady of Csejthe), a gothic novel written in a series of episodes.

1962: Valentine Penrose publishes *La Comtesse Sanglante*, a historical novel that celebrates the exploits of the Countess.

1975: French writer Maurice Périsset publishes, *Comtesse de Sang*.

1983: Raymond T. McNally writes, *Dracula was a Woman: In Search of the Blood Countess of Transylvania*.

1996: Andrei Codrescu writes, *The Blood Countess*.

EXCERPT FROM LÁSZLÓ TURÓCZI'S BOOK, *Ungaria*
suis cum regibus compendio data, **THAT RE-INTRODUCED**
THE COUNTESS TO EUROPE:

"(Thurzó, along with...) the sons in-law of the mistress, Niklas Zrínyi and György Drugeth, and their appointed servant, then the guardian of the orphaned Pál Nádasdy - Imre Megyery - , along with numerous soldiers and servants, went to the castle in the village of Csejthe. Immediately upon entering, he (Thurzó) was convinced of what the witnesses confessed. A girl named Doricza was found dead as a result of beatings and torture, as well as another girl who was already dying. Here was the sight of such a horrible and bestial madness and cruelty, of which so deeply shocked him that he declared Mrs. Nádasdy to be a bloodthirsty and blood-sucking godless woman, to have been caught red-handed, and sentenced to perpetual imprisonment in the castle Csejthe, her helpers, arrested."

Portrait of Countess Erzsébet Báthory

Portrait of Countess Erzsébet Báthory

Portrait of Countess Erzsébet Báthory

Portrait of Ferenc Nádasdy

APPENDIX

Portrait of Ferenc Nádasdy

Portrait of György Thurzó

APPENDIX

Portrait of King Mátyás II

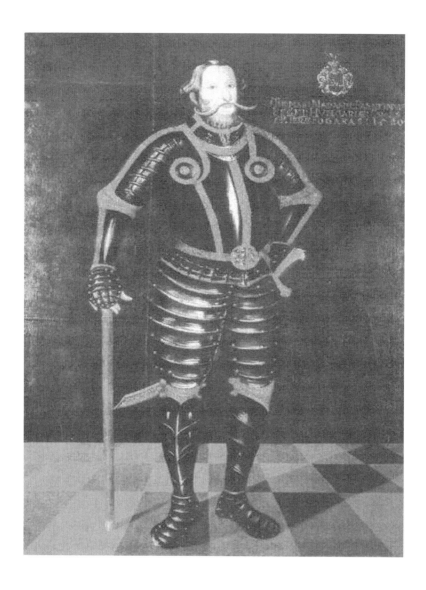

Tamás Nádasdy

Orsolya Nádasdy

Erzsébet's Uncle, István Báthory, King of Poland

APPENDIX

Erzsébet's Cousin, Gábor Báthory

Portrait of Krisztina Nyary, 1625, likely by the same artist who painted the copy of the Erzsébet Báthory portrait (note resemblance and similarities)

APPENDIX

Báthory family church and mausoleum, Nyírbátor, Hungary

Woodcut of Erzsébet Báthory's family home at Ecsed.

APPENDIX

Castle Csejthe as it appears today.

Castle Sárvár in Erzsébet's day.

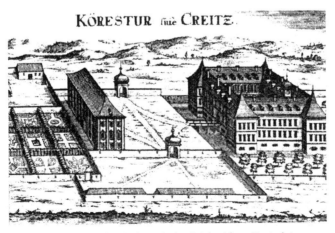

Sopronkeresztúr, a kastély és kertje. Matthias Greischer rézkarca, 17. század vége

Castle Keresztúr in Erzsébet's day.

Castle Csejthe (19th century photograph)

APPENDIX

KNOWN STAFF OF COUNTESS BÁTHORY

Benedikt Desëo	Court Master
Gergely Páztorny	Sárvár Judge
Janós Ficzkó	Personal attendant, Csejthe
Ilona Jó Nagy	Nursemaid, Sárvár; personal attendant, Csejthe
Dorottya Szentes	Personal attendant, Csejthe
Katalin Beneczky	Personal attendant, Csejthe
Anna Darvolia	Personal attendant, Sárvár/Csejthe
Ilona Zalay	Lady in Waiting
Jacob Szilvassy	Administrator, Leka and Keresztúr
István Martonfalvy	Castellan, Leka
Janós Desëo	Castellan, Keresztúr
Janós Zamabory	Provost and paymaster, Keresztúr
Lady Barbara Bixi	Attendant to the Lady
Ferenc Symanoffy	Castellan, Beckó
Michael Herwoyth	Provisor, Csejthe
Mátyás Sakathyartho	Cellar Master, Csejthe
Michael Horwath	Castellan, Csejthe
Janós Andachy	Castellan, Csejthe
Martinus Gablyowych	Staff
Dániel Vas	Stablemaster, Csejthe
Benedict Bicserdy	Castellan, Sárvár
Imre Megyeri	Tutor and guardian, Sárvár
Gregor Paisjártó	Vice Castellan, Sárvár
Benedikt Zalay	Paymaster, Sárvár
Ferenc Török	Squire, Sárvár
Baltasar Poby	Castellan, Sárvár
György Tarnoczky	Judge in Beckó
István Vagy	Administrator, Csejthe
Pál Beöd	Vice Castellan, Sárvár
Bulia, Barbera, Käte	Servants, Csejthe
Susanna	Servant, Sárvár and Csejthe

Sara Baranyai	Staff
Helena Kotsis	Staff
Anna Geonczy	Staff
(István ?) Kozma	Staff

KNOWN CONTRACTORS

Dr. Martinus	Pharmacist
Nicolaus Krestyan	Carpenter
Adam Pollio	Craftsman
Ambrosius Borbély	Plaster/paving
Erzsébet Miava (Majorova)	Occultist

KNOWN VICTIMS

Kata Berényi
Kata Fekete
Lady Zsuzska Zelesthey
Lady Anna Ztubyczay
Susanna Tukynzky
Anna Barbel
Elizabeth Jezernyczky
Lady Zichy
Szabattkay girl
Draskóczy girl
Lady Sittkey
Ms. Modli
Lady Nagyvathy
Lady Belanczky
Jánosi girl
Szabo girl
Szoltay girl

APPENDIX

KNOWN CLERGY

Rev. Michael Fabri	Pastor, Kosztolány
Rev. Nicolaus Barosius	Pastor, Verbo
Rev. János Ponikenusz	Pastor, Csejthe
Rev. Michael Zvonaric	Pastor, Sárvár
Rev. István Magyari	Pastor, Sárvár
Very Rev. Élias Lányi	Superintendant
Rev. Phythiaräus	Pastor, Keresztúr
Rev. Andreas Barosius	Pastor, Csejthe
Rev. Zacharias	Pastor, Leszetice

SOME OF THOSE PRESENT ON THE NIGHT OF THE ARREST (along with Thurzó, Megyeri, Zrínyi, and Drugeth de Homonnay)

Rev. Nicolaus Barosius
Martinus Waychko
Rev. János Ponikenusz
Rev. Zacharias
János Krappmann (church servant)
Andreas Butora
Andreas Pryderowyth
Stephanus Bobochay
Michael Horwath (Csejthe Castellan)
György Kubanovich
Martin Jankovich
Martin Krsskó
János Valkó
Andreas Ukrovich
Ladislas Centalovich
Tamás Zima

NAMES: HUNGARIAN TO ENGLISH

Erzsébet	Elizabeth
Ferenc	Francis
György	George
Ilona	Helena
Janós	John
Dorottya	Dorothy
Katalin/Kata	Catherine
Miklós	Nicolas
Mihály	Michael
Mátyás	Matthew
Pál	Paul
András	Andreas/Andrew
Orsolya/Orsika	Ursula
Tamás	Thomas
István	Stephen
Benedek	Benedict
Imre	Emmerich/Emory
Márton	Martin
László	Ladislas/Laslo
Gergely	Gregory
Gábor	Gabriel

APPENDIX

SOURCES OF ORIGINAL DOCUMENTS; ARCHIVES; AND CHRONOLOGICAL AND GENERAL BIBLIOGRAPHIES:

Reviczky, Bertalan v., *Elisabeth Báthory*, Piestány (1903), pp. 18-19.
*   *Thurzó Letter to his Wife, December 30, 1610*

Károlyi, Á., and Szalay, J., *Nádasdy Tamás nádor családi levelezése*, Budapest (1882), pp. 242-45.
*   Two Letters of Erzsébet Báthory to Ferenc Nadasdy, 1596
*   Letter of Orsolya Nádasdy to E. Báthory, 1604

Statny oblastny archiv Presov, Packet Drugeth Humenné, inv. C. 718.
*   *Chronicle of Castle Csejthe*

Magyar Országos Levéltár (MOL), Budapest, Packet E 142. Act. publ. fasc. 28. No. 18.
*   Letter of Mátyás II to Thurzó, Jan. 24, 1613, and Thurzo's reply from Feb. 5,   1613
*   Letter of Thurzó to András of Keresztúr, March 5, 1610
*   Report of András of Keresztúr, September 19, 1610
*   Letter of Thurzó to Mózes Cziráky, March 5, 1610
*   Report of Mózes Cziráky, October 27, 1610
*   Letter of Mátyás II to András of Keresztúr, Jan. 14, 1611
*   Report of András of Keresztúr to Mátyás II, July 28, 1611
*   Report of Mózes Cziráky, December 14, 1611
*   Report of the Court at Újhely, Jan. 9, 1612
*   Last Will and Testament of Erzsébet Báthory, Sept. 3, 1610, *Id.,* at Act. publ. facs. 44 no. 25.

* Letter of Ponikenusz to Lányi, January 1, 1611, *Id.*, Packet E 196. Rksz. 3. Fasc. 7. no. 69.
* Mátyás's Letter to Thurzó, January 14, 1611, , *Id.*, Packet E 196. Act. publ. fasc. 8. no. 7.
* Letter of Mátyás II to Thurzó, Feb. 26, 1611, *Id.*, at publ. fasc. 8. no. 40.
* Letter of Mátyás II to Thurzó, March 18, 1611, *Id.*, at publ. fasc. 18. no. 9.
* Letter of Mátyás II to Thurzó, April 17, 1611, *Id.,* at publ. fasc. 23. no. 22.

Statny oblastny archiv Bytca (SOBA), Faszikel OK-Thurzovska korespondenicia, sign. II-Z/24.
* Zrínyi Letter to Thurzó, December 12, 1610
* Thurzó Letter to His Wife, December 30, 1610, *Id.*, at sign. III-T/12
* Zrínyi Letter to Thurzó, February 12, 1611, *Id.*, at sign. II-Z/24
* Nádasdy Letter to Thurzó, Feb. 23, 1611, *Id.*, at sign. II-N/2
* Letter of Stanislas Thurzó to György Thurzó, Aug. 25, 1614, *Id.*, at sign. II-T/22

R.A. v. Elsberg, Elisabeth Báthory, Breslau (1904), pp. 262-69.
* Letter of Thurzó to Mátyás II, March 30, 1611
* Letter of Hungarian High Chamber to Mátyás II, March 31, 1611
* Letter of Mátyás II to Thurzó, April 17, 1611
* Second Testament of Erzsébet Báthory, August 3, 1614

Hesperus, Prague (1817), vol. 1, No. 31, pp. 241-48 and July 1817, vol. 2, no. 34, pp. 270-73.
* Trial transcripts of January 2nd and 7th, 1611.

APPENDIX

Tóth, István György, *Literacy and Written Culture in Early Modern Central Europe*, Central European University Press (2001).
*   Letters of Tamás and Orsolya Nádasdy

ARCHIVES

Országos Széchényi Könyvtár, Budapest
Magyar Orsazágos Levéltár, Budapest
Magyar Nemzeti Múzeum, Budapest
Státni Knihovna Ceske Socialisticke Republiky, Prague
Státny Oblastny Archiv, Bytca
Státny Oblastny Archiv, Presov
Österreichische Nationalbibliothek, Vienna
Österreichisches Staatsarchiv, Vienna

CHRONOLOGICAL BIBLIOGRAPHY

1575

Franciscus Hipolytus Hildensheim, *Euchai gamikai Apollinis et Musarum. Ad spectabilem et magnificum dominum, D. Franciscum de Nádasd, sponsum: Et generosam ac magnificam virgiem Elisabetham de Báthor, sponsam.* Viennae Austriae ex officina Stephani Creuzeri, Anno MDLXXV.

1609

Protestaria Elisabetha Bathory, fol. 210 liber II, Archives of the Cathedral Chapter of Graner (1609)
Civitate libera regia Tyrnavense feria II, proxima ante festum S. Martini episcope et confessoris 1609. Archives of the Cathedral Chapter of Graner (1609).

1729

László Turóczi: *Ungaria suis cum Regibus compendio data,*
Dum Illustrissimus, Rev. ac Doctissimus Comes Franciscus
Barkoczi De Szala, Tyrnaviae, Typis Academicis Soc. Jesu per
Fridericum Gall. Anno MDCCXXIX. Mense Septembri, 8.,
245, pp. 188-193.

1735

Mátyás Bel, *Apparatus ad Historiam Hungariae,* sive collectio
miscella, Monumentorum ineditorum partim; partim editorum,
sed fugientium, Posonii, Typis Joannis Paulli Royer, A.
MDCCXXXV, pp. 353-80, pp. 366-67, and p. 370.

1817

Abschrift des Zeugen-Verhörs in Betreff der grausamen That,
welcher Elisabeth v. Báthory, Gemahlinn des Grafen Franz
Nádasdy beschuldiget wird. 1611. Hesperus, Prague, vol. 1, No.
31, pp. 241-48 and July 1817, vol. 2, no. 34, pp. 270-73.

1876

Zichy, Edmund, *Bethlenfalvi gróf Thurzó György Levelei,* Budapest (1876).

1894

Ferdinand Strobl von Ravelsberg (R.A. v. Elsberg), *Die Blut-*
gräfin. (Elisabeth Báthory) Ein Sitten- und Characterbild. Mit
Illustrationen. Breslau: Schlesische Buchdruckerei, Kunst- und
Verlags-Anstalt v. S. Schottlaender 1894, rev. ed. 1904.

APPENDIX

1899

Chronik der Burg Csejte. Történelmi tár (1899), p. 722f.

1908

Dezsö, Rexa, *Báthory Erzsébet Nádasdy Ferencné (1560-1614)*, Benkö Gyula Udvari Könyvkereskedése, Budapest (1908).

1912

Sándor, Payr, *Magyari István és Báthory Erzsébet*, Protestáns Szemle, Budapest (1912), pp. 185-203.

1924

History of the Transdanubian Evangelical Church, Vol. 1, Székely & Társa Könyvnyomdájában, Sopron (1924).

1932

Níznánszy, Jozó, *Cachtická pani*. Prague (1932). Four Parts.

1965

Penrose, Valaentine, *Die blutige Gräfin. Erzsébet Báthory*. Verlag der Europäischen Bücherei H.M. Hieronimi, Bonn (1965) (English version, 1969).

1975

Périsset, Maurice, *La comtesse de sang. Erzsébet Báthory*. Editions Pygmalion, Paris (1975).

1976

Keller, Paul Anton, *Burg Lockenhaus: Landschaft und Geschichte.* Lockenhaus im Burgenland (1976).

1984

McNally, Raymond T., *Dracula was a Woman: In Search of the Blood Countess of Transylvania*, Robert Hale, London (1984).

1985

Katalin, Péter, *A Csejtei Várúrnö: Báthory Erzsébet*, Helikon Kiadó, Budapest (1985).

1989

Farin, Michael, *Heroine des Grauens: Elisabeth Báthory*, P. Kirchheim Verlag München (1989).

1997

Ammer, Vladímir. Cachtice. Bratislava: Alfa-Press (1997).

2001

Katalin, Péter, *Beloved Children: History of Aristocratic Childhood in Hungary in the Early Modern Age*, Central European University Press (2001).

Tóth, István György, *Literacy and Written Culture in Early Modern Central Europe*, Central European University Press (2001).

APPENDIX

GENERAL BIBLIOGRAPHY

Baring-Gould, Sabine. The Book of Werewolves. Orig. London: Smith Elder, 1865. repr. New York: Causeway Books, 1973.

Bathory Al Babel, Gia. The Trouble with the Pears (fiction) Bloomington, Ind.: Authorhouse, 2006.

Bloodcult, The: The Magazine for Dark Souls and Vampire Lovers. Crete: The Nocturnal Summoning V.S., 2001

Burtinshaw, Julie: Romantic Ghost Stories. Edmonton, Alberta: Ghost House Books, 2003. Contains "Love Gone Astray: Castle Csejthe, Hungary."

Cachtice 1248-1998. Multimediálne CD o obci Cachtice. Nové Mesto: Visgra s.r.o., 1998.

Canale, Ray. Nightfall: The Blood Countess. (fiction) Paperback Audio, 1990 (text) 1998 (recording).

Carillo, Carlos. Para Tenerlos Bajo Llave. (fiction). 1994. (Contains Legado de los Carpatos).

Codrescu, Andrei. The Blood Countess. (fiction) (manuscript); publ. New York: Dell, 1996.

Elsberg, R. von. Elizabeth Bathory (Die Blutgräfin). Breslau, 1894; 1904.

Glut, Donald F. True Vampires of History. New York: HC Publishers, 1971.

Farin, M. Heroine des Grauens. Wirken und Leben der Elizabeth Báthory. Munich, 1989.

Farkas, I. Cséthe vár véres asszonya (Báthory Erzsébet töténete). Budapest, 1936.

Glut, Donald F. The Dracula Book. The Scarecrow Press, Inc., Metuchen, N.J.: 1975 Republished as The Truth About Dracula, New York: Stein and Day.

Kocis, Jozef. Alzbeta Báthoryová a palatín Thurzo: Pravdo a cachtickej panej. Vydavatel'sto Blaha, 1996.

McNally, Raymond T. Dracula Was a Woman. New York: McGraw-Hill, 1983.

Manguel, Alberto, ed. Other Fires. (fiction) New York: Clarkson N. Potter, 1986. (Contains The Bloody Countess by Alejandra Pizarnik)

Melton, J. Gordon. The Vampire Book: The Encyclopedia of the Undead. Detroit: Visible Ink Press, 1994.

Newton, Michael. Bad Girls Do It! Port Townsend, Washington: Loompanics Unlimited, 1993.

Niznánsky, Jozo: Cachtická Pani. Bratislava: L Mazac Praba, 1932

Penrose, Valentine. Erzsébet Báthory, La Comtesse Sanglante. Paris, 1962. Eng. trans. The Bloody Countess. London, 1970. New edition: Creation Books, 2000.

Pérez, Carlos D.: Siete Lunas de Sangre (fiction). Buenos Aires: Topía Editorial, 1999.

Perisset, Maurice. La Comtesse de Sang: Erzsebeth Bathory. Paris: Pygmalion, 1975.

APPENDIX

Peters, Robert. The Blood Countess. Cherry Valley, N.Y.: Cherry Valley Editions, 1987.

Pirrotta, Luciano: Erzsébet Báthory: Una Visione - Incubo Rosso (play). [no city], Italy, Sallustiana, 2003.

Requiem: Archives du vampirisme Montpellier: Cercle d'Études Vampiriques, 1998.

Rexa, Dezso. Báthory Erzsébet Nadasdy Ferencne. Budapest, 1908.

Ronay, Gabriel. The Truth About Dracula. London: Gallancz, 1972. Repr. New York: Stein and Day, 1972.

Seabrook, William. Witchcraft. New York: Harcourt, 1940. Repr. New York: Lancer Books, 1968.

Szádeczky-Kardos, I. Báthory Erzsébet igazsá 1983.

Thorne, Tony: Children of the Night: of Vampires and Vampirism. London: Indigo, 2000.

Thorne, Tony: Countess Dracula. The life and times of the Blood Countess, Elisabeth Bathory. London: Bloomsbury, 1997.

Turoczi, Lászlo. Báthory Erzsébet. Budapest, 1744.

Turoczi, Lászlo. Ungaria suis cum regibus compendia data. Nagyszombat, 1729.

Twiss, Miranda: The Most Evil Men and Women is History. London: Michael O'Mara Books, 2002.

Wagener, Michael. Beiträge zur Philosophischen Anthropologie. Vienna, 1796.

About the Author

Kimberly Craft, Esq. holds bachelor and master's degrees in the humanities as well as a juris doctorate. An attorney and legal historian, Craft spent years researching the history of Countess Erzsébet Báthory, including more than a year devoted solely to translating original source material. As she put it, this project is one of the few times in which her love of the law, history, European languages, and a good horror story can all come together in one place.

Made in the USA
Lexington, KY
05 October 2011